Alexander Garden, Thomas Warren Field

Anecdotes of the American Revolution, Illustrative of the Talents and Virtues...

Vol. I

Alexander Garden, Thomas Warren Field

Anecdotes of the American Revolution, Illustrative of the Talents and Virtues...
Vol. I

ISBN/EAN: 9783337078645

Printed in Europe, USA, Canada, Australia, Japan

Cover: Foto ©ninafisch / pixelio.de

More available books at **www.hansebooks.com**

ANECDOTES

OF THE

AMERICAN REVOLUTION.

Illustrative of the Talents and Virtues

OF THE

HEROES OF THE REVOLUTION.

WHO ACTED THE

MOST CONSPICUOUS PARTS THEREIN.

By ALEXANDER GARDEN, of Lee's Legion

VOL. I.

REPRINTED:
BROOKLYN, NEW YORK
1865.

One Hundred and Fifty Copies printed, of which Thirty are on large paper.)

No. 118

PREFACE.

It was designed that this edition of Garden's Anecdotes should be accompanied by a sketch of the life of the author, and the publication of the work has been delayed in the expectation of discovering sufficient data for the performance of that design.

No probable source of information has been neglected, and no labor of investigation among the minutest narrations of Southern life has been spared in seeking information regarding Major Garden.

It is scant justice to one who has done so much to secure fame, and popular regard for others, to receive such meagre tribute to his memory. Nor has the task been rendered easier of accomplishment, by the singular fact, that while the name of Alexander Garden has few representatives in this country, no less than three remarkable and talented men who bore it, should have resided in Charleston. Incidents in the life of each, have been confusedly narrated in allusions to the others: and the dates of events which belong to one have been transferred to another.

Col. Benjamin Garden who commanded a regiment in South Carolina during the revolution is often referred to in the collections and histories, and not always by his distinctive title and name, thus adding another element of confusion to what was already so difficult.

The first Alexander Garden was a clergyman, officiating in Charleston as the commissary of the Bishop of London, a learned and pious man, who died in 1756, aged 70 years. The second Alexander Garden was eminent as a Physician, and naturalist, performing the arduous services of the first among the citizens of Charleston, and contributing by his zeal in pursuits of the last to the learning of the world for a period of more than thirty years. His death occurred at London in the year 1791, to which place he returned soon after the departure of the British from Charleston.

That Major Garden resided in Europe during the earlier period of the Revolution, whither he was sent for the purpose of obtaining an education at a college the name of which is not given, that it was by the commands of a parent that he was prevented from taking part in the first resistance to British arms—and that as soon as age freed him from legal obligation to parental authority he returned to share in the fortunes of his countrymen, and thereby sacrificed them to his patriotism: are particulars of which he himself informs us. If Alexander Garden the physician, were that parent it would not be difficult to conjecture other reasons, than the education of his son, for the exercise of paternal authority in preventing his participation in the conflict. This gentleman so justly celebrated for his learning and scientific labors (among which was the introduction of the Virginia pink root into the Materia Medica) was an adherent to the British Government. To him, it is narrated by Major Garden, Lord Rawdon applied for a certificate of inability to perform military service, and the application met with a prompt refusal. This rebuff was afterwards made more emphatic by declining to sign, and boldly protesting against the presentation of a complimentary address to Lord Rawdon, designed as Garden says by many tories.

That he would not have been solicited for his signature unless his loyalist sympathies were well known is evident. His relationship however to Major Alexander Garden has only the very unsatisfactory basis of conjecture.

But little better source could the writer of the article on Garden in the American Encyclopædia have possessed.

"Alexander Garden an officer of the American Revolution, in Lee's famous legion, died in Charleston, S. C., about 1825, at an advanced age. He was for a time aide-de-camp to Gen. Greene."

What unsafe materials for history such compilations are, may be seen when it is stated that during the year, which is thus authoritatively announced to be that of his death, Major Garden delivered an eulogium on the life and services of Gen. C. C. Pinckney, and that his second series of these anecdotes was not published until the year 1828. As Garden was precluded by non-age from military service until about the period of the formation of Lee's Legion, which was only effected in the latter part of 1780, he would have reached his sixty-fifth year in 1825, a period of life which can scarcely be termed an advanced age. He was an officer in the infantry section of Lee's Legion, and we learn from his anecdotes that he was a confidential aide-de-camp to Gen. Greene. His selections on several occasions as an eulogist of deceased members of the Society of the Cincinnati, indicates the esteem in which he was held by his comrades, as the character of his works does his literary ability. His printed works, so far as they are known are limited to those already mentioned.

His Anecdotes have everywhere been received with gratification and perused with pleasure. The simplicity of the style of their narration, the honesty and candor of his statements, and the high toned sentiment and fervent patriotism of his sentiments, have met with universal applause.

The author of a book entitled Records of Patriotism has used the Anecdotes as texts for the several chapters of his work, and constantly speaks of them as eminent examples of devotion to a country's good.

A careful examination of the literature relating to the Revolution in the Southern Colonies, enables the reader of Garden's Anecdotes to trace the origin of them in the author's mind. This literature, so prolific in the early part of this century, of works minutely tracing the progress of the War for Liberty and Independence emanated from the minds of men who had been active and potent in that cause, and events which they narrated were familiar as the daily routine of life to a generation which had not then forgotten the forms and features of the principal actors in that great drama. It was to illustrate those events then so familiar, and to preserve minuter incidents in the lives of those noble men, that Garden collected his interesting anecdotes, only vaguely referring to other sources of information regarding them. These other collections of memorable events and incidents, then so familiar, as scarcely to need a reference to their contents, have now become so rare, and of such high price that the reader of Garden's works can seldom gratify the curiosity excited by its perusal, without consulting works found only on the shelves of a Historical Society, or of some curious and fortunate book collector.

It was to these books that Alexander Garden constantly referred in his own mind, without often noting in his work that reference, and to them his work is properly, what doubtless he intended it, a laborious collection of addenda.

These had become somewhat obscure in their allusions to characters and incidents, and none who perused Garden's anecdotes could fail of a desire for a minuter narration of those stirring events to which he only made a tantalizing reference.

The notes illustrative of this work, which are given in this edition, are the result of a minute investigation of the History of the Revolution in the South, and from a portion of an essay upon Gov. Rutledge and the Carolinas during that period, now in press. If the notes shall be found to exhibit a design of depreciating the patriotism of the Carolinas in our Revolutionary struggle, it is a result produced by sad conviction after a patient study of all the sources of information within the writer's reach.

The numerous histories of the War for Independence in the South, have all been written by her citizens, whose sectional pride and ambition of local esteem, combined to warp their judgment, or induce suppression of unpopular and humiliating facts.

The sources from which these additional anecdotes have been derived, are not, however, all included in the number to which Mr. Garden had access. Since his death there have been many accessions to the Historic Literature treating of that period. Johnson's Traditions of the Revolution in the South—Caruther's Revolutionary Incidents in the old North State—Frazer's Reminiscences of Charleston—O'Neal's Biographical Sketches of the Bench and Bar of South Carolina—O'Neal's Annals of Newberry—Gibbs' Doc. His. of S. C.—Letters of Eliza Wilkinson.—Carrol's His. Collections of S. C.—S. Carolina His. Soc. Collections.—Wheeler's His. of N. C.—Fanning's narrative—and other incidental sources of information. have been consulted.

To have arranged these additions in the usual form of notes, would have interfered somewhat more with the original structure of Garden's work than the collector felt warranted in doing, and it is also due to candor that it should be said, that although the idea of some addition was conceived before the work had gone to press, yet no satisfactory plan had then suggested itself.

It is hoped that while the integrity of the original work has been faithfully preserved, yet its value has been enhanced by the additions.

T. W. FIELD.

ANECDOTES

OF THE

REVOLUTIONARY WAR

In America,

WITH

SKETCHES OF CHARACTER

OF

PERSONS THE MOST DISTINGUISHED, IN THE SOUTHERN STATES, FOR
CIVIL AND MILITARY SERVICES.

BY ALEXANDER GARDEN,

OF LEE'S PARTISAN LEGION; AID-DE-CAMP TO MAJOR GENERAL GREENE; AND
HONORARY MEMBER OF THE HISTORICAL SOCIETY OF NEW-YORK.

"I cannot but remember such things were."—*Shakspeare.*

CHARLESTON:
PRINTED FOR THE AUTHOR, BY A. E. MILLER,
NO. 4, BROAD-STREET.

1822.

District of South-Carolina, to wit:

BE IT REMEMBERED, That on the first day of April, Anno Domini, one thousand eight hundred and twenty two, and in the forty-sixth year of the Independence of the United States of America, Major Alexander Garden deposited in this office the title of a book, the right whereof he claims, as author and proprietor, in the words following, to wit:

"Anecdotes of the Revolutionary War in America, with Sketches of Character of Persons the most Distinguished in the Southern States, for Civil and Military Services. By Alexander Garden, of Lee's Partisan Legion; Aid-de-Camp to Major General Greene; and Honorary Member of the Historical Society of New-York. ——" I cannot but remember such things were."— *Shakspeare.*

In conformity with the act of Congress of the United States, entitled, " An Act for the Encouragement of Learning, by securing the Copies of Maps, Charts and Books, to the authors and proprietors of such copies, during the times therein mentioned;" and also to the Act entitled, " An Act supplementary to an Act entitled, 'An Act for the encouragement of Learning, by securing the Copies of Maps, Charts and Books, to the authors and proprietors of such copies, during the times therein mentioned," and extending the benefits thereof to the arts of designing, engraving and etching historical and other prints."

JAMES JERVEY,
Clerk of the District of South Carolina.

TO

Maj-Gen. Charles Cotesworth Pinckney,

PRESIDENT GENERAL

OF

THE SOCIETY OF THE CINCINNATI.

TO

Maj. Gen. Thomas Pinckney,

PRESIDENT,

AND THE OTHER MEMBERS OF THE SOCIETY

OF THE CINCINNATI IN SOUTH-CAROLINA.

IN GRATITUDE

FOR LONG EXPERIENCED TESTIMONIES

OF THEIR FAVOUR AND CORDIAL REGARD,

THIS WORK

IS AFFECTIONATELY DEDICATED,

BY THEIR BROTHER AND FRIEND

THE AUTHOR.

TO THE READER.

The Author of the following pages would be deficient in gratitude, did he fail to return his warmest thanks for the liberal patronage received from the Public. The rapidity with which his Subscription Lists have been filled up, is not only flattering to his effort to give to society a Work, that properly executed, may, to the rising generation, prove of some utility; but, particularly so, as it evinces, that an attachment to Revolutionary principles, is cherished in the bosoms of his fellow-citizens, with pristine ardour and admiration. It is not, however, numbers, so much as honorable names, that he would possess; and when on his lists he sees the signatures of many of those distinguished Ladies, whose firmness and exemplary conduct in the day of trial, dignified their sex, and adorned the annals of their country; and of venerable Patriots, whose wisdom in council, and valour in the field, essentially contributed to fix the Independence of America, he claims a right to be proud, and has only to hope, that his performance may justify their partiality.

To the Honorable Judge DESAUSSURE, and Mr. KEATING SIMONS, he acknowledges himself particularly indebted for much information respecting Generals DAVIE and MARION. To Colonel ROBERT Y. HAYNE, for the sketch of the life and services of Dr. DAVID RAMSAY; and to Colonel ARTHUR P. HAYNE, for his interesting account of the Battle of the 23d December, before New-Orleans. To the Honourable Judge PETERS of Pennsylvania, he is indebted for many interesting Anecdotes; and feels particular obligation for the politeness with which, though a stranger to him, they were generously presented. To his brother soldiers, the Honorable Judge PETER JOHNSON of Abingdon, Virginia, and Dr. MATTHEW IRVINE, of Charleston, he feels peculiar gratitude for the details of the services of the Legionary Officers and Soldiers, and many of the occurrences connected with the Army of the South. Nor is he less obliged to Dr. WILLIAM READ, for his interesting statement of the sufferings of the Continental Army, and of the heroic fortitude with which those intrepid Sons of Freedom supported them. Finally, it affords him great pleasure to express his thanks to his friends, Mr. STEPHEN ELLIOTT, THOMAS S. GRIMKE, and MITCHELL KING, for their judicious advice during the progress of his Work, and aid in its arrangement when preparing for the press.

INTRODUCTION.

"WHILE I YET LIVE, LET ME NOT LIVE IN VAIN."—*Addison.*

FREE from unwarrantable prejudice, I have invariably maintained, that the citizens of America during the war of our Revolution, had exhibited as splendid examples of heroic gallantry, as firm and honourable adherence to the cause of Liberty, as ever adorned the annals of any age or country. If facts sanction this opinion, we cannot but deeply regret, that from the encroachments of time, perpetually removing, not only the actors in many a brilliant achievement, but even the witnesses of them, they will be in the course of a few years irretrievably lost. To diminish the evil, I have anxiously endeavoured, to engage some youthful patriot, to collect and preserve for the benefit of future generations, as many anecdotes relative to the war of 1776, as appear worthy of record, and particularly, such, as have escaped the attention of Historians. —My effort has proved fruitless, and although I anticipate very partial success, yet confident of meeting the indulgence of my fellow citizens, who must approve my motive, I have at length resolved, myself to undertake it.

To the public I am bound by peculiar ties. In adversity they honoured me with their confidence, and rewarded my zeal with distinguished marks of favour, whatever I possess, is derived from their generosity, I feel the obligation in all its force, and know, that death, come when it may, must find my debt of gratitude uncancelled.*

I wish it were possible in pursuing my plan, to arrange the facts in chronological order, but this I consider, from the nature of the work, impracticable, and the reader must therefore receive them, without such connection. The anecdotes are indeed of so diversified a nature, that they ought to appear as they are, independent of each other. Many are of a serious cast, and can hardly fail to excite corresponding sentiments, and deep reflection, while others detailing sallies of wit, or scenes of mirthful adventure, are fitted only to amuse.

In such a work I am bound by a double sense of duty. *First* to save from oblivion, many acts of courage or magnanimity, that honour the patriots of our Revolution, and *secondly* to excite in the bosoms of our youth, a laudable desire to emulate them.

The spontaneous impulse of every heart is my best auxiliary. How grateful to my young countrymen must it be, to read the encomiums bestowed on their ancestors, to dwell on the merits of those great men, who had wisdom to plan the deliverance of the United States from a foreign yoke, resolution to attempt it, and valour to insure their independence. In contemplating the dignified firmness of their characters, the extent of their sufferings and the splendor of the actions achieved in the accomplishment of their momentous undertaking, the heart expands with gratitude, the soul with admiration. Liberty so honourably gained, appears with more fascinating charms; is cherished with imperishable affections, and the bosom of patriotism feels with full force, how sacred the obligation to trans-

---

* The author cannot sufficiently lament that he had but little share in the achievement of those important events which fixed the independence of the United States. His heart from the earliest dawn of the Revolution was devoted to the cause of his country, and he would have been first in the ranks of her armies but the Revolution found him a youth in Europe, in pursuit of his Collegiate studies, and a parent's mandate forbid it. When age permitted his return to America, his fortunes without a murmur were sacrificed to his principles, and his life, to have promoted the interests of America, would have been yielded without a sigh. The public witnessed his zeal and liberally rewarded it. His general gave him his confidence and promotion. His fellow soldiers, what he must ever consider his highest honour, their friendship and esteem.

mit such a blessing, with undiminished lustre, to posterity. It can only be necessary, to present to view the characters whose achievements I would celebrate.

> "And by their light,
> Shall every valiant youth with ardour move,
> To do brave acts." SHAKSPEARE.

> "For who shall lightly say,—that Fame,
> Is nothing but an empty name,
> While in that sound there is a charm,
> The nerves to brace, the heart to warm,
> As thinking of the mighty dead,
> The young from slothful couch shall start,
> And vow with lifted hands outspread,
> Like them to act, a noble part." BAILIE.

I am still further induced to persist in my undertaking, that I may both by precept and example bear testimony against a practice, in my judgment, decidedly prejudicial. With such instances of every public and private virtue, as the history of our own country affords, I consider it a serious error in our system of education, that our youth receive their *first* ideas of patriotic excellence, from the annals of other nations. Familiar with the achievements of the heroes of ancient times, the virtues and services of the worthies of their own country, are seldom or but imperfectly known. They will tell you of the retreat of *Xenophon*, before a horde of barbarians, while ignorant of the masterly manoeuvring of *Greene* retiring before the superior and victorious army of *Cornwallis*. They will dwell with delight on the sufferings, energy, and zeal of the virtuous *Alfred*, successfully resisting the ravagers of his country; while the difficulties and dangers surmounted by the inflexible *Marion* labouring under tenfold disadvantages, are altogether unknown. They admire *Fabius* as the *shield*, *Marcellus* as the *sword* of Rome, but unless it is acquired incidently, they either know not at all, or very imperfectly, that *Washington* by his wisdom and discretion in the cabinet, his skill and valour in the field, may still be more justly called, both the *sword and shield* of his country. By this injudicious system, a prejudice arises, which from the strength of early impressions, it is ever difficult to shake off. Comparisons are made altogether to the advantage of antiquity, and an ambition to arrive at excellence impaired, by a seeming confession of inability to attain it. I rejoice to think that this cannot be an evil of long continuance. The lives of the illustrious patriots of our Revolution, presented to view by the pen of intelligence, a natural consequence must ensue:—They will learn to "hold honour far more dear than life." If candidates for *fame*, admiring the heroes of *Rome*, will they not with greater enthusiasm revere and emulate the valour of their immediate ancestry? If the *justice* and *magnanimity* of Grecian worthies delight them, it is impossible not to conclude, that these virtues will be aspired to, with still higher admiration, when exemplified in the history of their own country.

Agisilaus king of Sparta, being asked, " what ought children to learn," replied, " that which they ought to practice, when they become men." No sentiment was ever expressed more conformable to the principles of our government. Next to their duty towards God, there is not a parent who ought not to impress upon the minds of his children, the devotion which is due their country; and how can this be more effectually done, than from the dawn of reason, to keep in their view, those virtues, which have raised the benefactors of the republic, to immortality. It is not my intention to attempt a history of the southern war. In freely offering strictures on the mode in which it was conducted, opportunity is afforded of attaining the end at which I aim. A delineation of the injustice and oppression, of wanton insult and ruthless severity, exercised on the one part, will afford ample occasion to relate the firmness with which they were met, and to detail the animating examples of patient suffering, inflexible perseverence and intrepidity, by which they were surmounted on the other. In animadverting on the cruelty and impolicy of the measures pursued, I shall be led to criticise the conduct of the commanders by whom they were adopted; and this will bring into view, the prominent characters who opposed them.—I would further observe, that as it is my plan *to collect Anecdotes*, I shall not endeavour by indulging fancy, to give them the advantage of attractive dress. I shall studiously aim at simplicity in detail, and laying no claim to originality, be content, if the merit is allowed, of making them useful and acceptable to my countrymen. This is the only reward I desire, and it is my trust that I shall receive it.

ANECDOTES

OF THE

REVOLUTIONARY WAR IN AMERICA.

MOULTRIE.

THE first conflict of the Carolinians with the enemy, gave such reputation to the character of the country, and was so highly creditable to General Moultrie, who commanded the post attacked on that memorable day, (the 28th of June) that it may be considered an act of justice in detailing the Anecdotes of the Revolutionary War, to commence with giving the particulars of the action. The defence of the pass at Sullivan's Island, may be compared with many of the splendid achievements which Grecian eloquence has rendered illustrious.—Impressed with prejudices as strong as Xerxes ever cherished against Greece, the commanders of the British forces approached our coast, not to conciliate, but subdue. Exulting in the supposed superiority of their discipline and valour, they spoke in the language of authority, and would listen to no terms short of unconditional submission. They too had been taught by the insinuations of insidious flattery, to entertain a thorough contempt for their enemy, and to brand them with the harshest appellations of infamy and reproach; and the extraordinary delay of their military operations, can alone be accounted for, by their belief, that it was only necessary to allow the Americans a sufficient time to reflect on the critical situation in which they were placed, to induce them to abandon the pass without a struggle, and seek safety by flight. On the other hand, the gallant Moultrie, commanding a corps, formidable only by their boldness and resolution, impatiently waited their approach. He was not insensible of the insufficiency of a work hastily constructed, and in every part incomplete, to afford the shelter requisite against a force so formidable as that before him. The advice of the experienced veteran Lee, called for its abandonment.* A necessary supply of ammunition was withheld, but seconding the bolder wishes of President Rutledge,† and considering himself pledged to give a proof to the enemy of American valour, he scorned the disgrace of relinquishing the post he had sworn to defend, and heroically prepared for action.—The attack was commenced by the British with intrepidity, and maintained throughout the course of twelve hours, with a gallantry that would have dignified a better cause, but naught could subdue the firmness of the garrison; resolved to repel the foe, or nobly perish, they received the tremendous fire of the shipping with composure, and returned it with terrible effect, till valour accomplished, what prudence had declared impracticable, and the retreat of the assailants, adorned the brows of every individual concerned, with laurels that can never fade.

The subsequent good conduct of General Moultrie, increased his military reputation and secured to him the perfect confi-

* General LEE styled the post at Sullivan's Island a slaughter pen, denounced its defence and pronouncing disgrace on the measure, should it be persisted in, earnestly requested the President to order it to be evacuated.

† Happily for the nation, its destinies were at that period, guided by that inflexible patriot JOHN RUTLEDGE, who confidently relying on MOULTRIE, and his intrepid band, heroically replied to LEE. "That while a soldier remained alive to defend it, he would never give his sanction to such an order." The result proved the accuracy of his judgment. The following laconic note was at the same time forwarded to Colonel MOULTRIE. "General LEE wishes you to evacuate the fort. You will not without an order from me. I will sooner cut off my hand than write one.   JOHN RUTLEDGE."

dence and respect of his fellow soldiers, and warm applause of his country. He engaged a British force, on Port Royal Island, with brilliant success, and conducted the retreat of a division of the army on the invasion of Provost, with an ability that saved the capital. His correspondence with Lord Charles Montague, while a prisoner at Haddrell's, sufficiently proves the steadiness of his principles and incorruptible integrity. The Eulogy to his memory,* published by order of the State Society of the Cincinnati, of which he was President, gives ample testimony of the veneration and affection entertained towards him by its members, and as it contains a just estimate of his private virtues as well as of his public utility, will not I hope be considered irrelevant, nor prove unacceptable to the admirers of patriotic virtue.

Eulogy.

THE 27th of September, 1805, will long be remembered with interest by every virtuous citizen of South-Carolina. On that day, deeply regretted by every individual who had sense to appreciate, and gratitude to acknowledge the pre-eminence of his patriotic virtues, died, in the seventy-fifth year of his age, the venerable Major General Moultrie, who, by uniform suffrage, had presided over this Society from its first institution. —As a revolutionary character, his steadiness in principle, his valour in the field, were particularly conspicuous. As a soldier, it was his fortune to check, and with an effect that paralized every subsequent exertion, the first efforts of a powerful and inveterate foe, for the subjugation of his country. Bold as Leonidas, he defended the strait committed to his charge, against a superior force, that had been deemed irresistible; and more fortunate than the Spartan hero, lived in honourable old age, under the shade of his laurels, to share with a grateful nation, the liberty his successful exertions had so happily contributed to establish. As a patriot it was equally his glory, disdainfully to reject the bribes of a nation, who, repeatedly foiled by his valour, hoped with better success to corrupt this integ-

* Written by the Author.

rity, and like another Fabricius to show to the admiring world, how insignificant the power of gold, to shake the principles of a heart, warmed with the genuine glow of heaven-born liberty. In private life, his disposition was frank, liberal, sincere, his manners simple and conciliating. Duplicity and disguise were odious to a nature fixed on the firmest basis of candour and truth. As a husband, father, master, he was affectionate, gentle, most indulgent; in short, as has been said of a great statesman, and distinguished patriot, " he was every thing to his family, but what he gave up to his country." When in future ages men shall seek examples of distinguished worth and excellence, Fame with delight, shall tell the unshaken faith, and gallant deeds of MOULTRIE. While, as brother soldiers, we offer this sincere, though inadequate tribute of respect to his memory, it is with pleasure we reflect, that the artillery, cavalry, and several volunteer corps of the city, together with a considerable concourse of the most respectable and patriotic of our citizens, attended his body to the grave, testifying their respect for his virtues, and unfeigned sorrow for the event, which deprived his country of one of its most distinguished, and estimable public characters."

The happy escape of the General during the siege of Charleston, deserves to be recorded. The fatigue experienced by severe duty on the lines, had so much overcome him, that to renew his energies, he took up his quarters for one night, in Elliott's buildings, near the centre of the city, where there was the least chance of interruption to the rest he sought for. A tremendous fire about the dawning of day, roused him from his slumbers, he started from his bed, and was hurrying on his regimentals, when a shot striking the house, entered the apartment, and lodged in the bed from which he had risen. The delay of a few moments, must have proved fatal to him.

The venerable Captain Richard Bahon Baker, now residing on Sullivan's Island, within view of the scene of his early achievements, and Mr. David Adams, of Charleston, who served as a cadet, in the company commanded by Captain Shubrick, alone remain of the intrepid band, who fought under Moultrie, on the memorable 28th of June, 1776.

Anecdote of John Rutledge.

It was my good fortune, many years after this celebrated victory, to meet Governor Rutledge on the spot, where the action of the 28th of June was fought, when the recollection of the triumphs of the day, filling his soul with enthusiastic delight, he exclaimed: "I remember the engagement as if it were fought but yesterday! I remember my perfect confidence in Moultrie! I have all the scene before me too, when I visited the post, to express the thanks of the country to the heroes who had defended it. *There* stood Moultrie, *there* Motte, *there* Marion, Horry, and the intrepid band, whom they commanded. I addressed them with an energy of feeling, that I had never before experienced, and if ever I had pretension to eloquence, it was at that moment."

I will not dwell on a subject, to which it is impossible for me to do justice, but briefly state, that inspired by it, and animated as if the objects of his commendation were immediately before him, he delivered himself in an eloquent and impressive strain of eulogy, so perfectly fascinating, that had his first address but borne a shadow of resemblance to it, there could not have been a man among his auditors, who would not have been proud to die, for liberty and his country. I have often heard of the strong impression made at the moment of delivery by this celebrated harangue. Certain it is, that under its animating influence, new honours crowned the valiant defenders of the post, and to the last, the gallant Second Regiment, were covered with glory.

The Second Regiment.

Proud of the encomiums bestowed on their valour, encouraged by the animating address of the governor, to aim at the achievement of new honours, the feelings of the gallant Second

Regiment, were still more highly excited, when *Mrs. Barnard Elliott*, presenting an elegant pair of colours, thus addressed them:

"*Gentlemen Soldiers*,

"Your gallant behaviour in defence of your country, entitles you to the highest honours! Accept of these two standards as a reward justly due to your Regiment, and I make not the least doubt, but that under Heaven's protection, you will stand by them as long as they can wave in the air of liberty."

Her anticipations were fully justified in the sequel. During the assault at Savannah, they were both planted on the British lines. The statement which I am about to give of the event, differs widely from that which has been generally received; but that it is correct, cannot be doubted, as it was afforded me by Lieutenant James Legare, whose services and character, entitle him to all credit. He was present in the action, and immediately in front of the colours at the time that the officers who bore them were killed. Lieutenant Brush, supported by Sergeant Jaspar, carried the one, Lieutenant Grey, supported by Sergeant McDonald, the other. Brush being wounded early in the action, delivered his standard to Jasper, for its better security, who, already wounded, on receiving a second shot, restored it. Brush at the moment receiving a mortal wound, fell into the ditch, with the colours under him, which occasioned their remaining in the hands of the enemy. Lieutenant Grey, receiving a mortal wound, his colours were seized by McDonald, who planted them on the redoubt, but on hearing an order to retreat, plucked them up again, and carried them off in safety.

It is highly grateful to me, to recollect an occurrence which strongly evinces how deeply the love of country is impressed on the human heart. Meeting an officer in the British service, who was a native of Carolina, in the streets of Edinburgh, shortly after the accounts of Moultrie's gallant defence of his post had reached Europe, he said, as he approached me: "I see triumph in your countenance, and do not wonder at it. I cannot but lament that His Majesty's fleet has been beaten, but as the event has happened, I rejoice that the victory has been gained by *Carolinians*."

LETTER FROM LORD C. MONTAGUE TO GENERAL MOULTRIE.

"*March* 11*th*, 1781.

"Sir,—A sincere wish to promote what may be to your advantage, induces me now to write; and the freedom with which we have often conversed, makes me hope that you will not take amiss what I say. My own principles respecting the commencement of this unfortunate war are well known to you, and of course, you can conceive what I mention is out of friendship. You have fought bravely in the cause of your country for many years, and, in my opinion, fulfilled the duty every individual owes to it. You have had your share of hardships and difficulties, and if the contest is still to be continued, younger hands should now take the toil from you. You have now a fair opening of quitting that service, with honour and reputation to yourself, by going to Jamaica with me. The world will readily attribute it to the known friendship that has subsisted between us; and by quitting this country for a short time, you will avoid any disagreeable conversations, and might return at leisure, to take possession of your estates for yourself and family. Appointed to command a regiment, the proof I can give you of my sincerity is, that I will quit that command to you with pleasure, and serve under you. I earnestly wish that I could be the instrument to effect what I propose, as I think it would be a great means towards promoting that reconciliation we all wish for; a thousand circumstances concur to make this a proper period for you to embrace; our old acquaintance—my having been formerly governor of this province; the interest I have with the present commanders.

"I give you my honour, what I write is entirely unknown to the commandant, or to any one else; so shall your answer be, if you favour me with one. Think well of me. Yours sincerely,

CHARLES MONTAGUE."

"*General Moultrie.*"

TO LORD CHARLES MONTAGUE.

"*Haddrell's Point, March* 12*th*, 1781.

"My Lord,—I received your's this morning by Fisher. I thank you for your wish to promote my advantage, but am much surprised at your proposition. I flattered myself, that I stood in a more favourable light with you. I shall write with the same freedom, with which we used to converse, and doubt not you will receive it with the same candour. I have often heard you express your sentiments respecting this unfortunate war, when you thought the Americans injured; but am now astonished to find you taking an active part against them; though not fighting particularly on the continent, yet seducing their soldiers away, to enlist in the British service, is nearly similar.

"My Lord, you are pleased to compliment me with having fought bravely in my country's cause for many years, and in your opinion, fulfilled the duty every individual owes to it. I differ very widely with you, in thinking that I have discharged my duty to my country, while it is still deluged in blood, and overrun with British troops, who exercise the most savage cruelties. When I entered into this contest, I did it with the most mature deliberation, and with a determined resolution, to risk my life and fortune in the cause. The hardships I have gone through, I look back upon with the greatest pleasure and honour to myself. I shall continue to go on as I have begun, that my example may encourage the youths of America to stand forth in defence of their rights and liberties. You call upon me now, and tell me I have a fair opening of quitting that service with honour and reputation to myself, by going with you to Jamaica. Good God! is it possible that such an idea could arise in the breast of a man of honour. I am sorry you should imagine, I have so little regard for my own reputation, as to listen to such dishonourable proposals; would you wish to have the man whom you have honoured with your friendship play the traitor? Surely not. You say by quitting this country for a short time, I might avoid disagreeable conversations, and might return at my own leisure, to take possession of my estates for myself and family; but you have forgot to tell me how I am to get rid of the feelings of an injured honest heart, and where to hide myself from myself; could I be guilty of so much baseness, I should hate myself and shun mankind. This would be a fatal exchange from my present situation, with an easy and approved conscience of having done my duty and conducted myself as a man of honour. My Lord, I am sorry to observe, that I feel your friendship much abated, or you would not endeavour to prevail upon me to act so base a part. You earnestly wish you could bring it about, as you think it will be the means of bringing about that reconciliation that we all wish for. I wish for a reconciliation as much as any man, but only upon honourable terms. The repossessing of my estates; the offer of the command of your regiment, and the honour you propose of serving under me, are paltry considerations to the loss of my reputation; no, not the fee simple of that valuable Island of Jamaica, should induce me to part with my integrity. My Lord, as you have made one proposal, give me leave to make another, which will be more honourable to us both; as you have an interest with your commanders, I would have you purpose the withdrawing the British troops from the continent of America, allow the independence, and propose a peace. This being done, I will use my interest with my commanders to accept of the terms, and allow Great Britain a free trade with America. My Lord, I would make one proposal,* but my situation as a prisoner, circumscribes me within certain bounds, I must therefore conclude, with allowing you the free liberty to make what use of this you think proper. Think better of me. I am my Lord, your Lordship's most obedient humble servant,

WM. MOULTRIE."

* "Which was to advise him to come over to the Americans; this proposal I could not make when on parole."—*Moultrie's Revolution.*

The publication of this note has greatly mortified me. I had always believed that nothing but the restriction imposed by his parole, had prevented General Moultrie from making an appeal to the sword to convince Lord C. MONTAGUE, how keenly he felt the insult of his degrading offer.

LIEUT. COL. ISAAC MOTTE.

MOULTRIE, on the 28th of June, was nobly supported by his companions in arms. Lieut. Col. Motte, the second in command, educated as a soldier, had served with distinction in Canada, in the war of 1756, and in the engagement with Sir Peter Parker, gave a spirited demonstration of what might have been expected from his subsequent exertions. His influence and abilities, were considered by the enemy, of the highest importance, and bribes, such as might have tempted any other than an inflexible patriot, were offered to induce him to join the standard which he had often with gallantry supported. But having embraced and sworn devotion to the cause of America, they were indignantly rejected, and to the last, his enthusiasm received the most unlimited applause. It is much to be lamented, that so meritorious an officer should at an early period of the war have quitted a service to which he did great honour. But, with the public weal continually in view, we find him in the civil department of government an active agent, and so much to the increase of his reputation, that on the establishment of the Federal Union, he was immediately appointed by President Washington, to a post of trust and emolument, which he enjoyed to the end of his days.

GENERAL MARION.

Among the companions of Moultrie, there was none who, at a future day, attained as much celebrity as Francis Marion. To an officer of so ardent and honourable feeling, the accident* which prevented his acting with his gallant associates of the Second Regiment in defence of the capital, must have proved peculiarly afflicting. He had shared with them, the toils and dangers of battle, and fully partaken of their well earned fame. To be separated, therefore, at a moment when new difficulties presented themselves, and a threatening cloud overshadowed the destinies of a community, whose hopes of security, rested on their exertions, and those of their companions in arms, must necessarily have excited his deepest regrets. Yet, great as the affliction must have been to individual feeling, it cannot be otherwise considered, than as the event that more than any other, gave ultimate security, happiness, and independency, to his country. I never undertook an essay, with so little hope of executing it with satisfaction to myself, and justice to the hero, whose actions I would celebrate, as in attempting to delineate the character and chivalric gallantry of General Marion.

Fortunately neither the pure exalted traits of his patriotism, nor the brilliant achievements of his sword, need the aid of embellishment. His virtues speak directly to the heart. His victories are emblazoned in their momentous consequences to

---

* Lieut. Col. Marion had dined a few days previously to the siege of Charleston, with a friend residing in the house next to Roupell's, in Tradd-street, and to the east of it. A mistaken idea of hospitality had occasioned his entertainer, according to the universal practice of the day, to turn the key upon his guests, to prevent escape, till each individual should be gorged to a surfeit with wine. Marion, attempting to make his escape by a window, fell into the street and dislocated his ancle in a shocking manner. The accident saved him from captivity. Non-effectives were ordered to retire from the city. His freedom gave safety to his country. From his active spirit arose that determined opposition to the British power, that blasted their fondly cherished expectation of supremacy, and ultimately caused their expulsion from the state.

his country. What greater praise can be bestowed on his character, than to say,—and where is there a man that will deny its justice,—that to the most exalted sentiments, he united the most charming simplicity of manners; and, to the courage of a soldier, an inexhaustible fund of humanity. Of his pre-eminent ability as a partizan officer, successfully opposing an active and enterprising enemy, with an inferiority of force that is scarcely credible—there can exist no doubt. He entered the field without men—without resources of any kind, and at a period, when a great proportion of the inhabitants of the district in which he commanded, either from a conviction of the inutility of resistance, or the goadings of unceasing persecution, had made their submission to the enemy. To concealment, he was indebted for security—and stratagem supplied the place of force. Yet always on the alert—striking where least expected—retiring when no advantage could be hoped for by exposure, he progressively advanced in the career of success, till a superiority was obtained that put down all opposition. Far more disposed essentially to benefit his country, than to give, by brilliant enterprize, increase to his own military reputation, his first care was the preservation of the troops whom he commanded, by studiously avoiding an unnecessary hazard of their lives. It was this prudential conduct, that so frequently occasioned a temporary retirement into fastnesses, where pursuit was rarely ventured on, and if persisted in, invariably attended with discomfiture and disgrace.—But, did occasion invite to victory—did carelessness in command, or the idea of security arising from distance put the enemy, though but for an instant, off their guard,—the rapidity of his movements, the impetuosity of his attacks never failed to render the blow inflicted decisive, and their destruction complete. Victory afforded additional claim to applause. Giving the rein to the most intrepid gallantry, and in battle exhibiting all the fire and impetuosity of youth, there never was an enemy who yielded to his valour, who had not cause to admire and eulogize his subsequent humanity. The strictness of the discipline invariably maintained, prevented every species of irregularity among his troops. His soul, was his country's—his pride, the rigid observance of her laws. His ambition, to defend her rights, and preserve immaculate her honour and her fame. "It would have been as easy to turn the Sun from his course, as Marion from the paths of honour." A memorable instance of his attachment to an honest fame, is thus recorded in an Oration, delivered on the 4th of July, 1797, before the Revolution and Cincinnati Societies.*

"A motion being made in the Legislature, immediately subsequent to the war, to exempt from investigation the conduct of the partizan corps of militia, who from the nature of the service in which they had been engaged, were supposed necessarily to have committed irregularities, the venerable Marion, the flush of virtuous indignation overspreading his countenance, nobly demanded that his name should be expunged from the bill. "For if," said he " in the course of command, I have in a single instance departed from the strict line of propriety, or given the slightest cause of complaint to any individual whatever, justice requires, that I should suffer for it."

Of his military prowess, innumerable instances crowd upon my memory. But, before I attempt to detail them, I would gladly speak of his uniform forbearance, tenderness, and attention to the unfortunates who had in the unguarded moments of despondency, swerved from the strict line of duty—and appeared to have forgotten the devotion pledged to their country. He was never heard to upbraid them. He sought not by the exercise of implacable resentment to drive them to desperation. He knew the frailty of human nature, and made proper allowances for it. He was sensible that many an individual, to save his family from the impending encroachments of absolute want —to protect them under the ravages of disease, likely to rob him of the children of his affection, the wife of his bosom, his friends, his fortune—had reluctantly given his promise of submission, while every sentiment of his heart, every wish that it cherished, was in unison and coincided with the patriotic principles of his country. He blamed their errors, but attempted not to correct them by coercion. The impolicy of the enemy he justly counted upon as a powerful auxiliary, and making

* By the Author.

mercy and gentleness the guides of his conduct, by the suavity and conciliation of his manners, not only reconciled them to themselves, and revived the hopes of a pardon despaired of, but added greater increase to the strength of the armies of his country than could have been obtained by the most decisive victory. The simplicity of conduct, preserved under all circumstances was above praise; the cheerfulness with which he endured privations, surpassed encomium. An anecdote is related of him, of the authenticity of which, many of his followers can still give testimony. I name one of them, Lieut. J. H. Stevens, of Mayham's regiment, who was an eye-witness of the occurrence.

A British officer was sent from the garrison at Georgetown, to negotiate a business interesting to both armies; when this was concluded, and the officer about to return, the General said, "If it suits your convenience, Sir, to remain for a short period, I shall be glad of your company to dinner." The mild and dignified simplicity of Marion's manners, had already produced their effect; and, to prolong so interesting an interview, the invitation was accepted. The entertainment was served up on pieces of bark, and consisted entirely of roasted potatoes, of which the General eat heartily, requesting his guest to profit by his example, repeating the old adage, that "hunger was an excellent sauce." "But surely General," said the officer, "this cannot be your ordinary fare." "Indeed it is, Sir," he replied, "and we are fortunate on this occasion, *entertaining company*, to have more than our usual allowance."

It is said, that on his return to Georgetown, this officer immediately declared his conviction, that men who could without a murmur endure the difficulties and dangers of the field, and contentedly relish such simple and scanty fare, were not to be subdued; and, resigning his commission, immediately retired from the service.

To the honour of his humanity, it may be further added, that he never suffered insult to aggravate the misfortunes of the families of the Tories steadily adhering to the British cause; but, on the contrary, assuaged their sufferings, and used every effort to reclaim the deluded enthusiasts, by whom they were abandoned. By such conduct, a number of inveterate enemies were converted into useful citizens, and many a hardy soldier given to the republic, whose services had otherwise been irretrievably lost. Independent of the glory obtained in partizan warfare, General Marion acquired great increase of reputation by the assistance bestowed and judicious conduct exhibited, in conducting the sieges of the captured posts held by the enemy. At Georgetown, Fort Watson, Fort Motte and Granby, his activity was rewarded by the most flattering encomiums of his commander. The blow inflicted on the cavalry of the enemy, drawn into an ambuscade near Parker's Ferry, so effectually checked their spirit of marauding, that in that vicinity they were never known to appear again. His gallantry at Eutaw, gave increase to his fame, and there exists not a doubt, but that naught but that their rapid retirement to the vicinity of Charleston, saved their entire army from captivity. When such a succession of military achievement, such a display of exalted virtue, was daily shown, it is not necessary to bestow the homage of higher admiration. One fact however cannot be forgotten, and is truly worthy of record. With the end of the war, the political animosities of General Marion expired. His magnanimity spurned the thought of adding to the miseries of men who were no longer in a situation to do injury, and whose punishment compelled to forego the delights of cherished home, to wander exiles in a foreign land, was fully proportioned to the extent of their offences. While, therefore, to the retiring refugees, the supplies were uniformly denied, which could contribute to the comfort of their families, General Marion, through the interposition of their friends, generously permitted every comfort and necessary refreshment to be conveyed to them, and the blessings of the afflicted rested on him.

Of the conduct and character of so good and great a man as General Marion, some further details will not, I trust, prove unacceptable.*

The friends of loyalty, adherents to the British armies, closely united, and possessing unbounded influence betwixt the

* They were furnished me by the venerable patriot, Mr. KEATING SIMONS, who acted as his Brigade Major, and whose word is a sufficient testimony of their correctness and authenticity.

two Pedee rivers, were always on the alert and caused so much annoyance, that the Whig inhabitants in their vicinity, who would otherwise have been actively employed against the enemy, were compelled to remain at home, to check their depredations, and give security and protection to their families. To paralyze their activity, which was a perpetual source of anxiety, more especially as their numbers were three times as great as those of his own troops, General Marion with judicious policy, entered into a truce for a year, by which it was stipulated, that neither party should use aggression towards the other, nor pass certain limits which were distinctly marked. Freed from the apprehension of immediate hostility, he now hoped to be enabled, to essentially aid the operations of Gen. Greene. But the moment that distance had lulled their fears, the enmities of his opponents were revived, they crossed the bounds prescribed, and became as before both troublesome and dangerous. Petitions were now presented to General Marion, soliciting, that he would march his brigade into the neighbourhood, and at the expiration of the treaty, reduce these disorderly men to submission. These he immediately forwarded to Governor Matthews and General Greene, who approving the measure, furnished him with letters to the Governor of North-Carolina, who was solicited to give every possible aid to his operations. General Marion who had deeply reflected on the object in view, had already formed his plans, and three parties were ready to enter the truce ground, in opposite quarters, with orders to strike with a decision, that should at once crush every thought of future resistance. At his approach these deluded people, who were well acquainted with his firmness, and fully apprized of his humanity, became panic struck, and though thrice his number, flocked in crowds to his camp, tendering submission, and demanding *written protections*. The consumption of paper on the occasion was so great, every individual claiming a certificate of pardon, that the supply at head-quarters and that of every individual in camp, was exhausted, and even the parts of letters not written on, were put in requisition to indulge their wishes. The period of the truce being nearly expired, the brigade was halted at Burch's Mills, on the Pedee. It was at that spot that a Captain Butler, who headed a marauding party under a British commission, surrendered himself on the terms held out to the disaffected, by a recent proclamation of Governor Matthews. A more sanguinary being did not exist. He had cruelly oppressed the Whig inhabitants; and but a little before, murdered some of the Americans, whose friends were then in camp. Irritated to madness, and to a disregard of all sense of duty, at the thought, that such a man, was, by submission, to escape the just reward of his crimes, a hasty and intemperate message was sent to the General, purporting, that such a villain as Butler should not receive protection. To this insulting communication, General Marion calmly replied:—"Confidently believing, that the pardon offered by Governor Matthews, would be granted, the man whom you would destroy, has submitted. Both law and honour sanction my resolution. I will take him to my tent, and at the hazard of my life, protect him." A second message now informed him, that Butler should be dragged from his tent and put to death—since it was an insult to humanity, that such a wretch should be defended. The honourable feeling of Marion was now exalted to the highest pitch, and calling the gentlemen of his family together, he exclaimed:—"Is there a man among you, who will refuse his aid, in defending the laws of his country? I know you too well to suppose it! Prepare, then, to give me your assistance; for, though I consider the villainy of Butler unparalleled, yet, as an officer acting under orders, I am bound to defend him; and I will do so, though I perish." He then collected a guard around the tent, into which he had introduced him, and at an early hour after night-fall, had him conveyed to a place of security.

Major Ganey, who commanded the British adherents within the truce ground, thought it now high time to negotiate; and having sent in propositions for that purpose to General Marion, commissioners were appointed to form a treaty. Unhappily, some allusions in conversation, to the escapes which one party had made in conflicts from the other, excited all the irritation of deadly animosity, and they separated with unabated resentments. Marion was grievously mortified by the failure of his commissioners; and feeling great anxiety to move to the lower country, the better to protect the families and property of those who had joined him, now left at the mercy of the British, determined to meet Ganey personally. Appointing, therefore, the gentlemen of his family as commissioners, to aid him in negotiation, Ganey was invited, with such of his associates as he chose to name on his part, to cross the river, under the sacred pledge of protection, and a treaty was speedily perfected, that put a final termination to all opposition in the interior. The basis of this treaty was, that all who wished to join the British standard, were to receive safe conduct for person and property, till arrived within their lines. That all who wished to be reconciled to their country, were to obtain pardon for past offences, and be received as citizens; and that persons found within the limits of the truce ground, after an appointed day, without having submitted themselves, were to be regarded as enemies. Ganey removed with those who preferred adhesion to the British; but, before his departure, said to General Marion—"Honour requires that I should surrender my commission to Colonel Balfour, from whom I received it. But, having done so, I shall immediately return to the country, and seek your protection." He strictly performed his promise; and it is remarkable, that at Watboo, placed in the ranks with about forty of his men, at the very point on which the British cavalry made their principal attack, greatly contributed to their discomfiture and repulse. Several of General Marion's principal officers were impressed with the opinion, that he had committed his dignity, in personally treating with Ganey, whom they regarded in no better light, than a leader of banditti; but he silenced their censures, by asserting—"That the only dignity he aspired to, was that of essentially serving his country."

About this period the celebrated marauder, Fanning, of North Carolina, arrived in the truce ground. He was a most determined enemy; resolute and sanguinary, and possessed such distinguished talents for partisan warfare, that much apprehension was entertained, that he would again stir up the spirit of revolt, and induce Ganey to break his engagements.

But an end was speedily put to suspense. A flag arriving from him, with a request, that General Marion would grant safe conduct to his wife, and some property, to the British garrison, in Charleston. Compliance was the immediate consequence. Most of the officers believed it bad policy, but the General justified his conduct, by saying: "Let but his wife and property reach the British lines, and Fanning will not fail to follow them; but force them to remain—deny the flag required, and we fix a serpent in our bosoms." Fanning finding no hope of exciting insurrection, fled the country, and was nearly as soon as his wife within the garrison. The General, moving into the truce ground, now busied himself in securing the persons of every individual, who, declining to retire within the British lines, still refused submission to American authority. In the execution of this duty, a hint was given to the General, that irregularities had been indulged that were highly disgraceful to the military character, which occasioned him, with his usual frankness, to declare, at table, "I have heard insinuations of conduct exercised, that would disgrace my command; no regular accusation has been made; but I wish it to be clearly understood, that let officer or soldier be proved guilty of crime, and he shall hang on the next tree." His inflexible firmness was known, and not a whisper was ever breathed of further irregularities. The brigade was soon after marched to Watboo; and after having beaten a party of horse, sent from Charleston for the purpose of surprising it, remained there till the evacuation of Charleston. While the British were preparing for embarkation, a party were sent to Lamprier's Point to procure water. A hint was given to Marion that this would afford a fair opportunity of inflicting a parting blow; to which he replied—"My brigade is composed of citizens, enough of whose blood has already been shed; if ordered to attack the enemy, I shall obey; but not another drop shall, with my consent, be lost, though it should procure me the greatest honours that, as a soldier, I could aspire to. Certain, as I am, that the enemy are at the point of departure, so far from offering to molest, I would rather send a party to protect them." Had such been the humane policy of Kosciusko, many valuable lives would have been spared, and Wilmott and Moore might, at this day, have lived to add new honours to the annals of their country. Next to Henry Lee, perhaps altogether his equal, no man could be more expert than General Marion, in obtaining information of every movement of the enemy, and anticipating the events that might be expected from their activity and enterprize. He was, when necessary, secret as the grave; appeared, generally, thoughtful, and was approached by his officers with reverential awe; but when out of reach of the enemy, and at liberty to give indulgence to the natural cheerfulness of his disposition, he was familiar with his intimates, and the gentlemen of his family, even to playfulness. In private life he was distinguished by the strictest integrity in all his dealings. He was the executor of several estates, and guardian of many children. Every duty was performed to perfection. No man lived more beloved—none ever died more universally and justly lamented. I shall close my eulogy with one anecdote, which I consider highly characteristic of his unerring virtue. A friend, to whom he was attached by the warmest affection, who had shared all his dangers, had transgressed the law by refusing to submit to the regular process of justice, hoping, by the interposition of friends, and his high reputation, to escape censure. "Deliver yourself," said Marion, "into the hands of the sheriff; submit to be conducted to gaol, and my hand and heart are yours. Refuse to do so, and trust, by the influence of friendship, to elude justice, and the line of seperation is for ever drawn betwixt us."

AMONG the companions of Moultrie, I will mention two other individuals, who afterwards were associated in arms with Marion, and, therefore, properly noticed in this place.

COLONEL PETER HORRY.

THIS officer was a descendant of one of the many Protestant families who removed to Carolina from France, after the revocation of the edict of Nantez. He early took up arms in defence of his country; and through all the trials of peril and privation, experienced by Marion's brigade, gave ample proof of his strict integrity and undaunted courage. The fame which he acquired, as one of the band of heroes who defended the post at Sullivan's Island, was never tarnished. For, although in a moment of despondency he once said to his General—" I fear our happy days are all gone by;" it was not the consequences that might accrue to himself, but the miseries apprehended for his country, that caused the exclamation; for never were his principles shaken; never, even for a moment, did the thought of submission enter his bosom. No man more eagerly sought the foe; none braved danger with greater intrepidity, or more strenuously endeavoured to sustain the military reputation of his country. A ludicrous story is told of him, that, though probably varied in the narration, has its foundation in truth. Colonel Horry was once ordered to wait the approach of a British detachment in ambuscade; a service he performed with such skill, that he had them completely within his power; when, from a dreadful impediment in his speech, by which he was afflicted, he could not articulate the word—"*fire.*" In vain he made the attempt—it was, *fi, fi, fi, fi*—but he could get no further. At length, irritated almost to madness, he exclaimed—" *Shoot,* damn you—*shoot*—you know very well what I would say—*shoot, shoot,* and be damn'd to you!" He was present in every engagement of consequence, and on all occasions increased his reputation. At Quinby, Colonel Baxter, a gallant soldier, possessed of great coolness, and still greater simplicity of character, calling out, " I am wounded, colonel!" Horry replied—" Think no more of it, Baxter, but stand to your post." " But, I can't stand, colonel—I am wounded a second time!" " Then lie down, Baxter, but quit not your post." " Colonel," (cried the wounded man) " they have shot me again, and if I remain any longer here, I shall be shot to pieces." " Be it so, Baxter, but stir not." He obeyed the order, and actually received a fourth wound before the engagement ended.

COLONEL MAYHAM.

If Colonel Mayham had never rendered any other service in the field, than the judicious invention of the tower, to facilitate the reduction of the posts held by the British, and afterwards distinguished by his name, he would, as a soldier, have been entitled to distinction. But, the fact is, that in no situation did he ever fail to increase his military fame. Expert in stratagem, he was equally alert in enterprize; and in hardy daring, second to no officer in the service. By the construction of his tower, the British post at Wright's Bluff, which, from its elevated situation, and the want of cannon, had been deemed impregnable, was so completely overtopped, and the American riflemen thereby enabled to fire with such deadly effect, that the besieged dared not show themselves, and were compelled to capitulate and make an immediate surrender. Lee saw the advantage accruing from it, and by a similar construction, obtained a superiority over Browne at Augusta, whose activity and resolution, had baffled ever previous attempt to injure him. Distinguished throughout the whole of Marion's campaigns, by his zeal and activity, it was the good fortune of Colonel Mayham, to close his military career by a partisan stroke, greatly to the discomfiture of the enemy, attacking, with invincible impetuosity, a detachment at Monk's Corner, within view of their main army, and carrying off eighty prisoners, without the smallest loss.

PARTISAN COMMANDERS OF MILITIA.

GENERAL SUMTER.

In relating the military acquirements of Sumter, I should feelingly lament the disasters attending his early career, had he not, like Antaeus, gathered strength from misfortune, and arose after every fall, with renovated powers of action. In the school of adversity, he learnt circumspection and was more than once, compelled to fight under the greatest disadvantages. He became, ultimately, so guarded in his attention to the security of his camp, and so happy in choice of his positions, that every attempt to injure him, on the part of the enemy, proved abortive, whilst the enterprizes which he conducted, were, for the most part, productive of the most brilliant success. No man was more indefatigable in his efforts to obtain victory; none more ready, by the generous exposure of his person, and the animating example of intrepidity, to deserve it. His attacks were impetuous, and generally irresistible. He was far less inclined to plan, than to execute; and on many occasions, by an approach to rashness, accomplished what prudence would have forbidden him to attempt. It was his supreme good fortune, to give the first check to the British successes in South Carolina after the fall of Charleston, by completely routing on the 12th of July, 1780, at Williams' plantation, a marauding detachment of their army, commanded by Captain Huck, a miscreant who, by his cruelty and profanity, appeared equally, the enemy of God and man. During his predatory excursions, he had perpetrated every species of barbarity, and excited the resentments of the inhabitants, still more by his words, than by his actions. With him, the exclamation was common—"God

Almighty has turned rebel; but, had the Americans *twenty Gods*, instead of *one* on their side, they should *all* be conquered."

General Sumter's attacks upon the posts of Rocky Mount and Hanging Rock, where, in the first instance, he was completely successful, did him great credit; and could he have restrained the insubordination characteristic of irregular troops, and destroyed their avidity for plunder and liquor, in both instances, his victory must have been complete. He, shortly after, captured a convoy of stores passing from Ninety-Six to Camden; but, most unfortunately, encamping within striking distance of the enemy, (now at liberty, by the complete defeat of Gates, to send forth large detachments,) he was attacked by Tarleton, when unprepared for resistance, and routed, with the loss of many men, and all the prisoners and valuable stores that had recently fallen into his hands. He was next attacked near Broad River by Wemyss, who, calculating on his former inattention to the security of his camp, hoped to surprise him. In his expectations, however, he was severely disappointed; his troops were repulsed, and himself wounded and taken. It has often been said, and universally believed, that in a pocket-book found on him, was not only an accurate list of the houses he *had* burnt, but of those also that he *intended to destroy*. Lord Cornwallis, writing immediately after this to Colonel Tarleton, to give energy to pursuit, says—"I shall be glad to hear that *Sumter* is in no condition to give us further trouble —he certainly has been our *greatest plague* in this country."

From a man of Lord Cornwallis' enterprize, such praise was the highest encomium. Tarleton now rapidly advanced, anxious to strike a blow that would annihilate him, before he could cross the Tiger River; and, stimulated by the impetuosity of his temper, attacked his strong position on Blackstock-Hill, with such imprudence, that, after severe loss, both of officers and men, he was compelled to quit the field, leaving his wounded to the mercy of his conqueror. To the credit of Sumter, his attention and humanity to them, has always been acknowledged. To the misfortune of Carolina, a severe wound received in the action, put a stop, for a considerable time, to his brilliant career; but, he was no sooner able to take the field, than he again appeared as an active partizan, breaking up the British posts in the lower country. On one occasion, Lieutenant Colonel Hampton, commanding under him, dispersed a large body of Tories near Dorchester. Placed at the head of the light troops, both regulars and militia, Sumter next compelled Lieutenant Colonel Coats to destroy his stores at Monk's Corner, and abandon the position, and would have made the entire 19th regiment, commanded by him, prisoners, had he not by the rapidity of his flight, passed the bridge at Quinby, and by throwing off the plank, prevented pursuit, till he had established himself in a strong position, from which, the want of artillery rendered it impossible to dislodge him. Important services were again performed by him at Eutaw. After which, the enemy retiring within their lines, seldom ventured beyond the gates of Charleston.

GENERAL PICKENS.

A truer patriot, nor more intrepid soldier than General Pickens, never trod the soil of liberty; and there are few characters of our Revolution to whom Carolina is more highly indebted. At the commencement of the war, great diversity of opinion existed among the inhabitants of the interior country, not only with regard to the practicability, but propriety also, of resisting the power of Britain. Attachment to former prejudices, and a belief of the perfection of the ancient system, were strong; and the spirit of opposition, encouraged by the new government, regarded if not unjustifiable, at least, rash and inconsiderate, and leading to consequences the most disastrous to the peace and happiness of the community. The exertions of Colonel Pickens, to counteract those fallacious principles, and to induce the inhabitants of his district to adopt opinions similar to those which animated the bosoms of every true friend to his country, were indefatigable. He was constantly on the alert; vigilance, indeed, became indispensable; for, although the Tories would oftentimes show a disposition to temporize, yet it was evident from their murmurings, and secret caballing, that they only waited a favourable opportunity to declare their sentiments, and to engage in open and decided hostility. No sooner therefore, did the British appear in force in the South, than their smothered resentments burst into flame. Several hundreds of them embodied, and committing every species of depredation on their route, marched forward to join the royal army in Georgia. Colonel Pickens, apprized of their movements, and irritated by their rapacity, pursued them with rapid steps, and overtaking them at Kettle Creek, attacked them so vigorously, that in less than an hour, forty of their number, and among them their leader, Boyd, were killed, and the rest so completely dispersed, as to leave no apprehension of any further trouble.

When Charleston fell, and the victorious Britons spreading themselves over the country, advanced into the interior, the revived resentments of the royalists, compelled Colonel Pickens, and the steady adherents of the cause of freedom, to abandon their habitations and country, and seek for refuge in North-Carolina. So soon, however, as General Greene had taken command of the army, and ordered General Morgan to enter the western division of the state, to check the aggressions of the enemy, and to revive the drooping spirits of the Whig inhabitants, Colonel Pickens was found the most active among his associates, seconding his enterprizes, and by gentleness and conciliation, attaching new adherents to the cause. Of his intrepid conduct at the battle of the Cowpens, it is scarcely necessary to speak. It is a well known fact, that he not only prevailed upon his riflemen to retain their fire till it could be given with deadly effect, but when broken and compelled to retreat, that he rallied them; and what had never before been effected *with militia*, brought them a *second time* to meet their enemy, and by continued exertion, to accomplish their final surrender.

Ordered by General Greene, after his retreat into Virginia, to recross the Dan, and in conjunction with Lee, to check the spirit of revolt which had manifested itself in many parts of North-Carolina, he aided, effectually, the infliction of that salutary punishment which rendered abortive every future effort of Lord Cornwallis to bring recruits to the royal standard.

When the British were subsequently compelled to retreat to Wilmington, and General Greene resolved to return to South-Carolina, Pickens, now a Brigadier, was directed to precede him, and to collect the militia of his brigade, and particularly to prevent supplies from being thrown into the garrisons of Ninety-Six, and Augusta. This service was effectually performed, and being joined by Lee, the combined force sat down before Augusta. Greater skill in defence, nor more intrepid resistance, was never shown than by Colonel Browne, which cannot but enhance the glory of the commanders who compelled him to surrender. At the Battle of Eutaw, where he was wounded, he acquired additional glory; and finally, completed his military achievements, by conducting an expedition in 1782, against the Cherokee nation with such decided effect, that with the utmost humility, they solicited peace, and promised never again to rise in opposition to our government.

GENERAL DAVIE.

At the commencement of the Revolutionary War, General Davie was a student at Princeton College, and feeling a strong desire to encounter the dangers of the field, marched as sergeant of a company of his associates, who had embodied themselves contrary to the wishes of their tutors, to join a detachment of the army stationed at Elizabethtown. How long these patriotic enthusiasts remained together is uncertain; but becoming disgusted more with the fatigues than the dangers of service, they justified the prognostic of Dr. Witherspoon, and gradually returned to their studies. When they first left the college the faculty spoke of expulsion, and other punishments, as the merited reward of disobedience. Dr. Witherspoon simply said,—"Let them alone; opposition to their purposes will only increase their desire to adhere to them; exposure to the fatigues of service will effect all that you desire; it will not be long before we have them all back again." Young Davie, and one other student named Brown, remained with the army. His taste for a military life was now confirmed; and we find him at the battle of Stono, as Brigade Major of cavalry, covering the retreat of Lincoln's army, and immediately afterwards an inmate of the hospital, severely wounded. He has often mentioned to a friend, an occurrence that plainly shows, how deplorable the situation of the continental army must have been with respect to the essential comforts which were never wanting to the British. Thrown into a stupor by the loss of blood, and the agony of his wound, the poor young soldier, on the recovery of his senses, found that his shirt had been stripped from his back to make bandages for the wounded who surrounded him, and having no change to replace it, acknowledged that, for a time, he felt all the pains of the most perfect despondency. At the period of Gates' defeat his zeal and activity had advanced him to the command of a legionary corps of militia. He was on detachment at the moment of defeat, but hastening forward as soon as he was informed of it, he was essentially serviceable, not only in preventing pursuit, but in recapturing several waggons, one of which, most fortunately, contained the hospital medicine chest. Convinced that the enemy would anxiously seek and strike at Sumter, he, with laudable zeal, immediately despatched a confidential soldier with intelligence of the disaster, and then reluctantly retired. He had previously, under the command of Sumter, fought both at Hanging Rock and Rocky Mount. At the first he cut off three companies of Bryan's regiment, took sixty horses and one hundred rifles and muskets; at the last, by a well directed charge, made great havoc among the loyalists, and had not some liquor, found in the enemy's camp, been *too attractive*, would have enjoyed a complete victory; but intoxication destroyed subordination, and every advantage was lost. After the battle of Camden his force, consisting of about two hundred men, was actively employed repelling predatory excursions, in harassing the enemy, and cutting off their supplies. Provisions were scarce in the British camp, and Lord Cornwallis was compelled to send out large detachments to procure them. One of these, stationed at Wahab's plantation, was struck at by Davie, and with complete success. Sixty of the enemy were left on the ground; ninety-six horses, with their equipments, and one hundred and twenty stand of arms, were taken, with the loss of but one man. Being now closely pressed, he retired to Charlotte, and joined by Major Grahame, made a stand that entitles him to the most exalted praise. Twice he repulsed the British legion, with considerable slaughter, and it was not till his flank was gained, and a third charge made under the influence of an animating address by Lord Cornwallis himself, that he relinquished his post, retiring without loss to Salisbury. General Davie was not only distinguished as an intelligent, but as an intrepid soldier. His delight was to lead a charge; and possessing great bodily strength, united with uncommon activity, is said to have overcome more men, in personal conflict, than any individual in the service. His knowledge of the country, and of its resources, induced General Greene, when pressed by the greatest difficulties, to intrust him with the charge of the quarter-master general's department. He afterwards employed him as a negotiator with the legislature of North-Carolina for supplies of men, the more effectually to resist the enemy, whose strength had increased by the arrival of three regiments from Ireland. In both these capacities he acquitted himself with consummate ability, and to the entire satisfaction of his General.

I do not think that I could find a better opportunity, than in this place, to point out the advantages of discipline. It may be remembered, that at the battle of Guildford, two North Carolina battallions of militia, advantageously posted behind a rail fence, were assured by General Greene, that if they would only preserve their station long enough to give their enemy two fires, they should obtain his free permission to retire from the field. They readily promised obedience, but the formidable whiskered Hessians, and athletic Guards, advancing with rapid motion, their courage forsook them, and they retired without firing a shot. As a punishment for their scandalous misconduct, they were, in compliance with the requisition made by General Greene, through the medium of Davie, placed under continental officers, and sentenced to serve for eighteen month in the ranks. The regularity of discipline soon taught them self-confidence; they actually panted for renown, and behaved with such gallantry at Eutaw, that of three hundred of their number that entered into the action, one hundred and ninety remained, at its conclusion, either killed or wounded on the field.

I had written this short sketch of the character and achievement of General Davie, when a packet was delivered to me from a friend in the interior country, above all other men qualified, from strict intimacy and just admiration of his talents and virtues, to furnish me with the information respecting him, that I required. To my readers I am confident I cannot offer too many particulars relative to a patriot who lived so much beloved—who died so universally lamented. And it would be an injustice to the friend, to whose communication I feel myself in the highest degree indebted, to make the communication in any other than his own words.

"At the bar, Colonel Davie soon rose to great eminence; and indeed, in a few years, became one of its principal leaders and ornaments. He was possessed of great sagacity, profound knowledge, and masculine eloquence. His manners were conciliatory, but imposing and even commanding. The late Alfred Moore, who was afterwards one of the Judges of the Supreme Court of the United States, and who was a very able lawyer, as well as an excellent man, was the intimate friend of Colonel Davie, and his rival, in their honourable career at the bar. Their practice and their labours were immense, and both made independent fortunes.

"Colonel Davie was appointed by the Legislature of North Carolina, to represent that respectable State in the Convention, called at Philadelphia, in the year 1787, to deliberate on the national embarrassments, and to form a national government, in order to correct the evils of a very loose confederation, and of a miserably weak and inefficient government.

"Being, at that time, a young man, he did not take a prominent part in the discussion which resulted in the formation of that constitution, which has been so severely tested, and found to be so admirably adapted to the government of our country. But, he there learnt the true foundations on which the government was laid, and the solid arguments in support of it.

"His name does not appear to that great instrument; the illness of his family having called him home before the labours of the Convention were concluded. But, when the constitution was submitted to the judgment of the State Convention in North Carolina, for adoption, he stood forth its most able champion, and its most ardent supporter.

"The University of North Carolina, is mainly indebted to his exertions, and to his labours, for its establishment, and for the assignment of permanent landed property for its support. Colonel Davie was extremely anxious upon this subject, and exerted the utmost powers of his persuasive and commanding eloquence, to ensure success. He was deeply sensible of the extreme importance of extending, as widely as possible, the advantages of liberal education, that there might be a perpetual succession of enlightened and liberal men, qualified to administer the affairs of this great and increasing people with wisdom and dignity. He considered the public liberty insecure, and liable to be disturbed by perpetual factions, unless education be widely diffused.

"Colonel Davie was now appointed a Major General in the militia of North Carolina; and some time after, in the year 1799, was elected Governor of that State; the duties of which station, he performed with his accustomed firmness and wisdom. He was not, however, permitted to remain long in that station. His country had higher claims on his talents and services.

"The venerable Mr. Adams, then President of the United States, anxious to make one more effort to put an end to the differences which subsisted between this country and France, associated General Davie with Mr. Ellsworth and Mr. Murray, as his Ambassadors in a mission to France, for that purpose. These gentlemen, on their arrival in France, found the tyrannical and corrupt government of the Directory, which had behaved so haughtily to General Pinckney and his colleagues, overturned by Buonaparte; who, though exercising more despotic powers than his predecessors, was, at that time, desirous to conciliate the United States. Commissioners were appointed to discuss the subjects of dispute, and their deliberations ended in a convention, which healed the breach, and saved the United States from being dragged into the vortex of European quarrels.

"General Davie always represented to his friends, Joseph Buonaparte, the ex-king of Naples and of Spain, then a minister in France, (now resident in the United States) as the person who, of all others connected with the French government, behaved most uniformly with liberality, disinterestedness and respect to the American commissioners. That gentleman, accordingly, always stood high in his esteem. Madame de Stael tendered civilities to the Commissioners, which it was deemed expedient to decline, that lady being then in disgrace with Buonaparte.

"It was impossible, for a man of General Davie's profound observation, to be in France, and to witness, for a considerable time, the workings of powerful minds in that agitated country, then just emerging from the most ferocious and bloody despotism of the mob, and tending to a more regular despotism of a single ruler, less bloody, but not less oppressive, without closely examining the state of public feeling, and acquiring an intimate knowledge of many of the principal actors in those eventful scenes. Of the history, character, and political connexions of many of those actors, he condensed the information he had collected, into short sketches, which were afterwards preserved and brought to this country. He saw and deplored, that the French Revolution could not terminate in the establishment of rational liberty and regulated authority; efficient only to all useful purposes, but powerless for all mischief. He saw, that each succeeding faction which acquired the supreme power, exercised it despotically, and with no other view, than to establish its own authority permanently, and without any regard to the rights of the citizen, the legitimate end of all government.

"Upon this subject, his conversation was always deeply interesting; and he endeavoured to impress upon all Americans, but chiefly upon young men of ardent minds, and promising talents, the vast importance of moderation and toleration in republican governments; without which, they can scarcely hope to escape the snares of ambitious demagogues, and the ruin of violent dissensions.

"General Davie contemplated the character of Buonaparte with great attention. He saw him often, and conversed with him freely. He considered him a man of first-rate talents as a warrior, and of great reach as a statesman. But he regarded him also, as a man of unbounded ambition, restrained by no principles human or divine. On one occasion, after an interesting conversation, Buonaparte concluded by saying, that he considered power as the only foundation of right; "*Enfin Monsieur la force est droit.*" General Davie's opinion of him was afterwards verified by his assumption of imperial and despotic power.

"Soon after his return to America General Davie lost his wife, a lady of lofty mind and exemplary virtues, to whom he was greatly attached; and not long after he took the resolution to retire from public life, and to become a farmer on his own fine estate at Tivoli, beautifully situated on the Catawba river, in Chester District, South Carolina. As a farmer he was active and intelligent, and endeavoured to improve the system of agriculture by the use of manures, rotation of crops, and rest to the land. He deplored the slovenly and wasteful system of farming in use throughout the the Southern States, which exhausts the soil without returning any thing to it. On the formation of an Agricultural Society at Columbia, he was appointed the President, and delivered a discourse, which for purity of style, sound observation, and clear exposition of the proper course of agriculture for this country, has never been excelled. It was admired equally by the scholar and the farmer.*

"Some years after General Davie's retreat to his farm, the belligerent governments of France and England, which had each endeavoured to draw our nation into their quarrel as a party, multiplied their aggressions on the commerce of the United States to such an extent, as furnished just cause of war against both; and it was even seriously proposed in Congress to declare war against both. But as that would have been an unwise exposure of the commerce of the country to the rapacity of both nations, it was abandoned; not, however, without strong declarations that the conduct of France and England gave us the right to choose our enemy. That choice was made, and it fell upon Great Britain, equally unjust with France in her conduct to our commerce, and coming more in collision with the personal feelings of American citizens, by her practice of impressing them into her naval service. In the formation of the army necessary for the defence of the country, on this emergency, the government, putting aside party distinctions,

* The address is printed in the 1st volume of the American Farmer, for the year, 1819, pages 217—225.

selected General Davie as one of the officers most fit to be entrusted with a high command. This was flattering to his military pride, and he would have been delighted to have rendered service to his country, in this his favourite profession. For though not entirely satisfied with all the measures of the administration, he felt that, as a citizen, he was bound to defend the country whenever it was in danger, however brought on it. But his increasing infirmities admonished him not to assume duties beyond his strength, which might prejudice the service, instead of promoting it. The wounds received in the Revolutionary War, and the rheumatism which, from long exposure during his service, became fixed on his constitution, rendered him incapable of those active exertions which his high sense of duty would have exacted from him as a commander. He, therefore, declined the honour offered him after a good deal of hesitation. But it is believed that he had several communications with the government upon subjects connected with the organization of the army, as to which his opinion was consulted; and the results of his experience and military knowledge were freely communicated.

"General Davie continued to reside at his beautiful seat, on the banks of the Catawba, to which travellers and visitors were constantly attracted by his open hospitality, his dignified manners, and elevated character. Occasionally he made excursions to the Warm Springs, in Buncombe County, North Carolina, for relief from the harassing rheumatism, which afflicted and wasted him. On those visits he was always greatly admired by the intelligent strangers who visited that place of resort from all the Southern and South-western States. The affability of his deportment gave easy access to all. But no person approached him, however distinguished by his talents or character, who did not speedily feel that he was in the presence of a very superior man. His great and varied information, combined with his profound knowledge of men and things, made him the most interesting of companions. The ignorant and the learned, the weak and the wise, were all instructed and delighted with his conversation, which had an irresistible charm for all. Although no man spoke more plainly his opinions and sentiments on proper occasions, he had the art of never giving offence. For, like the immortal Washington, "he was always covered with the mantle of discretion," a happy expression used by the late Mr. Ralph Izard, formerly a Senator in Congress from this state, and who served six years during President Washington's administration, knew him perfectly, and venerated him next to the Deity.

"At home, and in his own neighbourhood, Gen. Davie was revered with the highest filial piety. He was the friend of the distressed, the safe counsellor of the embarrassed, and the peace maker of all. His own character, free from every spot or stain, gave a power to his interpositions, which was irresistible.

"General Davie had a deep, and even an awful sense of God and his Providence; and was attached to the principles and doctrines of Christianity. But, he had not attached himself, as an avowed member to any particular sect. He thought they generally dogmatized too much, and shut the door of Christian charity too closely. He devised a proper site on his estate for the erection of a place of worship, to be erected by any Christian Society, which should choose to put up a suitable building thereon.

"He was a tall man of fine proportions; his figure erect and commanding; his countenance possessing great expression; and his voice full and energetic. Indeed, his whole appearance struck the beholder at once, as indicating no ordinary man; and the reality exceeded the appearance.

"Such was the man who has been taken from his afflicted family, his friends, and his country. He met death with the firmness of a soldier, and of a man conscious of a life well spent. His memory is cherished by his family and friends, with the most enthusiastic attachment. The good he did survives him; and he has left a noble example to the youth of his country, to encourage and to stimulate them in the honourable career of virtue and of exertion. May it be appreciated and followed."

BARNWELL.

No officer in the service, more resolved from principle, more anxious from patriotic enthusiasm, stepped forward to encounter all the dangers and difficulties of the field, while the freedom of his country was at stake, than General Barnwell.

At the commencement of the war, he commanded a company in the first Continental regiment of South Carolina; but, garrison and camp duty being less congenial to his disposition than partisan enterprize, he speedily quitted the regular, and received promotion in the militia service, as a Major of cavalry.

I have not been able to ascertain with accuracy, the time, or the particulars of an expedition, conducted by him at a very early period of the contest; but confidently assert, that a large and acceptable supply of powder was captured by him, and safely conveyed to the public stores.

At the battle of Port-Royal Island, he commanded, under the orders of General Moultrie, a small body of horse, and by throwing himself, during the engagement, into the rear of the enemy, greatly contributed to their defeat; taking many prisoners, and striking such a panic, that *sauve qui peut* became the general pass-word among the disorderly ranks, and the recovery of their boats the universal aim.

His conduct, during the invasion of Provost, entitles him to the highest honour. In watching the movements of the enemy, procuring intelligence, cutting off stragglers, and detached parties from the army, he was pre-eminently useful.

While Colonel Laurens, with a trifling command, was disputing the pass at Coosawhatchie, against the entire British army, Major Barnwell, having no field for action, remained at the head of the causeway that led to it; but, rendered him essential service, by sending to his aid, two volunteers of his corps. Mr. John Cuthbert, (since, General Cuthbert,) and Charles Freer, (at a subsequent period a Captain in the service) whose activity, in conveying his orders, and fearless exposure of their persons, gave animation to the exertions of a militia force, that had never before encountered an enemy. Soon as Laurens was ordered to retire, Major Barnwell, with alacrity, joined the army under General Moultrie, at Tulafinny-Hill, persuaded that so commanding a situation might insure effectual resistance; or, in the event of discomfiture, cause such a check to be given to the progress of the invaders, as to prevent their nearer approach to the capital. He considered retreat, as pregnant with the most disastrous consequences; and the loss of a battle, far less injurious, than the abandonment of the country. The event justified his opinion; for, by the time that the retiring army had crossed the Saltketcher River, the Southern militia had dispersed almost to a man. The terror excited by the Indians, who wore their war dresses, and wantonly displayed the instruments of torture, with which they were accustomed to agravate the sufferings of their prisoners, created the most appalling dismay. Whigs, of unquestionable patriotism, who would cheerfully have risked their lives in action, and used their utmost energies to have repelled the enemy, soon as retreat was commanded, sought their homes, choosing rather to perish with their families, or shelter them from danger by submission, than leave them exposed to the depredations of a ruffian banditti, led by M'Girth, and of savages, whose cherished object was to plunder, and destroy. It was at this disastrous period that many individuals, surprised in their habitations, and bewildered by their fears, sought and obtained British protections. Fatal, indeed, was their dereliction of duty, since left by the speedy and precipitate retreat of the invading army, to be reproached by their exasperated countrymen, for their weakness, and subjected to penalties very strongly indicating their abhorrence of it.*

---

* I know an instance of a gentleman of exemplary firmness of character, who, being upbraided for a departure from principle, because he had sought his home to share the fate of his family, said: "I would never have quitted the army, had the apprehension been removed from my mind, of the horrors which my wife and children were likely to experience from the ferocity of the savages. As the war advances, the opportunity may

It was then, that Major Barnwell, rising in his place on the floor of the Legislature, moved—"That to obliterate all unpleasant recollections, an act of amnesty for all who had transgressed, should be immediately passed." His proposition met with pointed, and even harsh animadversion ; and Mr. Thomas Ferguson, a distinguished patriot, exclaimed,—"Had you not, Major Barnwell, recently shown by your activity in the field, your perfect devotion to the cause of your country, I should not hesitate to pronounce you a traitor." Similar invective was used by other members ; when, finding conciliatory measures too unpopular to meet success, he turned with composure to his opponents, and said—"The danger which drove the unfortunates, in whose behalf I would plead for mercy, has never been brought to your own doors. Remember, that when it does reach you, that you swerve not from duty, nor forget the opinions you now support. From *you*, gentlemen, I shall, on every future occasion, look for unshaken firmness, and exemplary intrepidity." When, in after times, he found in the list of men soliciting British favour, the names of several who had affected to question his sincerity, it is not to be wondered at, that he gave indulgence to his resentments; and that he never failed, as often as they presented petitions to the Legislature, to have the penalties imposed on their misconduct, remitted, and memory of their political errors forgotten, to oppose them with the expression of the most marked indignation. I have always considered it a misfortune to this country, that his strictness in command, and unremitted efforts to render the militia as submissive to discipline as regular soldiers, rendered him so unpopular in his brigade, when advanced to the command of the Southern Division of the State, as to induce him, rather than give an excuse for non-performance of duty, to retire from active service. It is but too true, that great irregularities had been tolerated, by commanders more disposed to

still be mine, to show my perfect devotion to my country." His conduct at the siege of Charleston was exemplary. He was an inmate of the prison ships, and one of the inflexible patriots, who, preferring death to submission, requested General Greene, without regard to their situation, to avenge the death of Colonel Hayne. The promises and threats of the enemy, were equally held in contempt ; and he remained unshaken in his principles, to the conclusion of the war.

temporize than offend, and that the honour of the country required that they should be effectually checked. The resources of the state, for the maintenance of the army, were wantonly wasted, and the rights of property violated with impunity. A destructive system beyond question; but the curb which he wished to impose on licentiousness, was too suddenly applied, and too imperious. By the failure of the attempt, the service lost an officer of experience, whose courage, often tested in the field, gave invariably increase to his reputation, and the example of steady integrity and perseverence, that, imitated, could only have added to the respectability of the Republican character. But, though stern his resentments, against all who, regardless of their plighted faith to their country, sought favour with the British, and accepted their protection—to such as openly espoused their cause at the commencement of hostilities, he betrayed no symptom of inveteracy; more especially, if from a conviction of error, they expressed a desire to join and support the standard of their country. A very singular occurrence will amply prove this. Two brothers had embraced opposite opinions. The one was a decided Royalist—the other a professed Whig. In the eventful occurrences which attended the progress of the war, the first became a British Commissary, and in the hour of success, pressed six barrels of rice from his brother's plantation; who, yielding to the storm, and convinced that the resources of America were inadequate to effectual resistance, had become a strenuous admirer of kingly government. The successes of Greene, however, very speedily checked his enthusiasm; and taking the benefit of Governor Matthew's tender of pardon, he was again enrolled in the ranks of our armies. The Commissary, who had sufficiently witnessed the irregularities of the British, and frequent desertion of their adherents, about the same period made a confession of error, and was, by General Barnwell, admitted to all the privileges of citizenship. Peace being shortly after restored; the Whig wrote to his brother, reminding him of the impressed rice, and demanding payment for it, concluding with a threat, that in case of refusal, a suit would be immediately instituted for the recovery of the amount. General Barnwell's interposition was instantaneously solicited, to save him from ruin. One suit decided against him, would be the prelude to many; and the Commissary easily perceived, that the force of political prejudice, would prove him, on all occasions, an oppressor. Fortunately, the General had been looking over the papers of Colonel Lechmere, who had been made a prisoner at Pocotaligo, when commanding the district for the British, and found among them, from the professor of chaste principles, a letter to this purport—"I am solicitous, my dear Colonel, to show my zeal as a Loyalist—my devotion to the best of Kings. I am no soldier; but, as a magistrate, would ardently promote the good cause. Put me, I beseech you, on the list of Justices of the Peace, for here, I most solemnly aver, that the extinction of rebellion, and restoration of his Majesty's happy government, is to me, as a resurrection from the dead." "Send your brother a copy of this epistle," said General Barnwell, "and assure him from me, that the commencement of his threatened suit, shall be the signal to give it publicity." It is scarcely necessary to state, that the tranquility of the Commissary was never again disturbed. To the liberality of General Barnwell, many officers who held commissions under the Royal Government, were indebted for the support of their petitions, to become citizens of the United States. And from some of them, particularly *Mr. George Roupell*, the penalties of banishment, and every disqualification removed, even without an application for relief.

At the head of the list of voluntary martyrs, signing the requisition to General Greene, not to suffer any consideration relative to their safety to impede the fulfilment of his threat, to revenge the murder of Colonel Hayne, by retaliation on a British officer of equal rank, will be found the names of *John, Edward* and *Robert Barnwell*, alike distinguished by the steadiness of their principles, and exemplary intrepidity during the most trying scenes of the war. The last, after receiving seventeen wounds, was left as dead on the field, but sought for and conveyed to a neighbouring plantation, recovered.*

---

* The life of Mr. Robert Barnwell was saved by the affectionate and assiduous attention of his relative, Miss Mary Anna Gibbes, (the same who rescued from danger her in-

Turning his attention more particularly to literary pursuits, he appeared in the Legislative Councils of the State, and on the floor of Congress, with distinguished credit both to himself and his country. Nor will I neglect to mention the name of their nephew, *William Elliott*, who, though but a youth, after being severely wounded, was equally, with themselves, resolute to devote himself to his country, by signing the requisition to General Greene so highly characteristic of partriotic enthusiasm.

fant cousin, Fenwick, as will hereafter be related.) When considered by all around him, beyond the reach of mortal aid, she steadily persisted to bathe and dress his wounds, till exhausted nature recovered its faculties, and gave animation to his apparently lifeless corpse.

DISTINGUISHED CONTINENTAL OFFICERS.

Having endeavoured, with strict observance of truth, to detail the services of Moultrie, and briefly sketched the characters and achievements of the Partisan Commanders of Militia, who attained the highest celebrity, I turn, with peculiar interest, to the Officers of the Continental Line, the most distinguished in the annals of the Southern War; beginning with those, who, by their talents and intrepidity, so happily seconded the enterprize, and indefatigable exertions of Greene, till the expulsion of the enemy gave a stamp of excellence to his military character, that must for ever excite the applause and admiration of posterity.

ISAAC HUGER.

AMONG the patriots of South-Carolina, the Hugers were highly distinguished. *Daniel* was long a member of Congress. *John*, an able and industrious assistant in the state councils. *Francis* was numbered among the brave defenders of the pass at Sullivan's Island, when assailed by the British fleet. *Benjamin*, a soldier of the highest promise, closed a life of honour on the field, falling before the lines of Charleston, during the invasion of Provost. *Isaac*, of whom I would more particularly speak, as a bold and enterprizing commander, was preeminently distinguished. The cloud of misfortune did, it must be acknowledged, at one period obscure his fame; the disastrous surprise of Monk's Corner was highly injurious to his military reputation. But when it is recollected how extremely difficult the task to keep alive the vigilance essential to security, among troops newly initiated in military service, and how frequently the most judicious arrangements of the commanders of detachments are thwarted by the negligence of the patrols and videttes, whose unremitted attention alone counteract the energies of an enterprizing enemy, we cannot too harshly blame an officer for a single disaster, who, taught by misfortune, never a second time experienced discomfiture; and, who, in every subsequent rencounter with the British Army, by his zeal and intrepidity, acquired increase of reputation.

At the commencement of the war General Huger was commissioned as Lieutenant Colonel of the 1st Continental Regiment, and shortly after promoted to the command of the 5th. There was no battle of consequence fought in which he was not engaged, displaying on every occasion, great coolness, and invincible resolution. How highly he possessed the confidence of General Greene, is manifested by the trust reposed in him by that distinguished officer, when he was anxious to afford his personal aid to Morgan, who was endeavouring to elude the eager pursuit of Lord Cornwallis, and to conduct the prisoners taken at the Cowpens to a place of security. He committed the charge of the main army to General Huger, ordering him to conduct its retreat, and to join him at Guildford Court-House. Accompanied by a small escort of dragoons, General Greene then set out in search of Morgan, and happily joined him in safety. That Huger's conduct, on this occasion, was highly approved cannot be doubted, since we find him at the battle of Guildford, which immediately followed, intrusted with the command of the Continental Line. Here, supporting his character for exemplary bravery, he was severely wounded. At Hobkirk's Hill, he commanded the right wing of the army, and had made considerable impression on the line of the enemy, when an unfortunate movement, which threw Gunby's regiment into confusion, disconcerted all the measures of General Greene, and compelled him to relinquish a victory within his grasp, for a retreat, which, though not disgraceful, was necessarily attended with the deepest and most poignant mortification. The exertions of General Huger, in endeavouring to inspire courage by example, and to restore the order that had been lost, brought him so frequently to the muzzle of the enemy's muskets, that it was considered by all miraculous, that he escaped without injury. The abandonment of the interior country, by Lord Rawdon, very soon after this, allowed the General the happiness of embracing his family, from which he had been long separated. When General Greene was presented to them, he, with much emotion, said--" I would never, my dear Huger, have exposed you, as often as I have done, to bear the brunt of battle, and varied dangers of the field, had I known how numerous and lovely a family, were dependant on your protection."

GENERAL MORGAN.

This distinguished officer commenced his military career under General Braddock, but, in so inferior a station, as to have been subjected to coporeal punishment for some unguarded expressions towards a superior. It is painful to mention such a circumstance; and I should not have done it, had it not been recorded to his honour, that, incapable of entertaining lasting resentments, he had been distinguished, during the Revolutionary War, by the generous attention paid to every British officer who became his prisoner. Commanding a rifle company before Quebec, he was directed, under Arnold, to attack the lower town; and on the retirement of that officer, when wounded, taking the van of the assailing column, carried the first and second barriers. He even penetrated into the upper town, and was in possession of the main guard, giving paroles to the officers who surrendered, when, every prospect of success being baffled by the fall of Montgomery, and the enemy enabled to turn their entire force against him, he was surrounded and taken. His bravery well known, and his activity justly appreciated, an attempt was made by an officer of rank in the British service, to induce him, by the tender of wealth and promotion, to join the royal standard; but, with the true spirit of Republican virtue, he rejected the proposition, requesting the tempter—"Never again to insult him by an offer, which plainly implied, that he thought him a villain."

Advanced to the command of a regiment, his indefatigable activity greatly contributed to the capture of Burgoyne, being regarded, according to the repeated declarations of the enemy, as their greatest scourge.

General Gates considered it as an offence never to be forgiven, that Morgan had peremptorily refused to countenance the intrigues that were to remove the Commander-in-Chief, and to place *him* at the head of the army. He, therefore, never in the slightest degree mentioned his meritorious services in his official despatches, and appeared to exalt the claims of other officers to applause, the more certainly to mortify Morgan. Such malice, however, availed not to deprive him of his full share of glory. His country acknowledged the legitimacy of his title to fame; and the captive General declared, in allusion to the particular nature of the service in which he was employed, "That he commanded the finest corps in the world." His advancement to still higher command, gave increase to his reputation; and so long as the heart is susceptible of patriotic feeling, and capable of acknowledging, with gratitude, one of the most splendid and momentous achievements that was ever accomplished, the battle of the Cowpens will raise the heroic gallantry of Morgan to the highest pinnacle of Fame.

GENERAL OTHO HOLLAND WILLIAMS,

OF MARYLAND.

He was no less distinguished by the elegance of his manners, and politeness in private society, than by his chivalrous enterprize and exemplary constancy in the field. The services which he rendered as Adjutant General, in perfecting discipline and directing the manœuvrings of the light troops, covering the retreat of the army till the accomplishment of the memorable passage of the Dan, cannot be too highly estimated. Possessing the most perfect self-command, he put nothing at hazard, and frequently suffered the opportunity to escape, of acquiring advantages, which would have increased his own fame, rather than to risk, what might in its result, prove injurious to his country. Confining my observations to his conduct in the Southern War, it is due to his merit to say, that after the defeat of the army at Camden, and its abandonment by Gates, he conducted it to a place of security. His country is likewise indebted to him, for his judicious conduct in the retreat over the Dan, already alluded to, and for his exemplary intrepidity in the battles of Guildford, Hobkirk's Hill, and Eutaws. So close was the pursuit maintained by Lord Cornwallis, that the officers of the cavalry covering the rear, to relieve their hunger, have often, while holding the bridle with one hand, attempted to roast a piece of bacon, stuck on the point of a stick, with the other, and been obliged to eat it when scarcely warmed through, compelled, by the rapid approach of the enemy, to mount and retire. The character of General Williams may be drawn in a few words. In the field, he exercised caution, united with invincible intrepidity; in camp, the strictest discipline. In the cabinet, he distinguished himself by his perspicuity and profound intelligence—qualifications which secured to him, the confidence of his General, the esteem of his brother officers, and the love and respect of the soldiers he commanded.

JOHN EAGER HOWARD,

OF MARYLAND.

No man possessed, in a higher degree, the confidence of General Greene—none better deserved it. He had every requisite for the perfection of the military character—patience, judgment, intrepidity, and decision. To his memorable charge with the bayonet at the Cowpens, so nobly supported by Washington and his cavalry, that important victory is chiefly to be attributed. Nor do I regard his gallantry less worthy of admiration, when, at the battle of Guildford, following up the blow inflicted by Washington, he charged the second battalion of the British Guards, and nearly annihilated them. At Hobkirk's Hill, his efforts to rally the broken regiment of Gunby, did him high honour; nor did the bitterness of grief ever pervade the human bosom more keenly, than in his, when he found all his exertions to revive the courage of men, who, on every former occasion, were distinguished for intrepidity, was unproductive of the slightest effect. At Eutaw, he was severely wounded, but not till he had seen his regiment retrieve its tarnished reputation, and triumphantly drive the enemy before them. In concluding my encomiums on his merits, I do not consider it an exaggeration to say, in the words of General Greene—"Howard is as good an officer as the world affords, and deserves a statue of gold, no less than the Roman and Grecian heroes."

COLONEL CARRINGTON,

OF VIRGINIA.

I wish I could more particularly speak of the services of Colonel Carrington, as I am well apprized, that he enjoyed the entire confidence of General Greene; and by his judicious councils, and unremitted exertions as Quarter-Master-General, greatly contributed to the advantages gained over the enemy. It is an indisputable fact, that in a country exhausted, and deficient in all resources, he still contrived to provide such supplies for the comfort and support of the army, that he appeared to have achieved impossibilities, and not a murmer nor complaint impeded the progress to victory. A dispute, relative to rank, had called him to the North, before it had been my happiness to receive a commission in the service; but, previously to the evacuation of Charleston, he had rejoined the army, and resumed his former station; which gave me ample reason to believe, that wheresoever placed, his pre-eminent abilities must have been of the highest importance to his country.

LIEUTENANT COLONEL LEE,

OF THE LEGION.

FAVOURED with his friendship, and honoured by a commission in his regiment, in drawing a sketch of the character of this distinguished partisan, I may be suspected of indulging improper partialities. I disclaim any feeling that could produce them, and would far rather, that his reputation should depend upon a candid examination of his military services, than any commendation, that from grateful attachment, I might be inclined to bestow. General Charles Lee, who was, beyond question, a competent judge of military talent, averred—"That Henry Lee came a soldier from his mother's womb." General Greene pronounced him *The Eye* of the Southern Army; and to his councils, gave the most constant, implicit, and unbounded confidence. In the hour of difficulty, (and from the exhausted and distracted state of the South—the wretched and forlorn condition of the army—the superiority of force, and endless resources of the enemy, it was, to us, a war of difficulties,) was danger to be averted, was prompt exertion necessary to prevent revolt—crush insurrection—cut off supplies—harass the enemy, or pursue him to destruction—to whom did he so often turn as to *Lee?* That such preference should give birth to *Envy,* and cause the calumnies arising from it, to be propagated, and cherished with an avidity that would almost lead to the supposition, that they were believed correct, cannot, from the perverse propensities of the human heart, be considered surprising. Lee had his enemies, and they were not slow in giving currency to opinions injurious to his reputation. Measuring the extent of his powers, by the contracted scale of their own abilities, no allowance was made for the calculations of superior genius; and the acuteness of almost unerring discernment; and because he did not, on all occasions, engage with a blind precipitancy, according with their judgment, would have fixed on him the imputation of a shyness, that he never knew. In his memoirs, which, as a literary composition, do him high honour, it is remarkable, that he is so shy in claiming merit; and certainly, in various instance, has withheld pretensions, which he might have fairly made, to high distinction. He has not hinted, in the slightest degree, that the grand scheme, for the recovery of the two Southern States, when Lord Cornwallis, after the battle of Guildford, retired to Wilmington, was first suggested to General Greene by him; and that it would have been afterwards abandoned, but for his earnest remonstrances. Such, however, was the truth, and perfect the evidence corroborating it. In reply to my inquiries on the subject, the Honourable Judge Johnston, of Abingdon, Virginia, a meritorious and distinguished officer of the Revolution, says:—"I am perfectly satisfied, that the grand enterprize, for the recovery of South Carolina and Georgia, by marching into those States, when Lord Cornwallis retired to Wilmington, originated with Colonel Lee. Accident afforded me the view of a letter, written by General Greene to Colonel Lee, immediately after the second battle of Camden, fought on the 25th of April, 1781, in which the General expressed a determination to abandon the scheme of continuing his progress southwardly; and directed Lee to join him immediately with his corps, which had, about that time, reduced the post of the enemy at Wright's Bluff, on the Santee River. I shall never forget one expression, in that letter, which goes very far to prove, that I am right, in the opinion that I have ever since entertained. 'I fear, my friend, said the General, that I have *pursued your advice too far.* I have resolved to march back with the army towards Virginia, and desire that you will join me with your command as soon as possible.' Without a moment's delay, Colonel Lee left the Legion, and sought General Greene, doubtless to counteract the pernicious tendency of this hasty resolution, since he speedily returned, countermanded the orders to unite with the main army, crossed the Santee, and marched rapidly forward to lay siege to Fort Motte." This statement is fully supported by the testimony of Dr.

Matthew Irvine; and more satisfactory authority could not be desired, since he was actually the agent, the organ of communication betwixt the two, while the scheme was in agitation, and ripening for perfection. Communication, by letter, was considered as inexpedient and dangerous; and by personal interviews with the parties, delivering opinions reciprocally, and conveying the answers to them, he became the happy instrument of bringing to maturity, the plan that gave liberty to the South. The letter mentioned by Judge Johnston, my correspondent, was seen also by Dr. Irvine. He states, that the General added—"Although I am confident, that your wish was, to give increase to my military reputation; yet, it is evident to me, that by listening to your advice, I have forfeited my pretension to it for ever." Can further evidence be required? In the eyes of the unprejudiced, I should say, certainly not. Believing, then, that Lee's advice to General Greene, induced him to transfer the war into South Carolina, I shall briefly state the consequences resulting from the measure.

North Carolina became encouraged, by finding that her future security was not considered as endangered, and the Partizan Commanders of the South, Sumter, Marion and Pickens, who, *unsupported*, had already effected wonders, were now stimulated to give increase to activity and enterprize, from the conviction, that they would not only contend with the enemy upon more equal terms, but be enabled, more effectually, to maintain the advantages resulting from their valour and their victories. The fall of the military posts held by the enemy, followed in rapid succession. The surrender of Fort Watson, Fort Motte, Fort Granby, in South Carolina, and of Fort Cornwallis at Augusta, in Georgia, give the stamp of judicious foresight to the councils of Lee. Nor is less applause due to the skill and enterprize attributed to him, in their reduction. Had *he* directed the operations of the besiegers at Ninety-Six, instead of *Kosciusko*, different indeed would have been the result. On his arrival at the post, immediately after the capture of Fort Cornwallis, he, with the eye of a soldier, at once perceived, that the plan of operations, and point of attack, adopted and pursued by General Greene, had not been advantageous ly chosen. With that exquisite military sagacity, which cannot be denied him, he immediately satisfied the Commander-in-Chief, that the place would be easily carried, by obtaining possession of the western redoubt, a slight fortification at a distance from the enemy's main work, but of great importance, since it completely commanded the only fountain from which the garrison could procure water; and subsequent events incontestibly proved, that if his plan had been adopted in the first instance, the fort must have fallen, even though defended by the gallantry of Cruger, seconded by his able coadjutor, Greene.* In evidence of his services, and the extensive benefits resulting from them, it is only necessary to give an extract of a letter from General Greene, expressed in the following terms: " Lieutenant Colonel Lee retires for a time for the recovery of his health. I am more indebted to *this* officer, than to any other, for the advantages gained over the enemy, in the operations of the last campaign; and should be wanting in gratitude, not to acknowledge the importance of his services, a detail of which is his best panegyric." Dated February 18th, 1782.

Of the *horses* of his regiment, he has been frequently accused of being *too* careful; but, considering the advantages accruing from a precaution, by which a constant superiority of cavalry was maintained, how can he be blamed with justice, more especially, when it is known, that the number of prisoners taken in a single campaign, by the dragoons of the Legion, doubled their effective number; and that every individual of the corps, was armed with a *Potter's sword*, the weapon most highly estimated for service, taken in personal conflict from the enemy. Of the lives of his infantry he was never sparing. There was no action in which they were engaged, in which they did not perform a conspicuous part; while the lamentable fate of poor *Whaling*, and his followers, (fully detailed in another part of this work) evince, that their fall was regarded as a needless and unnecessary sacrifice. Of the free exposure of his person, where example was necessary to excite to gallant

---

* Major in a *Provincial* Regiment.

achievement, there can be no doubt. If there are any who cherish less charitable opinions, they must deny discernment to Greene, who employed him in the most hazardous enterprizes; and judgment to the immortal Washington, who, when the insurrection took place in the upper parts of Pennsylvania, placed him at the head of the army, with a declaration, that he considered him the man in the United States, the best calculated to suppress it, with promptitude, and effect. Towards his officers, he possessed the most friendly and affectionate feelings. To his soldiers, he was a parent—he was attentive to their wants, and indulgent to their wishes. His constant and assiduous care, was exercised to procure them comforts, and with such effect, that while other corps were almost entirely destitute of clothing, the Legion were enabled, invariably, to preserve a highly respectable appearance. I would mention, with particular commendation, the *vigilance* of Colonel Lee. Surprised, when a Captain in Bland's regiment, near Philadelphia, he profitted by experience, and was, to the end of the war, so attentive to the security of the force which he commanded, that, whenever within striking distance of the enemy, the Sergeant of the Quarter Guard, invariably, at midnight, woke up every officer and private soldier, who, by order, putting on their entire dress and accoutrements, might again seek repose, but in such a position, that on the firing of a musket, or tap of a drum, every man was at his post, prepared for action, or ready to retreat, as circumstances required. When surprised at the Spread Eagle Tavern, near Philadelphia, and surrounded by the entire British cavalry, he assured the dragoons under his command, who gallantly joined in defending the house, that he should consider their future establishment in life, as his peculiar care; and he honourably kept his word. They were all, in turn, commissioned; and by their exemplary good conduct, increased their own renown, and the reputation of their regiment.

GENERAL WILLIAM WASHINGTON.

WITH no less respect and admiration, would I record the gallant achievements of the modern Marcellus; the *sword of his country*—Lieutenant-Colonel William Washington, who, at the first call to arms, engaged in the military service, and to the termination of the war, appeared on the field of glory with pre-eminent distinction. He fought, with his gallant regiment, at York Island, and receiving merited applause, shared its difficulties and dangers on the retreat through New Jersey. At the surprise of the Hessians at Trenton, as a Captain in the line, he headed the van of one of the assailing columns; and, while leading on his company to the attack, was severely wounded in the hand. He was now transferred, with an increase of rank, to the cavalry; and having the good fortune to escape the slaughter at Tappan, with the remains of Bland's, Baylor's, and Moylan's regiments of horse, was detached to join the army of General Lincoln in South-Carolina. His first rencontre with the enemy, took place betwixt Ashley Ferry and Rantowle's Bridge, where he drove back the cavalry of the British Legion, commanded by Lieutenant Colonel Tarleton, and took several prisoners; but, being unsupported by infantry, gained little advantage from his success. The surprises at Monk's Corner, and Laneau's Ferry, which had nearly caused the entire destruction of the American cavalry, are in no degree, attributable to him, as he acted, in both instances, in a subordinate capacity; and at the last place, finding his advice to pass the river without delay, disregarded, he prepared for the castastrophe, and on the sudden attack of Tarleton, plunged into the river, and happily gained the opposite shore. These repeated disasters, compelling him to retire, with the remainder of his corps, to the borders of North-Carolina, he applied, but in vain, to General Gates, for the aid of his name and authority, to expedite its restoration and equipment. Severely did that infatuated General pay the penalty of his injudicious refusal. Had the request been attended to, the presence of a superior cavalry, led by so distinguished a soldier as Washington, might greatly have influenced the success of the battle, and, at all events, prevented the terrible slaughter that followed the defeat at Camden. While attached to the light corps commanded by General Morgan, he, by a very ingenious stratagem, carried the post at Rugely's, taking a large body of the enemy without firing a single shot. Apprized of the character of his opponent, Rugely, he fixed a pine log on the front wheels of a wagon, so as to make it appear, at a distance, as a field piece, and threatening immediate destruction should resistance be attempted; the affrighted Colonel requested, that quarter might be allowed, and surrrendered at discretion. It was on this occassion, that Lord Cornwallis, writing to Lieutenant Colonel Tarleton, laconically said—" Rugely will not be a Brigadier." He, in a high degree, contributed to the achievement of the brilliant victory at the Cowpens, although his too ardent zeal had nearly cost him his life; for, anxious by example, to increase the energy of pursuit, he was led so far in advance, as to be surrounded by several officers of the British Legion; and must have fallen, had he not been rescued by the gallantry of a sergeant, and his bugleman, *Ball*, who, by a well-aimed pistol-shot, disabled the officer, whose sword was raised for his destruction. In the retreat into Virginia, and in all the manœuvres subsequent to the recrossing of the Dan, he essentially aided to baffle the skilful efforts of Lord Cornwallis, to force General Greene, heading an inferior army, to battle. At Guildford, he acted a most conspicuous part. By a spirited and most judicious charge, he broke the regiment of Guards commanded by Colonel Steward, who fell in the action, and followed by the gallant Colonel Howard, leading on the Marylanders, with fixed bayonets, nearly annihilated them. Trifles have often, in the heat of battle, been productive of the most unlooked for consequences. Washington's cap fell, and while he dismounted to recover it, a round of grape, from the British artillery, fired by the order of General Webster, on friends as well as foes, the more effectually to check the success of the Americans, so grievously wounded the officer next in command that, incapacitated from managing his horse, the animal wheeled round and carried him off the field, followed by the rest of the cavalry, who unhappily supposed that the movement had been directed. This accident saved the remnant of the Guards, and, in all probability, the entire British army. I heard, from an officer of distinction in the army of the enemy, who was wounded in this action, the following interesting particulars: —" I was near General Webster, when the charge was made by Washington. The desperate situation of the Guards, had its effect on all around. An officer of rank, in the American army, quickly perceiving it, rode up to the British line, and called aloud, 'surrender, gentlemen, and be certain of good quarters.' Terrified by appearances, and concluding that defeat was inevitable, the soldiers of the regiment De Bose, were actually throwing down their arms. Confusion was increasing. General Webster, whose presence of mind could not be disturbed, exclaimed—' Unless that gallant fellow is taken off, we are lost.' A Lieutenant of artillery, bringing up a field-piece at the moment, was directed to fire into the throng, where the Guards now appeared to be greatly out-numbered, and did so with the happiest success—the cavalry wheeled off, the remains of the battalion rallied, and the army was saved." At Hobkirk's Hill, new honours awaited him. Gaining the rear of the British army, by judicious manoeuvring during the action, he captured and paroled eleven officers, and made prisoners of upwards of two hundred men—fifty of whom he brought off the field; the retreat of the American forces obliged him to relinquish the remainder. But, in the evening of the day on which the engagement took place, having decoyed Coffin, who commanded the horse of the enemy, into an ambuscade, he charged him with an intrepidity that could not be withstood, and compelled him, after the loss of half of his men, to fly and take shelter in Camden. At the battle of Eutaw, though unfortunate, no hero had ever, in a higher degree, merited success. His repeated charges on the British light infantry, would, probably, have disconcerted a corps less brave, or commanded by any other officer than Majoribanks;* but, they maintained their position with a steadiness that could not be subdued; and in a last effort for victory, Washington's horse being killed, he became entangled, as he fell, in the ranks of the enemy, and being unable to extricate himself, was bayoneted and taken. The intrepid conduct of his gallant followers, cannot be too highly extolled.—Captain Watts, the second in command, the Lieutenants Stuart, King, Gordon, and Simons, were wounded; Mr. Carlisle, a volunteer, killed, and half of the men destroyed. After which, the residue were drawn off by Captain Parsons, the only officer who escaped without injury. The action at the Eutaws, was the last in which Lieutenant Colonel Washington was engaged. Remaining a prisoner to the conclusion of the war, he married a lady equally distinguished by her virtues and accomplishments, and settled in South-Carolina. Possessing a very considerable property, he indulged in unbounded hospitality, receiving, with affectionate attention, his military associates, and maintaining the respectable character of a liberal and independent country gentleman.

The eclat of his military services occasioned his immediate election to the Legislature, where it soon became evident, that he possessed every requisite to render himself as much distinguished in Council, as he had been in the field. His intuitive knowledge was great; and by his assiduous application to business, received daily improvement. His friends, who clearly perceived that he possessed far greater claims to talent, than his extreme modesty would admit, were anxious to place him at the head of the State Government; but, it was in vain that

---

* This distinguished officer is still spoken of in St. John's with great respect. He was the foe to oppression, and guardian of the unfortunate. He suffered no severities within the reach of his command; nor withheld his beneficence where the power appeared of doing good, even from the families of his most decided opponents. He fell a martyr to disease, and is buried on the plantation of DANIEL RAVENEL. An old Negro, still living, has often pointed out his grave, and added, this is the officer who turned aside the soldier's bayonet, who would have killed Colonel WASHINGTON, when he fell at Eutaw. The fact which, I doubt not, gives him new claims to our admiration. The Commanding Officer had his grave enclosed, and a cypress board, (which still remains) placed at his head, with the following modest inscription:

JOHN MAJORIBANKS, Esquire.
Late Major in the 19th Regt. Inf., and commanding a flank battalion of his Majesty's army. Obit 22d Oct., 1781.

they essayed to excite him to become a candidate for the office. "My ambition is," he constantly said, "to devote my services to my country; but, there are two powerful reasons which render it impossible for me to aspire to the honour of governing the State. The first is, that till lately I was a stranger among you; and, in my opinion, the Chief Executive Officer should be a native of the land on which he presides. Nor would I, on the score of qualification, put my talents in competition with those of many able men, who are ambitious of the honour. My other reason is insurmountable. If I were elected Governor, I should be obliged to make a speech; and I know, that in doing so, without gaining credit in your estimation, the consciousness of inferiority, would humble me in my own—*I cannot make a Speech.*"

A report having reached Head-Quarters, that the author of "*Common Sense*" was in distress at Philadelphia, it was no sooner communicated to Lieutenant-Colonel Washington, than he said to a friend—"I cannot bear the idea, that the man, who, by his writings, has so highly benefitted my country, should feel the want of bread, while the power is mine to relieve him;" and without a sentence more on the subject, by the first post, remitted him a bill for one hundred guineas.

In the year 1810, I was appointed by the Society of the Cincinnati, to pronounce an Eulogy, expressive of their high sense of his meritorious services, and of their deep regret on the loss sustained by his death. Circumstances compelled me to decline the honour, though I have always considered it as the highest compliment that could have been paid me by my fellow-soldiers, that they deemed me worthy, to detail the services, and celebrate the virtues of so good a man.

Colonel Washington was tall and majestic in person, exhibiting a manly figure, with every indication of superior strength, and corresponding activity. His countenance was composed, and rather of a serious cast, but evinced the benevolence that characterized all his actions.

The sketch which I have given of his military career, falls, in my own estimation, far short of the encomiums which are his due. To compensate my readers for the insufficiency of the attempt, I offer, as a treat, the Resolutions published by order of the *Revolutionary Society*, on the melancholy occurrence of his death.

Resolutions of the Revolution Society of South-Carolina.

THE *American Revolution Society*, convened on the occasion of the recent death of Lieutenant-Colonel WASHINGTON, feel themselves prompted by duty and sensibility, to give utterance to their sentiments upon that calamitous event. They who knew the deceased, (and to many of this Society, of which he was a member, he was intimately known,) could not but have remarked in him, a felicitous combination of mind and heart, rarely united, which qualified him to be eminently distinguished as a soldier, and esteemed as a citizen: which produced in him great virtues untarnished by the association of correspondent vices; which rendered him modest without timidity, generous without extravagance, brave without rashness, and disinterested without austerity; which imparted firmness to his conduct, and mildness to his manners; solidity to his judgment, and boldness to his achievements; which armed him with an equanimity unalterable by the frowns of adversity, or the smiles of fortune; and steadiness of soul not to be subdued by the disasters of defeat, or elated by the triumphs of victory. When the Society also recollects, that he was a gallant soldier, enterprizing without ambition, encountering danger, not for his own renown, but for his country's independence; that he was a patriot, inflexible without obstinacy, warm without passion, and zealous without bigotry; that in private life he was useful without parade, liberal without ostentation, amiable without weakness, and honourable without fastidiousness, they cannot permit him to descend to the silent tomb, and refrain from expressing some mark of reverence and affection for his worth; however frail and evanescent these testimonials may be, it will nevertheless manifest that they honoured the deceased when living, and that they cherish the remembrance of his virtues and services after death.

Therefore, *Resolved*, That the members of this Society do wear crape on their left arm for thirty days, as a tribute of respect to the memory of General WILLIAM WASHINGTON.

Resolved, That the President be requested to transmit a copy of these resolutions to Mrs. WASHINGTON, and to express to her the deep regret of this Society for the great loss she has sustained.

Resolved, That the foregoing resolutions be published in the Gazettes of this city.

By Order of the Society.

WILLIAM CRAFTS, *President*.

JOHN CRIPPS, *Treasurer and Secretary*.

GENERAL GREENE.

To distinguish with commendation, equal to his merits, so good and great a man, is, confessedly, beyond my ability. Having been honoured by his friendship, and a member of his military family, the opportunity I enjoyed, of taking a more critical view of his character, strongly impresses the belief, that it was exalted beyond the reach of adequate praise. In presenting it to view, an opportunity will be afforded me, of exhibiting the sentiments of more competent judges, while I reserve to myself, the privilege of asking —" Whether such multiplied evidence, as I shall produce of private worth, and public utility, of captivating virtues, and superior talents, do not give to General Greene, an exalted claim to superior intelligence."

Great is my disappointment, that a gentleman, admirably well qualified to do justice to his memory—a soldier who had served under him—a friend, whom he loved, after having made considerable advances in the delineation of his life and character, withholds it from the public. Judge Pendleton, of New York, to whom I allude, shared with Gen. Greene, in all the dangers and difficulties of the Southern War, and had daily opportunity of witnessing the development and exercise of those brilliant talents, which caused him, like the Great Frederick, "to shine with greatest lustre, when hardest prest;" and, ultimately, to establish the liberty and independence of a large portion of the United States, on a basis that can never be shaken.

To speak of his military capacity—We are told, that, on his very first appearance in the camp at Cambridge, from the ardour of his zeal, unremitted activity, and strict attention to every duty, he was pronounced, by soldiers of distinction,[*] a man of real military genius.

---
[*] Colonel Pickering and others.

"His knowledge (said General Knox to a distinguished citizen of South Carolina,)* is intuitive. He came to us, the rawest, and most untutored being I ever met with; but, in less than twelve months, he was equal, in military knowledge, to any General Officer in the army, and very superior to most of them."

The British officer, who opposed him in Jersey, writes— "Greene is as dangerous as Washington; he is vigilant, enterprizing, and full of resources. With but little hope of gaining any advantage over him, I never feel secure when encamped in his neighbourhood."†

To speak of his disinterestedness, General Washington gives the following honourable testimony of his character:—"There is no officer in the army more sincerely attached to the interests of his country than General Greene. Could he but promote these interests in the character of a corporal, he would exchange, without a murmur, his epaulette for the knot. For, although he is not without ambition, that ambition has not for its object, the highest rank, so much as the greatest good."

In compliment to his brilliant successes, the Chevalier de la Luzerne, the Minister of France, who, as a Knight of Malta, must be considered a competent judge of military merit, thus speaks of him:—"Other Generals subdue their enemy by the means with which their country, or sovereign furnishes them; but, Greene appears to subdue his enemy by his own means. He commenced his campaign, without either an army, provisions, or military stores. He has asked for nothing since; and yet, scarcely a post arrives from the South, that does not bring intelligence of some new advantage gained over the foe. He conquers by magic. History furnishes no parallel to this."

Previous to his appointment to the command of the Southern Army, he had acquired a considerable share of professional reputation. The Commander-in-Chief, recommending him to Congress, says—"He is an officer, in whose abilities, fortitude and integrity, from a long and intimate experience of him, I have the most entire confidence."

---

*Judge Desaussure.   † Lord Cornwallis.

He had long been his intimate associate; and it has often been said, that he so highly approved the excellence of his heart, and was so fully satisfied of his pre-eminent talents, and ability to direct the operations of an army, that, in the event of his own death, he strongly urged that he should be advanced to the supreme command.

I shall now, more particularly, detail his services; for in all that regards so good and so great a man, I consider every circumstance of importance. General Greene contributed to the security of the army in the retreat through the Jerseys. He displayed the best conduct and most distinguished intrepidity at Trenton, Brandywine, Germantown, and Monmouth. He conducted the retreat at Rhode Island, with consummate skill, after having vainly endeavoured to procure the co-operation of the fleet of D'Estaing. Had his solicitation been successful, it must have placed the entire force of the enemy in our hands. But, it was in consenting to be placed at the head of the Quarter-Master General's Department, conformably to the earnest wishes of the Commander-in-Chief, that he rendered incalculable benefit to his country. His natural disposition led him rather to seek for laurels in the field of battle, than to the safer duty of providing resources for others. But, considering the benefit that would result to his country, as superior to every selfish feeling, he uttered no complaint; and so completely justified the expectations formed of his capacity and persevering industry, that, when retiring from the station, General Washington said to him—"You have rendered the path of duty in the Quarter-Master's Department, so broad and plain, that it will not be easy for your successors to mistake it."

On his arrival in Carolina, he found a country every where marked with outrage, desolation, and blood, and an enemy bold in enterprize, and flushed with success, prepared to crush him. The prospect was truly appalling. The remnant of the army, delivered up by Gates, consisted not only of inferior numbers, but was mostly composed of militia, dispirited by misfortune, and entirely destitute of every adequate means to sanction the hope of effectual resistance. Their provisions were exhausted—the comfort of decent clothing was unknown

—and the want of arms and ammunition so great and deplorable, as to render impracticable, every attempt to commence active operations. Yet, beneath such an accumulation of difficulty, his resolution sunk not. His immediate care was, to obtain a supply of subsistence and ammunition, to increase the comfort of his troops, and to perfect their discipline. This he so completely effected, that in a very short time, the condition of the army was so much ameliorated, that the recollection of misfortune was lost; and with the utmost confidence in his ability, they solicited their General to advance, declaring, that under his guidance, they considered victory as secure. But, though delighted with this propitious change in the disposition of his troops, his future hopes and high confidence were derived from the known characters of the officers under his command. Aided by the zeal, activity, enterprize, and varied talents of Huger, Morgan, Williams, Carrington, Howard, Washington, and Lee in the regular Line, and of Sumter, Marion, Pickens, and Davie, the Partizan Commanders of the militia, he looked forward, with no presumptuous hope, to the certainty of success. It is a tribute justly due to their merits, to say, that he was particularly fortunate in the choice of the Aids-de-Camp, then serving in his family. Burnett, Morris, Hyrne, Pierce, Pendleton, and Shubrick, were officers of no common character, and daily evinced, that they were worthy of the honour bestowed on them.*

* In addition to the advantages accruing to General GREENE, from the talents of the distinguished characters attached to his command, I consider him particularly fortunate, while in active service, in the selection he had made of his Aids-de-Camp. The attachment to his person, and devotion to his will, of Colonel MORRIS, Majors BURNETT, PIERCE, and HYRNE, and Captains PENDLETON and SHUBRICK, while grateful and flattering to himself, he proudly acknowledged essentially beneficial to the service; it gave energy to exertion, display to their abilities, and caused each, in succession, to be honoured with the thanks of Congress. To the watchfulness of Colonel MORRIS, to whom the General was most sincerely attached, he handsomely acknowledged his security from captivity, and, probably, his escape from death, at the battle of Guildford. BURNETT and PENDLETON, pre-eminently possessed the talents the best fitted for conducting the important business of Head-Quarters. PIERCE, admirably qualified to conciliate all who approached the General, with complaints or solicitation. He well knew how to give additional sense of obligation to favours granted, and parry, without offending, unreasonable requests; and even to give to direct refusal such an appearance of justice, as to prevent complaint. HYRNE excelled in negotiation, while his honourable scars evinced, that he was no less bold than intelligent. SHUBRICK was no less distinguished. To convey orders through every peril—to assail with the column he was directed to see advance—to charge with the troop commanded to fall on the enemy, no man possessed more chivalric gallantry than he did. He had constantly

Every necessary preparation being now made, for the commencement of hostilities, General Morgan was detached to enter South-Carolina, and take a position on the left of Cornwallis, while General Greene, at the head of the main army, moved to the Cheraw Hills, about seventy miles to his right.

It is not my intention to give details of the battles fought, and of victories gained; nor of the skilful manœuvres practized to avoid action, when, consequences too momentous, would have been put at hazard by defeat; but, looking to the results, I feel confident in saying, that greater prudence, more happy and accurate discernment in anticipating events—more promptitude to profit by favourable occurrences, were never displayed by any General, in ancient or in modern times, than by General Greene. I mention it to the honour of the gentlemen of his family, who were present at the battle of Guildford, that immediately previous to its commencement, they waited upon him in a body, earnestly to solicit—"That he would put their lives at every hazard; but that he would be careful of his own, as the service would not suffer by their loss, but that his fall would not only be fatal to the army, but, in all probability, greatly retard, if not destroy, every hope of securing the independency of the South." His ardour, however, was not to be

shown himself an officer of talent and enterprize; and not only will his name be enrolled among the heroes of the Revolution, from his own merits, but to future generations, shine with additional lustre, from the pre-eminent intrepidity of his gallant offspring. Six sons has he given to the service of his country. The two eldest died before the aggressions of an enemy, gave opportunity to evince their devotion to their native land. Of Captain JOHN TEMPLAR SHUBRICK, how shall I speak?—How, in terms sufficiently energetic, express my admiration of his exalted worth! The brave, the heroic youth, who, *thrice* in the space of twelve months, saw the flag of Britain floating beneath the banners of his country—"the Lion prostrate beneath the basilisk glance of the triumphant Eagle." His merits are beyond the reach of encomium. Imagination may lead us to conceive, of what might have been expected from him—but, alas!

"*He is gone—and idolatrous fancy
Must sanctify his relics.*"

The share which Lieutenant WILLIAM SHUBRICK had, in the capture of the *Cyane* and *Levant*, gave ample testimony of *his* merits. Lieutenant EDWARD SHUBRICK was less fortunate in the opportunity of displaying his gallantry, but not less eager to meet the foe; and in different cruizes under Commodore RODGERS, did an infinity of mischief to their trade, conveying many valuable prizes, with safety, into port. IRVINE SHUBRICK, the sixth brother, began his career under the cloud of misfortune. He was captured on board of the *President*, but lost no honour; and had the satisfaction of perceiving, by the complete discomfiture of the *Endymion*, that had the contending force been more equal, another naval victory had graced the annals of his country. From youths of such promise, what may not be expected, should war be again the portion of our country.

restrained. The exposure of his person was his least consideration; and it had nearly cost him his liberty; for a party of the British Guards, pursuing the flying militia, passed within a very few yards of him, but not till the warning voice of an Aid-de-Camp, had given him time to place himself in security. In writing, shortly after, to Mrs. Greene, he says—" To my friend Morris, I am indebted for my safety."

The loss of cannon, in action, has always been considered as the most certain testimony of defeat.—General Greene felt this; and when compelled to retire before the enemy, at Hobkirk's Hill, finding the horses belonging to the artillery, too much crippled to remove the pieces brought into the field, dismounted himself, and putting his hand to the drag-ropes, gave such animation to the exertions of the men, that they were carried off in safety.

And here I would mention, that his military occupations had made but little alteration in his principal habits, and that, in simplicity of his manners, he was still a Quaker.

Exertion being imperiously called for, after the battle of Guildford, and his own, as well as the wounded of the British, who had been left and recommended to his humanity, impeding his movements, he, in the style the best suited to his views, so pathetically addressed the Society of Friends, in the neighbourhood, that they immediately tendered their services, to give relief to the afflicted, and left him at full liberty to pursue the retiring enemy.

One talent he possessed, in the highest degree, beneficial to the service—an accurate discernment of the capacities and peculiar traits of genius, characterizing the officers under his command, and of applying them in the manner in which they promised to produce the best effects. *Lee*, he considered his *eye*—*Washington* his *arm;* now, although I have no doubt, but that Washington would have succeeded in conducting the sieges of the posts held by the enemy, (for he had shown at Rugely's, that he was not deficient in stratagem;) and am perfectly convinced, that Lee would have headed a charge of cavalry with the gallantry of a hero, yet, it will scarcely be denied, but that the former was more in his proper sphere, in causing the enemy to fly before the vigour of his attacks; the last, in the exercise of the fertile expedients that produced the end to be accomplished, more certainly, than if attempted by force and violence. To Sumter and Pickens, who commanded a bold and hardy race of men, who had never submitted, was peculiarly intrusted, the conduct of the enterprizes where bold and impetuous attacks were the most essential to success. To Marion, was assigned the more difficult duty of conciliating the disaffected; and by the gentleness and suavity of his manners, and perfect knowledge of the human heart, reconciling to themselves, and to their country, the men who, by the delusion of fair promises, or threats of violence, had yielded temporary obedience to the enemy. Not, however, confining the abilities of so distinguished a soldier, to such views alone, but encouraging him to pursue that mode of warfare so happily adapted to his genius--harassing detachments—cutting off supplies—exciting perpetual alarm—and striking, with effect, the points where he was least expected, till his name became so formidable, that, to pass the limits of encampment, was considered the immediate prelude to death or captivity. But in no instance, did he show greater accuracy of judgment, than in the appointment of Colonel Otho H. Williams, to the command of the light troops, who were to cover his retreat into Virginia; for never was man better suited to the happy discharge of such a trust. Perfect in military science, he kept an ardent temper under strict control; was vigilant and circumspect; always prepared to profit by occasion, but never to risk for slight advantage, or endanger the security he was strictly commanded to maintain.

Of General Greene's literary talents, I have little to say. His early education had not been conducted on an extensive scale; the knowledge which he possessed, was from the inspiration of natural genius and an uncommon strength of mind. When called upon to speak, or write with promptitude, on a subject that interested him, his ideas were sublime, his expressions forcible, and well adapted to the subject; but, when he aimed at elegance of style, and to give to his correspondence the beauty of well-turned periods, his compositions were of a different cast.

When the mutiny of the cavalry took place on the Hills of Santee, while Lieutenant Merriweather, who brought the intelligence, and waited his despatches to return, was snatching a hasty meal, I sat by the side of the General, transcribing a copy of his address to the revolters, as quickly as the sheets on which it was written, were thrown to me. At the conclusion, he left me, more forcibly to impress on the Lieutenant, the necessity of despatch, to overtake the corps, to read to them his address, and to endeavour to bring them back to their duty. In the interim, one of the most enlightened patriots, and distinguished officers of our army, entered the apartment. Delighted, myself, I asked his opinion of this hasty production, and was gratified to hear him declare:—" That he had never heard an address better calculated to produce the effect that might be hoped from it." The General's heart had been interested—he felt the disgrace that would tarnish the laurels so honourably attained; and writing under the influence of strong emotions, wrote well. But, as I said before, whenever he laboured to excel, he never succeeded.

To the gentlemen of his family, he was affable and kind, inspiring them with the warmest affection for his person, and admiration of his fame.

By his Officers he was beloved—by his Soldiers, idolized. They knew him brave, and believed him invincible.

Against such a man, the British Commander of the South, General Leslie, saw the folly of contention; and till the evacuation of Charleston, contented himself, for many months, to remain, tranquilly, within his lines.

OFFICERS WHO FELL IN THE SOUTHERN WAR.

It is impossible for me to notice, with just estimation of their talents and patriotism, the distinguished military characters who fell previously to my return to my native country and connection with the army. On the authority of others it is still delightful to record them; and where I fail to bestow the due meed of praise, I trust it will be attributed to the true cause,—the want of sufficient information for the proper performance of the duty.

COLONEL OWEN ROBERTS.

The untimely fate of Colonel Owen Roberts, who fell at Stono, was the cause of universal regret. He was an inflexible patriot, an excellent disciplinarian, and an enthusiast in pursuit of military fame. His son, who was in the action, hearing of his misfortune, hastened to him. The expiring veteran, perceiving in his countenance the liveliest sorrow, addressed him with great composure:—"I rejoice, my boy, once again to see and to embrace you. Receive this sword, which has never been tarnished by dishonour, and let it not be inactive, while the liberty of your country is endangered. Take my last adieu—accept my blessing, and return to your duty!"

LIEUT. COL. JOHN LAURENS.

It is with peculiar delight, that I mention, among the most distinguished worthies of the Revolution, Lieutenant Colonel John Laurens; for no man more highly merited the gratitude of his country, and by none was I ever so highly befriended.

His general character is so well known, and has been so ably depicted by others, that I have little to say that can increase its celebrity. His extensive information, and classical knowledge, obtained the respect of the learned. His polite and easy behaviour, insured distinction in every polished society. The warmth of his heart, gained the affection of his friends, his sincerity their confidence and esteem. His patriotic integrity commanded the veneration of his countrymen—his intrepidity their unlimited applause. An insult to his friend, he regarded as a wound to his own honour. Such an occurrence led him to engage in a personal contest with General Charles Lee, who had spoken disrespectfully of General Washington. The veteran, who was wounded on the occasion, being asked—" How Laurens had conducted himself?" replied " I could have hugged the noble boy, he pleased me so."

His gallantry, in action, was highly characteristic of his love of fame. The post of danger was his favourite station. Some, indeed, may style his display of intrepidity, at every risk, the height of rashness.—Strictly speaking, it was so. But, at the commencement of the war, when the British Officers were persuaded, or affected to believe, that every American was a coward, such total disregard of personal safety, on the part of Laurens, such display of chivalric intrepidity, that equally excited their surprize and admiration, was, essentially, beneficial to our cause. To deny that his anxiety to meet the foe, led him too often into unnecessary peril, is impossible. I had, too often, cause to see and to lament it. Let one instance suffice to prove it. A centinel on the bank of Ashley River, opposite to Dorchester, perceiving a Red Coat moving through the brush-wood on the other shore, gave the alarm that the enemy were without their lines. This being communicated to Lieutenant-Colonel Laurens, a troop of dragoons, and a company of infantry of the Legion, were ordered to cross the river and reconnoitre. But, the rapidity of the stream determined Captain O'Neal, who commanded, to wait till a boat, which had been sent for, should arrive. In the interim, Lieutenant-Colonel Laurens galloped up and demanded with warmth, "Why this halt, Captain?—were not orders given to cross?" "Yes, Colonel, but look to the current, and judge if it be practicable." "This is no time for argument," rejoined Laurens. "You, who are brave men, follow me." Saying this, he plunged into the river, but was instantaneously obliged to quit his horse, and with extreme difficulty reached the opposite shore. O'Neal, than whom a braver man did not exist, indignant at the speech of Laurens, replied, "You shall see, sir, that there are men here as courageous as yourself," and at the head of his troop, entered the river. I cannot do justice to the scene that followed. All was tumult and confusion; for, although no life was lost, several of the men were so nearly drowned, that it became necessary to use every means to make them disgorge the water they had swallowed; and all were so much exhausted, that a temporary halt was indispensably necessary. The infantry, by the aid of plank, and large doors torn from a neighbouring ware-house, passed over with less difficulty. In the mean time, Lieutenant-Colonel Laurens, attended by Messrs. Ralph and Walter Izard, and Mr. Wainwright, who ever accompanied him as his aids, hastened to the spot where the British regimental had been seen. It then was found, that a military coat had been hung up in a tree, by a soldier who had been whipped and drummed out of the 64th Regiment, for drunkenness, and whose lacerated back would admit of no covering.

The exposure of so many valuable lives, connected with other causes, induced the Officers of the Legion, at an after period, to resign their commissions rather than serve under Laurens.

To speak more particularly of his military achievements. His first essay in arms was at Brandywine. At the battle of Germantown, he exhibited prodigies of valour, in attempting to expel the enemy from Chew's house, and was severely wounded. He was engaged at Monmouth, and greatly increased his reputation at Rhode Island. At Coosawhatchie, defending the pass with a handful of men, against the whole force of Provost, he was again wounded, and was probably indebted for his life to the gallantry of Captain Wigg, who gave him his horse to carry him from the field, when incapable of moving, his own having been shot under him. He headed the Light Infantry, and was among the first to mount the British lines at Savannah—displayed the greatest activity and courage during the siege of Charleston—entered with the forlorn hope, the British redoubt carried by storm at York-Town, and received with his own hand the presented sword of the Commander; by indefatigable activity, thwarted every effort of the British garrison in Charleston, confining them for upwards of twelve months, to the narrow limits of the city and neck, except when under the protection of their shipping, they indulged in distant predatory expeditions; and unhappily, at the very close of the war, too carelessly exposing himself in a trifling skirmish near Combahee, sealed his devotion to his country in death.

I consider it highly to the honour of Lieutenant Colonel Laurens, that when requested to carry a message to Provost, on his approach to the lines of Charleston, proposing, "neutrality during the continuance of the war," he declined it with decision: "I will do any thing," said he, "to serve my country, but never bear a message that would disgrace her." When General Moultrie, who equally spurned the idea of entering upon terms with the enemy, declared, in Council, "that he would not deliver up his Continentals as prisoners of war," Laurens leapt from his seat, and exclaimed, "'tis a glorious resolve, General; thank God, we are on our legs again."

But there is one service rendered to his country, which, though little known, entitles him to its warmest gratitude. When sent by Congress to negotiate a loan from the French Government, although his reception was favourable, and encouragement given, that his request would be granted, yet the delays perpetually contrived by the Minister, the Count de Vergennes, afforded little prospect of immediate success. Convinced that procrastination would give a death-blow to Independence, he resolved in defiance of all the etiquette of the Court, to make a personal appeal to the King. Dr. Franklin, our Minister at Versailles, vehemently opposed his intention; and finding Laurens firm in his purpose, he said—" I most cordially wish you success, Colonel; but, anticipate so different a result, that I warn you —I wash my hands of the consequences." Accordingly, at the first levee, Colonel Laurens, walking directly up to the King, delivered a memorial, to which he solicited his most serious attention, and said—" Should the favour asked be denied, or even delayed, there is cause to fear, that the sword which I wear, may no longer be drawn in defence of the liberties of my Country, but be wielded as a British subject against the monarchy of France." His decision met with the reward it merited. Apologies were made for delays. The Minister gave his serious attention to the subject, and the negotiation was crowned with success.

From such a display of chivalric gallantry in early life, may not friendship be allowed to say, without the imputation of improper partiality—to auger from the achievements which the past had exhibited, had not death stopped the career of his glory, he would have proved a model, both of civil and military virtue, " a mirror by which our youth might dress themselves."

SERGEANT JASPER.

Second Regiment.

The gallantry displayed by the heroic Jasper, during the battle of Sullivan's Island, cannot be passed over in silence. It has been frequently recorded; but while I notice the achievements of men of superior grade, his intrepidity, enhanced by his extreme modesty, demands my warmest encomium. The flag-staff of the fort having been shot away very early in the action, Jasper leaped down upon the beach, took up the flag, fixed it to a spunge staff, and, regardless of the incessant firing of the shipping, mounted and planted it on the rampart.

Governor Rutledge, in testimony of his admiration of so distinguished an act of heroism, presented him a sword, and offered him a commission. The first he gratefully accepted, but declined the last. "Were I made an officer," he modestly said, "my comrades would be constantly blushing for my ignorance, and I should be unhappy, feeling my own inferiority. I have no ambition for higher rank than that of a Sergeant."

Through every subsequent period of the war, his conduct was exemplary; but, in the details which I have seen, carries too much the air of romance, to be dwelt upon. He was a perfect Proteus, in ability to alter his appearance; perpetually entering the camp of the enemy, without detection, and invariably returning to his own, with soldiers he had seduced, or prisoners he had captured.

During the attack at Savannah, he appeared at the head of the assailants, he seized the colours of his regiment, which had fallen from the hands of the lieutenant who bore them; but receiving, himself, a mortal wound, returned them, and retiring, but reached the American encampment to expire.

WILMOTT AND MOORE.

A FEW days previous to the evacuation of Charleston, a very rash expedition suggested by Colonel Kosciusko, occasioned the loss of Captain Wilmott and Lieutenant Moore, two of the most distinguished Partisans in the service. The object was, to surprise a party of wood-cutters from Fort Johnson, working in view of the Garrison of Charleston. So much was the accuracy of the information doubted, that many believed, that the negro who gave it, had been sent expressly to decoy the Americans. Certain it is, the party found their enemy prepared, and received so deadly a fire, that Wilmott and several of his men, fell lifeless, while Moore and many others remained on the field, covered with wounds. Kosciusko, although a spontoon was shattered in his hand, and his coat pierced by four balls, escaped unhurt. A British dragoon was in the act of cutting him down, when he was killed by Mr. William Fuller, a very young and gallant volunteer, who had joined the expedition.

This was the last bloodshed in the Revolutionary contest. The British buried Wilmott with the honours of war, and showed the greatest attention to Moore, who was removed to Charleston, to receive the best surgical assistance. The amputation of the limb, in which he received his principal wound, being indispensible, it was performed within a few days after the evacuation, by our own surgeons; but, mortification rapidly following, he died greatly and universally lamented. When first brought into town, great pains were taken by the British surgeons to extract the ball, but without success. Mrs. Daniel Hall, in whose house he lodged, and who had watched over him unremittingly, being apprized of the business which brought the most distinguished surgeons together, entering the apartment of Moore, as soon as they had retired, said—" I am happy to find, that you have not been subjected to as severe an operation as I had anticipated; you appear to have experienced but little agony. I was constantly in the next room, and heard not a groan." "My kind friend," he replied, "I felt not the less agony; but, I would not have breathed a sigh, in the presence of British officers, to have secured a long and fortunate existence."

Colonel Lee, in his memoirs, mentions a singular instance of an officer of the British Guards, Captain Maynard, distinguished, on many occasions, by his intrepidity, who, reluctantly, entering into the engagement at Guildford, foretold the death which he actually met.

I consider it, in like manner, remarkable, that Wilmott, whose courage bordered upon rashness, and who was never known to impede the progress of any enterprize, however hazardous, on being ordered by Kosciusko, to get ready for the expedition, said to Mr. John Gibbes, one of the youthful volunteers who served under him—"I have not my baggage at hand; you must lend me a shift of clothes, my young friend, for, if I fall, which is not unlikely, it would be a satisfaction to me, that the enemy should find me clad in clean linen." And a bowl of tea being presented to him, at the moment, by Miss Mary Anna Gibbes, (the same who had risked her life to save from danger her infant cousin Fenwick,) he gallantly said—"This attention is particularly gratifying. It is delightful to think, that the last refreshment that may ever pass my lips, was presented by so lovely and amiable a friend." In a few hours, he was numbered with the dead.

LIEUT. COL. RICHARD PARKER.

The fall of this excellent officer, is thus feelingly noticed by Lee:—" He was one of that illustrious band of youths, who first flew to their country's standard, when she was driven to unsheath the sword. Stout, intelligent, brave, and enterprizing, he had been advanced from the command of a company, in the course of the war, to the command of a regiment. Always beloved and respected, late in the siege of Charleston, he received a ball in the forehead, and fell dead in the trenches, embalmed in the tears of his faithful soldiers, and honoured by the regrets of the whole army."

CAPTS. T. MOULTRIE & PHILIP NEYLE.

During a sortie made by a detachment of the garrison of Charleston, under Lieutenant Colonel Henderson, with the hope of impeding the approaches of the besiegers, much gallantry was displayed, particularly by Mr. Daniel Wilson, and Benjamin Singleton, then a boy of sixteen, who, when volunteers were called for, was the first to offer his service. No advantage, however, resulted from it; a few of the enemy were killed, and eleven prisoners taken; while the service lost a zealous and brave officer, Captain Thomas Moultrie, who fell universally lamented.

Captain Philip Neyle, about the same period, a gentleman of high accomplishment, refined manners, and determined bravery, was killed by a cannon ball. He was Aid-de-Camp to General Moultrie, and was pressing forward to the lines, exulting in an order which he conveyed, to quicken the fire upon the enemy, when the catastrophe occurred, which deprived his country of one of its boldest defenders.

The battle of Eutaw, proved fatal to two officers of distinguished reputation:

LIEUT. COL. CAMPBELL,

Of the 1st Virginia Regiment, who had previously, under the command of General Greene, both at Hobkirk's Hill, and at the siege of Ninety-Six, gained high renown, fell in the decisive charge which broke the British line, and without a struggle expired.

LIEUTENANT DUVAL,

Of the Marylanders, at the same period, closed his brilliant career in death. The service did not boast an officer of more consummate valour, or higher promise. He was active, intelligent, and ever foremost in the pursuit of glory and renown. At Ninety-Six, he led the forlorn hope of Campbell, storming the Star Redoubt with exemplary intrepidity; and at Eutaw, had taken a field-piece from the enemy, when struck by the fatal ball which terminated his existence.

MAJOR BENJAMIN HUGER.

In Major Huger, the service lost an officer of great gallantry, and high promise. He fell, covered with wounds, before Charleston, while executing an important duty, during Provost's invasion; and, to increase the calamity, by friendly hands—the fire which destroyed him, proceeding from the American Lines.

The Marquis de la Fayette, and Baron de Kalb, on their first arrival on the shores of America, landed on North Inland, in Winyaw Bay, and were welcomed, with the most cordial hospitality, by the family of Major Huger, who made it their summer residence.

Anxious to pursue the object of their voyage, they speedily, under the guidance of their friendly host, removed to Charleston, and from thence to the army commanded by General Washington, in which they both, in a very short time, received honourable appointments.

It required but a short acquaintance with La Fayette, to feel interested in his success. He was greatly admired by his entertainers; and their sentiments in his favour, continually increased by his rising fame; it is not to be wondered at, that the son of the family, by constantly hearing the encomiums bestowed on his gallantry, and love of liberty, should have cherished that enthusiastic attachment to his character, that led to as noble an act of friendship and heroism, as adorns the page of chivalry.

The circumstances attending this generous exertion of friendship, are so highly interesting in themselves, and honourable to my gallant countryman, Colonel Francis Kinloch Huger, that I trust I shall rather be commended than blamed, for more particularly detailing them.

When, at an early period of the French Revolution, La Fayette discovered, that the Liberty which he had so zealously contended for, and which he had fondly hoped to see established in his beloved France, was insulted and trampled on; and that the government and destinies of the nation had passed into the hands of men, far more ambitious of self aggrandizement, than to promote the true interests of their country. When he saw, that the very individuals, who but a little before, had enthusiastically professed themselves to be the apostles of benevolence and philanthropy, bewildered by the wildest chimeras of imagination, and dreaming of perfections incompatible with the frailty of humanity, were now to be satisfied only by unlimited increase of power, and appeased in their resentment by the unceasing effusion of blood. When in the scowl of the giddy multitude, it was evident, that the life which he would have sacrificed with delight for the public welfare, was now to be aimed at by the dagger of the assassin. Distracted by the view of evils that he could not prevent, and foreseeing the miseries that would speedily fall on a deluded people, he retired a voluntary exile, to seek an asylum in a foreign land, where, unnoticed and unknown, he might pity and lament them. It could scarcely be imagined, that under such circumstances, showing no disposition to hostility, uttering no word that could offend, no sentence that indicated a wish to disseminate the principles of his own political creed, and from the reduced number of his adherents, incapacitated from doing injury, that he should have been regarded, either as an object of apprehension, or distrust; much less, that the effort to procure the inestimable blessing of freedom to his country, should subject him to penalties, that cannot be otherwise considered, when weighed in the scales of justice, than as outrages to every principle of honour and humanity. Yet, without the slightest commisseration for his forlorn condition, or sympathy in his unmerited disgrace, he had scarcely entered the dominions of the Sovereigns allied against France, before he was arrested and delivered up to Austria, and conducted to Olmutz, to suffer every rigour of persecution, in solitude, and in a dungeon. The world, however, viewed not his misfortunes with cold indifference. Petitions for his release were presented from all quarters; and in the British House of Commons, the motion made for the interposition of the Government, in the sufferer's behalf, must ever do honour to the memory of General Fitzpatrick. Unhappily, the Emperor's irritation was, at the moment, exalted to the highest pitch, and he remained inexorable.

The anxious wish to free from captivity, a man who had boldly stepped forward the Champion of Liberty, originated with Dr. Bolman, a young Hanoverian, active, intrepid, and intelligent, but communicated confidentially to his friend Huger, with an inquiry, if he was inclined to second the enterprize, was embraced with alacrity, and entered on with an ardour, that ensured his unremitted efforts to produce its accomplishment. The preparatory arrangements were speedily settled. Huger feigned indisposition, and Bolman, assuming the character of his attending physician, horses were purchased, and after visiting several German cities, the friends arrived at Olmutz. Constantly intent on the object of their association, an acquaintance was speedily formed with the gaoler, to whose custody the illustrious prisoner was committed, and without appearing to take too great an interest in his fate, by speaking occasionally of the severity of his treatment, which they candidly acknowledged, they thought disproportioned to his offence, obtained permission to send him books that might beguile the tedium of solitude, and afford some mitigation of his griefs. The gaoler, a simple, benevolent man, saw no impropriety in the transaction, while the books delivered were subjected to his inspection, and the opportunity afforded of ascertaining, that there was nothing improper in their contents. Thus, a correspondence was established. La Fayette, informed of the source of this unhoped for indulgence, at once conceived that more was meant than met the eye, he, therefore, carefully perused the book, and found, in different places, words written with a pencil, which being put together, gave him the names of the parties, and a clue to their designs, which, if approved, would at once determine them, at all hazards, to free him from his captivity. The book was returned with an open note, thanking them for their civility in sending it, and an assurance, that it had been read with *marked attention*, and that he was, in the highest degree, *charmed with its contents*. In this manner, and by the stratagem of writing in lemon-juice on the back of a note, in its visible contents, altogether trivial, with a hint in the book sent—" *Quand vous aurez lu ce billet mettez le au feu;*" which, when complied with, caused the intended communication distinctly to appear in legible characters, he was made acquainted with their arrangements, and the day fixed on to put their plans in execution. They had been already apprized by the gaoler, that his prisoner, though generally closely confined, was permitted, under the charge of proper attendants, to take exercise without the walls; that he rode in an open cabriolet, accompanied by an officer, and attended by an armed soldier, who mounted behind by way of guard; and that, when at a distance from the walls, that it was their custom to descend and walk together, for the better enjoyment of exercise.

On the day appointed, La Fayette was requested to gain as great a distance from the town as possible, and on their approach, by an appointed signal, to discover himself, as he was unknown to both.

Every preliminary being arranged, the friends quitted Olmutz, well mounted, Bolman leading a third horse, and in anxious expectation awaited the approach of the object of their solicitude.

The city is situated about thirty miles from Silesia, in the midst of a plain, which, taking the town as a centre, extends three miles each way, without the interposition of woods, rocks, or impediments of any kind. From the walls, every thing passing within these limits, could be distinctly seen. Centinels were posted at all points, to give the alarm, whenever a prisoner endeavoured to escape, and considerable rewards promised to all who contributed their aid to secure him. These were, indeed, appalling difficulties, but not sufficient to check the ardour of youthful enthusiasm, intent to break the chains of a hero, against whom no accusation rested, but an ardent and unceasing effort to better the condition of his fellow men.

La Fayette, at length, appeared, accompanied by his usual attendants. The preconcerted signal was given, and returned. A conflict speedily succeeded, which gave freedom to the prisoner. The led horse was presented by Huger, who exclaimed

—"Use the means, sir, that are offered for escape, and may Fortune be your guide;" but, before he could mount, the gleam of the sun upon the sword that had been wrested from the officer, startled the animal, who broke his bridle and fled. Bolman rode off in pursuit, hoping to overtake him. In the interim, Huger, with a generosity truly chivalric, insisted that La Fayette should mount the horse that he himself rode, and hasten to the place appointed as a rendezvous.—"Fly," he exclaimed—"the alarm is given—the peasants are assembling—save yourself!" The advice was followed, and in a little time, the fugitive was out of sight. Bolman, who had in vain pursued the frightened horse, now returned, and taking Huger up behind him, galloped away, following the route of La Fayette. They had gone but a little way, when the horse, unequal to such a burden, stumbled and fell, and Bolman was so terribly bruised, as to be scarcely able to rise from the ground. The gallant Huger, aided his exertions to remount, and superior to every selfish consideration, earnestly entreated him to follow La Fayette, declaring that he could easily reach the woods which bordered the plain, and in their recesses find security. Bolman, though with extreme reluctance, complied.

During the rencontre which had taken place, the soldier, who had remained with the cabriolet, instead of assisting his officer, ran off towards the town, but the alarm had been given long before his arrival there. The transaction had been seen from the walls, the cannon fired, and the country raised. Bolman evaded his pursuers by telling them, that he himself was in pursuit. Huger, less fortunate, was marked by a party who never lost sight of him, and being overtaken, was seized and carried back in triumph to Ohmutz. Meanwhile, La Fayette was rapidly advancing in his flight, and had actually progressed ten miles, when arriving at a spot where the road divided, he was at a loss which to choose, and unluckily took the wrong one. Its direction very speedily induced him to suspect the truth, and he stopped to make inquiry of a man, who, concluding that he was a prisoner attempting to escape, gave him a wrong direction, running to a magistrate to communicate his suspicion, so that La Fayette, at a moment that he believed himself regaining a road that would give him security, found himself surrounded by an armed force, and again a prisoner. To the interrogation of the magistrate, his answers were so apt and ready, and a tale invented to account for the rapidity of his movement, so plausible, and so satisfactory, that expressing his conviction of his innocence, he was about to dismiss him, when a young man entering the apartment, with papers which required magisterial signature, after fixing his eyes attentively on the prisoner, said—"This is General La Fayette! I was present when he was delivered up by the Prussians to the Austrian Commandant, at———. This is the man, I cannot be mistaken." This declaration at once settled his fate. He too, was triumphantly conducted to Olmutz. Bolman escaped into Prussian Silesia, but after two days, was arrested and again delivered over to the Austrian authorities.

On the arrival of Huger at Olmutz, he was carried before Count Archo, the Military Commandant of the City, a veteran of high respectability, who conducted himself, during the examination, with gentleness and humanity, but after some inquiries, delivered him over to the Civil Authority.

Three days after this, chained hand and foot, the dauntless enthusiast was again brought before the Commandant and Civil Officer, to be further interrogated. The temper and disposition towards him, seemed now essentially changed.

The Civil Officer, this day, took the lead in the examination; and when Huger complained with strong expressions of indignation, of his treatment, the Judge imperiously demanded—"Know you, sir, the forfeit of your conduct?" An answer being returned in the negative, he very solemnly and impressively replied—"Your life!" But, apparently in order to remove the impression that such a sentence was calculated to produce, Count Archo immediately turned the discourse into a panegyric upon the Emperor, telling him, that his youth, his motives, and conduct, could not but secure his clemency. "Clemency," said Huger; how can I expect it from a man, who did not act even with justice, towards La Fayette." A check was immediately given to the boldness of the prisoner, and Count Archo then mildly added—"I judge of others from my own feelings. The attempt to injure me I freely forgive; and if ever I shall need a friend, I wish that friend may be an American."

Count Archo's entire conduct, was probably intended, not only to encourage hope in the prisoner, but to beget some consideration for him, and to give him consequence in the eyes of the Civil Officer, which might induce him to treat him better, and with greater respect than he had at first seemed inclined to do. And it certainly had its effect. Yet, with what shadow of excuse, can the conduct of the Emperor be palliated? A heart, possessed of any claim to generous feeling, or capable of justly appreciating the enthusiasm of disinterested friendship, would have spurned the idea of treating with rigour, an intrepid youth, whose generous ardour, in a cause that he idolized, constituted the only crime alleged against him. But chains—a dungeon—restrictions both in food and clothing, were imposed by the imperious fiat of power, and his sufferings regarded with an apathy degrading to the character of man. Yet, the ardent spirit that gave birth to enterprize, did not, under such appalling circumstances, forsake him. His mind was at peace with itself, and his fortitude remained unshaken.

During a long and rigorous confinement, Hope embellished the anticipations of more propitious fortunes, and constancy enabled him, with firmness, to support the immediate goadings and pressure of calamity. Restored at last to freedom, he sought his native country—became conspicuously serviceable in a military capacity, and now, in tranquil retirement, possesses as much of happiness as domestic felicity, and the universal esteem of his fellow-citizens can possibly bestow.

SURVIVORS OF THE REVOLUTION.

Having presented to my young Countrymen, this brief Narrative of the achievements of their ancestors, and of the patriotism of the dead,
"By all their country's wishes blest,"
would it not be blameable, to withhold the tribute of applause from the living, who honoured in early life, with the love and confidence of their Country, give now to the world, in the vale of years, examples of every patriotic virtue, that can evince their devotion to it.

GENERAL C. C. PINCKNEY.

Very early after his appointment, to command a company in the 1st Continental Regiment of his native state, Captain C. C. Pinckney was sent into North Carolina to recruit. He had scarcely established himself in quarters at Newbern, when two persons arrived there as settlers, very evidently, both from personal appearance, and easy address, of superior rank and qualifications. The one was advanced in years; the other appeared in the bloom and vigour of life. Captain Pinckney immediately recollected, that an intercepted letter from General Gage to Governor Martin (which, as a member of the Secret Committee, he had read previously to his departure from Charleston,) assured him, "That a Highland Officer of ability, well calculated to conduct an enterprize successfully, would speedily appear in his province; and earnestly entreated him, till such a person should produce his credentials, and to his entire satisfaction, make himself known as a zealous Loyalist, that he would use his utmost endeavours to keep the Scotch emigrants quiet, lest, by premature insurrection, they might blight the existing hope, and favourable prospect of a counter Revolution." Conviction, struck forcibly on the mind of Captain Pinckney, that one of the persons who had attracted his attention, was the very individual alluded to in the letter of General Gage—the other, his assistant and counsellor. He, accordingly, repaired to the Committee of Public Safety, and having stated his reasons for believing that the strangers were hostile to the views and interests of the country, demanded their arrest. Hostility was, as yet, but in its dawn—Aggression, on the one part, had not excited inflexible resentment on the other. The Members of the Committee were timid, and declined interfering, choosing rather to run the risk of a great evil than do an act that might be found unjust and oppressive. " Besides," (it was alleged by one of them) " the intercepted letter spoke but of *one*, and here are *two* persons equally liable to suspicions." " I would recommend the arrest of both of them," replied Captain Pinckney. " Prudence demands it. The age of the one proclaims him the Monitor to advise; the vigour and activity of the other, the Leader to execute." " It is enough," it was replied, " that we will allow you to recruit. We cannot any further, while a glimmering prospect remains of reconciliation, oppose the Royal authority." " Then, gentlemen" rejoined the Captain, " prepare for the consequences."

The event very speedily evinced the clear and accurate perceptions of Captain Pinckney. The strangers repaired to Cross Creek, and speedily exciting the countrymen to arm in support of the Royal Government, appeared at the head of a very formidable force. General Moore immediately marched against them. M'Donald, the Chief, was intrusted by Governor Martin, with the supreme command, and justified the high opinion entertained of his courage and activity; but, the veteran M'Leod, his associate, being killed, and many other officers of his party, his men abandoned him, and he was compelled to surrender himself a prisoner.

After the repulse of the British Fleet at Sullivan's Island, little prospect appearing of immediate hostilities in the South, the anxiety of Colonel C. C. Pinckney, (now advanced to the command of the 1st Regiment) to serve his country, and to acquire an increase of military knowledge, induced him to join the army in the vicinity of Philadelphia. There he was immediately received into the family of the Commander-in-Chief, and appointed his Aid-de-Camp. In this capacity, he was present at the battles of Brandywine and Germantown, and by his intelligence, zeal, and activity, so successfully won the confidence of Washington, as to be honoured by him afterwards, both in the field and in the diplomatic corps, with the most distinguished and important appointments.

As soon as danger threatened the South, he returned to Carolina; and on the approach of General Clinton to Charleston, was intrusted with the defence of Fort Moultrie. Influenced by the recollection of former misfortunes, and intent only on gaining the command of the harbour, the British Admiral, profitting by the advantage of a favourable breeze, and flowing tide, passed the fort with rapidity, giving little opportunity to the garrison, to display either courage or skill. The disappointment was great, and the hopes of enhancing the reputation of our arms was completely frustrated. To remain an idle spectator of the siege, was to a soldier of enterprize, ardent in the pursuit of his country's glory, altogether impossible. He hastened with a part of the garrison, to the post of danger; and so long as a cheering ray of hope encouraged resistance, offered an animating example of courage and of constancy. At the Council of War, summoned during the siege, to deliberate on the propriety of surrendering the city to the enemy, Colonel C. C. Pinckney delivered his opinion to this effect:— "I will not say, that if the enemy attempt to carry our lines by storm, that we shall be able to resist successfully, but I am convinced that we shall so cripple the army before us, that although we may not live to enjoy the benefits ourselves, yet to the United States they will prove incalculably great. Considerations of self, are out of the question. They cannot influence any member of this Council. My voice is for rejecting all terms of capitulation, and for continuing hostilities to the last extremity."

The battle of Bunker's Hill, and the more recent and brilliant victory at New-Orleans, show how correct the views of Colonel Pinckney, and prove, how completely militia can cripple, or destroy the most veteran troops, when sheltered (however slightly) behind entrenchments, which, to them, supply the place of discipline.

Captured in Charleston, and a prisoner till the conclusion of the war, no further opportunity was afforded to Colonel Pinckney, of serving his country in the field.

An effort while yet in durance, in the cause of humanity, must not be passed over in silence. Major Hyrne, the Commissioner sent by General Greene into Charleston, for the purpose of negotiating an exchange of prisoners, indignant at the harsh treatment shown to Colonel Hayne, and anxious to prevent the infliction of the penalties denounced against him, proposed to Colonel Balfour, that the circumstances of his case should be discussed by Colonel C. C. Pinckney of the American Army, and Major Barry of the British Forces, intelligent officers, at that period engaged in settling some points of controversy betwixt the contending parties. This being assented to by Colonel Balfour, Major Barry, who probably thought that an American officer knew just as little of the Law of Nations, as of the Doctrines of Confucius, boldly quoted the opinions of Grotius, as decidedly favourable to, and supporting the justice of the British proceedings; which being instantaneously declared incorrect by Colonel Pinckney, who averred, that the sentiments of that great man were in direct opposition to the statement made by Major Barry, reference was made to the author—whose works being produced by Colonel C. C. Pinckney, Major Barry was compelled to confess, that he was in error, lamenting—"That he had not studied the passage with his usual accuracy." Grotius, however, was no longer his oracle—it was indeed farcical to have named him, for he well knew the resolve of Lord Rawdon, and that the Laws of the Medes and Persians, were not more immutable than his fiat, once pronounced.

As a member of the enlightened assembly which framed the Constitution of the United States, he assisted in forming our present Government, and afterwards in the State Convention, by the force of his reasoning, and clear demonstration of its excellencies, contributed amply to its adoption, by a considerable majority.

In 1794, his firm opposition to the arrogance of the French Directory, demanding *Tribute* as the price of *Peace*, obtained for him, the universal applause of his country; nor can it be forgotten, while the hallowed Standard, raised at the construction of the lines for the defence of Charleston, on the Pinckney redoubt, proclaims the cherished sentiment of America—'*Millions for defence, but not a cent for tribute.*'

Another trait of character, exhibited at a later period, I cannot withhold from view. An officer of rank, talent, and distinguished military services, having been nominated in 1794, to a command inferior to General Hamilton's, indignantly exclaimed—"Though my salvation depended on it, I would spurn the Commission, rather than serve under a man whom I had once commanded." When General C. C. Pinckney, on his return from France, was informed that General Hamilton, his junior in rank, had been placed above him, by the nomination of General Washington, in the true spirit of patriotism, he replied—"I am confident that the Commander-in-Chief had sufficient reasons for this preference. Let us first dispose of our enemies—we shall then have leisure to settle the question of rank."

It is a tribute due to the disinterestedness that I venerate, that I record one other occurrence of peculiar interest. It is a fact well understood, that at the period of the struggle of party, relative to the nomination of a President of the United States, in the year 1800, that General C. C. Pinckney, by consenting to unite his name with that of Mr. Jefferson, would have secured to himself, the unanimous vote of the Electors of South Carolina. But, consistent with his *decided principles*, such an association could not be entered into; and to relinquish them, satisfied as he was of *their purity and correctness*, with a view to *self-aggrandizement*, would have evinced a duplicity altogether repulsive to his nature. The scheme of union was, accordingly, dropped. The contest took place, and the dignity aspired to was obtained by Mr. Jefferson. The Ex-President Adams, writing to General Gadsden on the occasion, thus expresses himself—"I have been well informed of the frank, candid, and honourable conduct of General C. C. Pinckney at your State Election, which was conformable to the whole tenor of his actions through life, as far as they have come to my knowledge."

GENERAL THOMAS PINCKNEY.

APPOINTED by the Society of the Cincinnati of South-Carolina, at the commencement of the late war with Great Britain, to declare their satisfaction on the nomination of their President, General Thomas Pinckney, to the command of the Army of the South, it was particularly grateful to me to find, that the sentiments then expressed, were greeted with the perfect approbation of the public. The sketch of his character, which I shall now present, will, I trust, be received with equal favour, since more particular traits are given of his military career, and details of achievements that, in a high degree, exalt his claim to applause.

Pursuing his studies in Europe, previous to the Revolutionary War, the dawn of hostility towards his country no sooner appeared, than renouncing his professional pursuits, his whole attention was given to the acquisition of military knowledge, and so rapid was his proficiency, that the rudiments of discipline were first taught by him to the infantry of the South-Carolina line. A mutiny among the troops, at an early period of the war, afforded an opportunity of manifesting that firmness and decision, so characteristic of him as a soldier. Persuasion having been first employed, without avail, while other officers indulged in menaces and upbraidings, Major Pinckney, unawed by their threats, and regardless of personal safety, walked deliberately into the midst of the mutineers, and with a blow of his sabre cut down the ringleader. The effect was instantaneous —the cry for pardon was universal, and the order to disperse, obeyed without a murmur.

At the battle of Stono, his exertions, as second in command of the light infantry under Colonel Henderson, gained him the highest applause. Two companies of the 71st Regiment, the elites of the British Army, sallying out from their redoubts to support their pickets, were eagerly charged with the bayonet, and so completely routed, that nine only of their number returned within their lines. The credit of the corps was still further increased, by the bravery with which they covered the retreat of the army, enabling General Lincoln, not only to maintain order, but to carry off his wounded without loss.

At the attack at Savannah, he headed an assailing column of the Continental Army, and actually mounted one of the British Redoubts, but was compelled, after sustaining considerable loss, reluctantly to retire.

In the account given of the suppression of the mutiny in his regiment, there appears sufficient evidence of his firmness and decision. No trait of his character more highly entitles him to admiration, than the inflexible steadiness of his temper. The composure of his mind was never ruffled, either by the threatening of immediate danger, or pressure of continued misfortune. I was informed by my respected friend *Colonel D'Oyley*, that while with Major Pinckney, superintending the construction of a redoubt at the siege of Savannah, a shell from the enemy fell into the ditch, and burst so near them, that the earth was thrown with violence over them both, and in such a manner, as completely to blind them, when the Major, without changing his position, or showing the slightest discomposure, calmly said—" I think, D'Oyley, that must have been very near us;" and continued, with great animation, to encourage the workmen to complete their labours. I state on the same authority, that at this disastrous siege, when the assailing column which he led was repulsed, and a retreat ordered, some confusion arising from the desire of the van, to press forward and get out of the reach of a heavy and destructive fire, by which they were greatly incommoded, Major Pinckney hastening into the front, commanded an immediate halt. " Success, my brave fellows," he exclaimed, " though richly merited, has not crowned your exertions; yet, do not disgrace yourselves by precipitate flight; and though repulsed quit the field like soldiers." The effect of this address was instantaneously perceptible. Order was immediately restored, and the regiment, with deliberate step, regained their encampments.

At the disastrous battle of Camden, while acting as Aid-de-Camp to General Gates, he was desperately wounded and made a prisoner. His patience and fortitude remained unshaken. Conveyed into the town, it was night when he reached Mrs. Clay's house (then by the fiat of power, converted into a Hospital.) The family had retired, and Major Pinckney was placed on a table in the piazza, where he lay till morning, suffering under a compound fracture of both bones of his leg, as he would not permit the rest of an oppressed and patriotic female to be disturbed. This calm and happy temper of mind, contributed in no small degree to the preservation of his life, for an exfoliation of the broken bones following soon after his removal to quarters, and no surgical aid at hand, he was obliged to direct the dressing of his wound, and to point out to his anxious and intrepid wife, the splinters that occasioned the greatest agony, while with tenderness she removed them. The trial was, indeed, a severe one, to a lady of uncommon sensibility; but there is no exertion to which the female heart, under the influence of its affections, is not equal. The duty performed, the fortitude of Mrs. Pinckney was no more; her emotion, on seeing her husband's sufferings, so totally overpowered her, that she fainted and fell. The recollection of such tender and heroic conduct cannot be lost; it must ever command the admiration of the world, and to her sex, afford a fascinating example for imitation.

The Embassies of Major Pinckney, both in England and Spain, give ample proof, that the intrepid soldier was an able negotiator; while the flattering reception he met with, on his return to his native country, evinced the continued affection of his fellow-citizens.* He was shortly after elected to Congress, and there his talents always commanded the most respectful attention.

It is little known, but certainly worthy to be recorded, that during our negotiation with France in 1798, when the despatches of our Envoys, Generals Pinckney, Marshall, and Mr. E. Gerry, reached the United States, detailing the hostility of

* His fellow-citizens took the horses from his carriage, and dragged him in it, amidst loud plaudits, to the place of his residence.

the Directory, and the humiliating proposition of tribute, President Adams, apprehending, that their immediate publication might occasion further indignities to be offered to those gentlemen, still remaning in Paris, wished to withhold them for a time from public view. On consulting Major Pinckney, he gave a decided opinion, that they ought immediately to be made public, that the people might obtain a perfect knowledge of the insulting conduct of the French Directory. "And, sir," he feelingly added, "if the situation of my brother causes you to hesitate, I speak for him, as I know he would for me, were I similarly circumstanced. The glory of our country is at stake. Individual suffering must not be regard. Be the event what it may, life is nothing compared with the honour of America."

During the late war with Great Britain, he commanded the Southern Army, and his utmost efforts were unremittingly employed, in the first instance, to perfect the discipline of the troops, to give them a confidence in themselves, and an ardent desire for fame; and in the second place, to secure our coasts and cities by fortifications, at those points the most exposed to the enemy. The Indian War, brought to a speedy termination under his auspices, gives the best testimony of the wisdom of his measures. Before he assumed the command, victories were gained without the acquisition of permanent advantage, and triumph invariably followed by precipitate retreat. The want of means to maintain the superiority acquired, imperiously called for its relinquishment; but, by establishing Military Posts, with depots of provisions, arms, and ammunition, security was given to conquest, and no abandonment of the territory subdued, was ever after necessary. His ready discernment of the talents of General Jackson, who, at a very early period, was pointed out to the Executive as an officer in the highest degree, meriting the confidence of the Government, has proved of incalculable advantage to his country, while the happy employment of them, by increasing his ardour for enterprize, and skill in turning to profit every possible advantage, led to one of the most brilliant victories that ever adorned the annals of the world.

GENERAL JACKSON.

It is impossible for me to name this distinguished character, without offering to his merits, the tribute of applause so justly their due. Carolina proudly numbers him among her sons. The world allow him a degree of excellence, rarely attained, and never surpassed by the military characters of the highest celebrity. To speak of him with enthusiasm, is consistent both with justice and duty. My object, in giving publicity to the Anecdotes I would record, is, avowedly, to honour the Fathers of our Revolution, and to excite that emulation in their descendants, to imitate their example, that will best secure the benefits resulting from their valour, and their virtues.

General Jackson, at a very early period of life, aspired to obtain celebrity. At the age of fourteen, he commenced his military career, and shared the glory of the well-fought action at Stono. Made a prisoner in his native settlement at the Waxaws, shortly after the surrender of Charleston, his manly opposition to the orders of an unfeeling tyrant, who wished to impose on him the duties of a hireling, gave superior claims to applause. Wounds were inflicted, and increase given to persecution, but without effecting either the steadiness of his principles, or firmness of his resolution. He told his oppressor—"You may destroy, but can never bend me to submission."*

Pre-eminently distinguished by services of a later period, there is an emanation of glory, giving brilliancy to his achievements, which renders him peculiarly the object of admiration. Of the prudence of his conduct, and ardour of his intrepidity,

---

* The severity of his treatment, arose from his refusal to obey an officer who ordered him to clean his boots. The spirit of the youth, which ought to have called forth applause excited no sentiment, but that of unbridled resentment.

when placed in command, I consider it altogether unnecessary to speak, as they transcend all praise. But, there are traits in his character, which, though hitherto but little noticed, should be more particularly detailed, and brought into view. He has, in all his conversations, and on every occasion, appeared a stranger to the arrogance too frequently resulting from success, nor been tempted by it, to deny his obligations to the Commander-in-Chief, of whom he ever speaks with warm affection, candidly acknowledging, that to a seady adherence to his well arranged plans, and able advice, is greatly to be attributed, the success that brought the war to so speedy, and happy a termination. But, for no part of his conduct do I consider him more entitled to praise, than for his steadiness in resisting the recommendation of Governor Blount, in the campaign of 1813, who advised him to discharge a part of his force, quit the country he had subdued, and to retire for security to the settlements. The Governor hesitated with regard to the exertions of power, and feared reproach in enforcing orders, which, when given, had been altogether neglected, or disobeyed. I admire the manly reply of General Jackson! I admire the Republican feeling that laid aside all the formalities of ceremony, and taught him, in the firm language of truth, to say to the Governor—" If you would preserve your reputation, you must take a determined course, regardless of the applause or censure of the populace, and of the forebodings of that dastardly and designing crew, who, at a time like this, continually clamour in your ears. The very wretches who now beset you with evil council, will be the first, should the measure which they recommend, eventuate in disaster, to call down implications on your head, and load you with reproaches. Your country is in danger; apply its resources to its defence! Can any course be more plain? There are times when it is highly criminal to shrink from responsibility, or scruple about the exercise of our powers. There are times when we must disregard punctilious etiquette, and think only of serving our country. The Commander-in-Chief, General Pinckney, supposes me prepared for renewed operations. Shall I violate the orders of my superior officer, and evince a willingness to defeat the purposes of my Government? Shall I abandon a conquest thus far made, and deliver up the friendly Creeks, and Cherokees, who, relying on our protection, have espoused our cause, and aided us with their arms? What! retrograde under such circumstances? I will perish first! I will do my duty—I will hold the posts that I have established, until ordered to abandon them by the Commanding General, or die in the struggle! I would not seek to preserve life at the expense of reputation! What then is to be done? I will tell you what! You have only to act with the energy and decision that the crisis demands, and all will be well! Send me a force engaged for six months, and I will answer for the result; but, withhold it, and all is lost—the reputation of the State, and yours, and mine along with it."

This was, indeed, the language of a patriotic heart; nor did he swerve from it, but nobly persisting in his resolution—fought—was victorious, and gloriously terminated the Indian War. Yet, in how much higher a degree must his resentments have been excited, and patience tortured, when at a later period on his approach to Orleans, where he was appointed to command, the Governor informed him—" That the Legislature, instead of discharging with alacrity, diligence, and good faith, the duties which had been confided to them by their constituents, had, under the garb of privilege, endeavoured to mar the execution of measures the most salutary for the defence of the country." And when he found, that on a requisition for their services, the militia resolutely resisted the call to rise in its defence, his indignation was roused to the highest pitch; and feeling conviction, that without a change of system, and the adoption of measures, energetic in proportion to the danger which threatened, that the country could not be saved, he promptly, and with decision, proclaimed Martial Law, calling on every individual, under the threat of the heaviest penalties in case of refusal, to step forward and defend his country. " He thought, at such a moment, (a powerful, ambitious, and enterprizing enemy ready to invade the soil) constitutional forms should be suspended for the preservation of constitutional rights; and that there could be no question, whether it was better to depart for a moment, from the enjoyment of our dearest privileges, or have them wrested from us for ever." It is not for me to detail the discussions which followed, nor the irritation eventuating from them, betwixt the civil and military power. I look to results. Disaffection was paralyzed. The spirit of the Commander was communicated to every division of the army. Hope and confidence animated every bosom. General Jackson knew, as he himself expressed it— "That he possessed the best defence, a rampart of high-minded and brave men." He knew, that his well-tried troops were equal to the most daring enterprizes; and that the less experienced levies were ambitious to emulate their glory. He led them to action with success, and when in turn assailed, defended his lines with a degree of skill, and display of intrepidity, that added a victory to the annals of his country, that will, to the end of time, do it honour, while it exalts his name to immortality. The blessings of a grateful nation, are the reward of Jackson.

It may, perhaps, be considered as a departure from my original plan, to give the details of an action of a recent date. But, the battle of the 23rd of December, 1814, fought at night before New-Orleans, appears to me so highly characteristic of the clear perceptions and intrepidity of General Jackson, and of such momentous importance, by its influence on subsequent events, that I shall present it as communicated to me, by the gallant Lieutenant Colonel Hayne, whose services on that, and every other occasion, cannot be too highly commended.

A brief account of the battle that took place before New-Orleans, on the night of the 23rd December, 1814, written by Colonel ARTHUR P. HAYNE, *at the particular request of Major General* ANDREW JACKSON.

ABOUT 2 o'clock P. M., on Saturday, the 23d of December, 1814, his Excellency the Commander-in-Chief, was informed by Major TATAM, that the enemy had effected a landing at the extreme point of Villery's canal, and from thence had reached the left bank of the Mississippi, six miles below the city of New-Orleans. The Commander-in-Chief, with much foresight had anticipated the probability of an attack from that quarter, and had, but one hour before, ordered five hundred men, under the command of Inspector-General HAYNE, to take post on Villery's Canal. Major TATAM and Mr. LATOUR, had been ordered to precede this command, for the purpose of reconnoitering. They were in the execution of this order, when to their astonishment, and that of the whole country, they found the British in the possession of the left bank of the Mississippi, only six miles below the city. In conformity with previous arrangements, and with which commandants of corps were made acquainted, signal guns were fired, and all the troops of the different cantonments were placed under arms, and ready to move against the enemy. The Commander-in-Chief, whose firmness in danger, and promptness in execution, eminently distinguish him, with a calmness and intrepidity which all must remember, *determined to meet the enemy.*

But he was well aware, from the manner in which his army was cantoned, that the city might be surprised before he was able to concentrate his forces. In order, therefore, to frustrate such an event, he determined to push the light troops in advance. These troops consisted of the Mississippi dragoons and two companies of riflemen. He had orders to proceed forth-

* " To prevent this, Colonel HAYNE, with two companies of riflemen, and the Mississippi dragoons, were sent forward, to reconnoitre their camp, learn their position, and in the event they were found advancing, to harass and oppose them at every step, until the main body should arrive."—*Life of Jackson, p. 287.*

with against the enemy, to reconnoitre his position, ascertain his strength, and if possible, to check his advance, so as to enable the Commander-in-Chief to collect and concentrate his forces. This duty was promptly performed, and without meeting with any opposition. It was supposed that the enemy's forces amounted to two thousand men, and a report to that effect was made to the Commander-in-Chief. The troops in advance then halted within a short distance of the enemy, and were joined by the main body of the army, a little after sunset. It was about this time that the order for battle was given, and the plan of attack explained. Commodore PATTERSON and Captain HENLY were directed to drop down the River with the schooner *Caroline*, come to anchor opposite the enemy's position, and at half-past seven o'clock, to bring on the action. The main army, under the immediate direction of the Commander-in-Chief, was to attack him in front at eight o'clock; and Brigadier General COFFEE's mounted riflemen, supported by Major HINDS' dragoons, had orders to turn his flank and gain his rear.

The following was the disposition of the main army:—The advance guard, led on by Lieutenant M'CLELLAND, had orders to proceed in as wide a column as the road would admit, and to attack the enemy's main picket, which was only three hundred yards in advance. He was also charged to make his men reserve their fire, to wait that of the enemy, and to continue his attack for fifteen or twenty minutes, as it would take that time to enable the artillery, whose position was immediately in rear of the advance, to form *battery*. After the execution of this order, the advance was to form in the rear of the artillery.

Our main line was only separated from the advance and the artillery, by a post and rail fence. It was composed of the 7th and 44th regiments of regulars, and Majors PLANCHE's and DAQUIN's city volunteers. These troops were drawn up in the avenue leading to La Rond's house, and had orders to break off by double files, from the heads of companies, and in that order to proceed against the enemy, dress to the right by the head of the artillery column, and thus to advance till our men should come in contact with the enemy. The line of battle was then to be promptly formed, by filing upon the right of companies. The enemy's position was some distance in advance of our line, his right toward the swamp, his left resting on the Mississippi, with a chain of centinels very closely posted in front of his camp, supported by strong pickets.

Our arrangements preparatory to action being all complete, and every thing ready, at half-past seven o'clock the battle was brought on by Commodore PATTERSON and Captain HENLY. This attack produced a very happy diversion in our favour, causing much confusion in the enemy's ranks, and compelling him to throw his whole line immediately under the Levee, thereby exposing his right flank to our main army, and his rear to Brigadier General COFFEE's command. At eight o'clock, the main army advanced in line of battle upon the right flank of the enemy, causing him to place his army somewhat in the form of a *crotchet*, in order to meet our attack, and still oppose the *Caroline*. At about half-past eight o'clock, Brigadier General COFFEE's men commenced their attack, taking the enemy in right flank and rear, and involving him in much confusion. The firing of General COFFEE's command was distinctly heard by our men. At about nine o'clock, the engagement became general. After an obstinate conflict of about one hour, the enemy was drawn from all of his positions. The heavy smoke occasioned by excessive fire, and a thick fog, induced the Commander-in-Chief to resume his former position, otherwise there can be very little doubt, that we would have succeeded in capturing the whole army of the enemy. Our series of attacks, in regular succession, had involved their ranks in so much confusion, that they were unable to recover themselves. Our loss was great, but that of the enemy was much more severe.

In the midst of Brigadier General COFFEE's engagement, Colonel REUBEN KEMPER, a man of sound and vigorous mind, and of uncommon coolness, courage and perseverance, found himself almost surrounded by the enemy. Perceiving his perilous situation, and that his only chance of escape was in stratagem, he exclaimed in an audible voice, to a group of the enemy —"What the Devil are you doing there? Where is your regiment? Come along with me immediately!" and they all followed him into the American lines, and were made prisoners.

Ensign LEACH also deserves particular mention. He received a severe and dangerous wound through the body, but never quitted his post till victory was secured. He then retired to the city; but the first gun that was fired in the lines, recalled him to the post of danger, where he remained till the final overthrow of the enemy.

The Americans engaged in the battle, may be estimated at about fifteen hundred regulars and irregulars; that of the British at about five thousand.

The Commander-in-Chief, apprehending a double attack, by way of Chef-Monteur, directed Major General CARROLL to take post on the Gentilly road.

The result of the battle was the saving of New-Orleans. The pride of an arrogant foe was humbled, the first time that he dared to profane the soil of Freedom by his hostile tread. It produced confidence in our ranks, established unanimity, and at once crushed disaffection. It is thought to be the most finished battle fought during the late war. The *ensemble* of the general movement, was maintained throughout the whole affair. It was not a mere exertion of physical strength, *as is often the case*; but in every stage of it, we clearly perceive the effects produced by the admirable arrangements of the Commander-in-Chief; and like Cæsar, he might have exclaimed—*Veni, vidi, vici.*"

CHARACTER AND CONDUCT OF THE OFFICERS OF THE LEGION.

I feel too proud of the partial friendship experienced from my brother Officers of the Legion, not to be ambitious, in some degree, to acquit myself of my debt of gratitude, by recording the successes resulting from their exemplary good conduct, and the achievements that gave to many of them, peculiar claims to celebrity. Where merited praise is not bestowed, I can truly aver, that it will not proceed from intentional neglect. The title of most of them to distinction, has been repeatedly acknowledged by their General, and confirmed by the flattering concurrence of their confederates in arms. I can only speak particularly of those with whom I was most familiar, and best acquainted. Major JOHN RUDOLPH, *the Captains* ARCHER *and* HURD, *the facetious Captain* CARNS, *bold in action, in quarters the delight of his associates;* GEORGE CARRINGTON, WINSTON, SNOWDEN, LOVELL, POWER, HARRISON, LUNSFORD, *and* JORDAN, *performed every duty with alacrity, and with the highest advantage to the service.*

CAPTAIN JOSEPH EGGLESTON.

CAVALRY.

This meritorious officer was endowed with superior powers of mind, but decidedly better qualified to gain celebrity in the cabinet, than in the field. He had the most perfect knowledge of duty, and was ever prompt in its performance; but the spirit of enterprize particularly requisite in a partizan, was foreign to his nature. There occurred, however, one rencontre with the enemy, in which he acquired distinction, both for talent and intrepidity. On the retreat of the British army from Ninety-Six, Lee, knowing that the rich settlement South of Fridig's Ferry, could alone afford the forage which they would require, determined to avail himself of the probable chance of striking a blow, which should paralyze every future movement, Eggleston was detached for the purpose, to the expected scene of action, and choosing an advantageous position, anxiously awaited their approach. A party of sixty British dragoons, and some foraging wagons speedily appeared, evidently intending to reach the very farm he occupied. The charge was immediately sounded. The Legionary Cavalry rushed forward with irresistible impetuosity, the enemy were at once put to rout, the wagons taken, and forty-five dragoons brought off prisoners, without the loss of a single man.

It is painful to state, though the imputation of blame rests not on him, that the opportunity of totally destroying the British cavalry at Eutaw was lost, by his having, from his ardour to perform his duty, obeyed an unauthorized order to engage. Foiled, and compelled to retire, when summoned to advance by Lee, he was too far distant to support Armstrong, who was ready to engage, but unequal with a single troop to meet the superior force of Coffin. On the day following the battle, however, he rendered very essential service, charging the retiring enemy, and taking from them several wagons containing stores and baggage. On this occasion, his horse was killed under him—he himself escaping without injury, though five balls pierced his clothes and equipments.

At the conclusion of the war, turning his attention to literary pursuits, he was returned a Member of Congress, in which respectable body he obtained applause and distinction.

Of warm and impatient temper, while yet in the flower of his age, tormented by the irritation of a disordered leg, and insisting on amputation, mortification ensued, which caused his immediate and untimely dissolution.

CAPTAIN JAMES ARMSTRONG.

CAVALRY.

There was no officer in the service of the United States, whose feats of daring intrepidity, had made a more salutary impression on the minds of the enemy, than those of Armstrong of the Legion. The British did justice to his merits; they admired his valour; they gratefully acknowledged his humanity; and when he, by an accident, became their prisoner, behaved towards him with marked and flattering attention. Had they displayed the same generous conduct towards others, which they exercised towards him, the asperities of the war would have been softened, and nothing heard of those acts of intemperate violence, which debased their character as men.

The details of his achievements are to be met with in every history of the war; it would be superfluous again to repeat them. But, one instance of his attention to a brave and unfortunate soldier, has not, in my judgment, been sufficiently dwelt upon. Lieutenant Colonel Lee was certainly a man of strong prejudices; but, where admiration was excited towards a gallant enemy, his generosity was unbounded. Fascinated by the consummate skill and bravery of Colonel Browne, in the defence of his post at Augusta, his resolution was immediately fixed, to save him from the fury of an exasperated population, and the better to effect it, put him under the safeguard of Armstrong, to conduct him to Savannah. The precaution was the more necessary, as the inveteracy of party, in the neighbourhood of Augusta, had given birth to a war of extermination, and he saw that without such interposition a gallant soldier, who had committed himself to his enemy, on their plighted faith, would otherwise have been sacrificed. Colonel Grierson of the British militia, had already fallen by an unknown hand; and to have risked a repetition of the crime, would have subjected the victorious commanders to merited censure and reproach.

I have often heard the gallant Armstrong declare, that he never had, in his own opinion, encountered equal peril with that which he experienced on this trying occasion. At every turn preparation was made for death—in every individual who approached, was seen the eager wish to destroy. Resentment was excited to the highest pitch, and called aloud to be appeased by blood. Yet, by dint of good management, by the gentleness of persuasion—by forcibly portraying the duty of humanity to a captured and unresisting foe, and occasionally well applied threats, he saved the contemplated victim, and delivered him in safety to his friends in Savannah.

A remarkable scene is said, by Dr. Ramsay, to have occurred on this occasion, which well deserves to be recorded, as exemplifying the firmness of a female, labouring under the deepest affliction of grief. Passing through the settlement where the most wanton waste had recently been made by the British, both of lives and property, a Mrs. M'Koy, having obtained permission to speak with Colonel Browne, addressed him in words to the following effect :—" Colonel Browne, in the late day of your prosperity, I visited your camp, and on my knees supplicated for the life of my son—but you were deaf to my entreaties! You hanged him, though a beardless youth, before my face. These eyes have seen him scalped by the savages under your immediate command, and for no better reason than that his name was M'Koy. As you are a prisoner to the leaders of my country, for the present I lay aside all thoughts of revenge; but, when you resume your sword, I will go five hundred miles to demand satisfaction at the point of it, for the murder of my son."

While Armstrong remained a prisoner, he was treated, as I have stated, with distinguished politeness. To Colonel Thompson, afterwards Count Rumford, I have heard him express great obligation; and still more to Commodore Sweeny, whose attentions were such, as none but a generous enemy could have known to bestow. I have only to add, that ever high in the esteem and affection of his associates, admired and respected in every society, he lived beloved, and died lamented.

CAPTAIN O'NEAL.

CAVALRY.

O'NEAL was one of the officers of the Legion, who rose to rank and consideration by the force of extraordinary merit. He entered the army a private trooper in Bland's regiment, and was one of a gallant band who, when Captain Henry Lee was surprised at the Spread-Eagle Tavern, near Philadelphia, resolutely defended the position against the whole of the British cavalry, and ultimately compelled them to retire. Lee, on this occasion, addressing his companions, and strenuously urging them rather to die than surrender, added—"Henceforth, I consider the fortune of every individual present, as inseparably connected with my own! If we fall, we will fall like brothers! If successful in repelling the enemy, (and it needs but a trifling exertion of your energies to effect it) my fortune and my interest shall be uniformly employed to increase your comforts, and secure your promotion." Nor did he ever swerve from his promise. Appointed, shortly after, with the rank of Major, to the command of a corps of horse, O'Neal and Winston, another of his faithful adherents, received commissions, and to the last hour of the war, by uniform steadiness of conduct, and exemplary intrepidity, gained increase of reputation. It was said, on this occasion, that Tarleton, making his first essay as a military man, but for the accidental snapping of O'Neal's carbine, would have fallen a victim to a bold effort, which he made to enter by a window at which he was posted, the muzzle of the piece being, at the time, within a foot of his head. Tarleton behaved with great calmness; for, looking up, he said with a smile, "You have missed it, my lad, for this time;" and wheeling his horse, joined his companions, who, deceived by a false alarm, were retiring with precipitation.

CAPTAIN MICHAEL RUDOLPH.

INFANTRY.

There was not, in the Southern Army, an officer of the same grade, whose activity and daring spirit produced such essential advantages to the service as Michael Rudolph; yet, in the page of history he is scarcely named. I never knew a man, so strictly enforcing the observance of discipline, who, at the same time, maintained so perfect an ascendancy over the affections of his men. He was their idol; and such was their confidence in his talents and intrepidity, that no enterprize, however hazardous, could be proposed, where he was to be the leader, but every individual in the regiment became anxious to obtain a preference of service.

His statue was diminutive; but from the energy of his mind, and personal activity, his powers were gigantic.

Fully to detail his services, is beyond my ability; but that he merited the grateful applause of his country, must be allowed, when it is recollected, that he led the forlorn hope, when the post at Paulus' Hook, in full view of the British garrison at New York, was surprised and carried by Lee; and that the same perilous command was assigned him at the storming of the Stockade Fort at Ninety-Six; that he bore a pre-eminently distinguished part in conducting the siéges of the several forts reduced in the interior country, and particularly directed that against Fort Cornwallis at Augusta; that at Guildford his conduct was highly applauded, and that he was conspicuous from his exemplary ardour, leading the charge with the bayonet, which broke the British line at Eutaw; that shortly previous to the evacuation of Charleston, he, with sixteen men, took and burnt the galley protecting the left of the

British line at the Quarter House, bringing off twenty-six prisoners; and that, finally, about the same period, fighting hand to hand, he dismounted and made a prisoner of one of the boldest black dragoons employed by the enemy.

Such were the Revolutionary services of the Captain, under whose auspices I entered the army, and whose virtues were no less estimable than his public utility.

At a later period in the war with the Western Indians, he served with distinguished reputation; but, anxious to provide for an increasing family, he left the service to engage in trade, and sailing on a voyage of speculation to the West Indies, was heard of no more.

CAPTAIN HANDY.

INFANTRY.

ANIMATED by principles as pure and patriotic, Captain Handy gained distinction by his zealous performance of every duty, and the invincible coolness with which he encountered danger. His activity contributed very essentially to the reduction of several of the forts held by the enemy in the interior country, particularly that at Augusta, where his vigorous charge on the British, who had, by a bold sally, actually possessed themselves of the trenches of the besiegers, caused their expulsion, and precipitate retreat into their posts, from whence they never ventured again. On the retreat of Lord Rawdon from Ninety-Six, while Lee was endeavouring to gain his front, Handy, deviating a few paces from his command, was seized and carried to a distance by a party of *banditti*, who robbed him of his watch, money, and every article of his clothing, leaving him in a state of perfect nudity, to find his way back to his party. The appellation which I have used is not too harsh; the ceremony of a parole was, indeed, insisted on, and given; but on application at an after period, to the British commander for the exchange of Handy, he candidly acknowledged, that he was not known as a prisoner, and that his captors, must have been a set of lawless marauders, of whom the British had no knowledge. Captain Handy, again restored to the service, by patient endurance of all the miseries and privations of the last campaign, had great influence in tranquilizing the minds of men, driven almost to desperation by famine and disease. The departure of the enemy, at length, closed the scene of calamity.

Handy led the van of the troops taking possession of Charleston, and having the command of the main guard, by his arrangement of patrols, and the correct conduct of his men, preserved a tranquility that could scarcely have been expected, from soldiers so long deprived of every comfort, who had now a town, rich in spoil, and many of their most implacable enemies, altogether within their power. To his credit I can assert, that no irregularity was committed—not a murmur heard.

LIEUTENANT PETER JOHNSTON.

INFANTRY.

Imbibing, at a very early period of the Revolutionary war, an enthusiastic attachment to the cause of Liberty, and sensible, that the opinions of his father, whose political creed sanctioned the pretensions of Britain, would militate against his ardent ambition to serve, Peter Johnston, at the age of sixteen, eloped from his college, and avoiding successfully the pursuit of his tutors, joined the Legion as a volunteer. His eagerness to acquire military knowledge, and unceasing efforts to obtain distinction, very speedily attracted attention, and obtained for him the commission to which he aspired, while the whole tenor of his conduct evinced, that it could not have been more judiciously bestowed. He was brave, enterprizing, and where duty called, exemplary in its performance. I will give no further proof of it, than his intrepid conduct at the siege of the post at Wright's Bluff, where the removal of the abbatis, under the immediate fire of the British riflemen, connected with the appalling erection of the Mayhem Tower, struck the enemy with so great a panic, as to cause an instantaneous surrender.

To the end of the war, he still acquired an increase of reputation, and so completely gained the favour of the parent he had offended, as to be received, on his return to the domestic circle of his family, not only with affection, but pride. Pursuing the study of the Law, he rapidly obtained professional reputation; and now promoted to a seat on the bench of Judges, is equally admired for the wisdom and justice of his decrees.

JOHN MIDDLETON,

CORNET IN THE LEGION.

Of Middleton, I would speak with justice, equal to his merit. It would, indeed, be a sacred duty were I competent to perform it. He was ever "the man nearest my heart." Brought up together from infancy, and united in our progress through life, by ties of the most disinterested friendship, he was to me as a brother; and I can with truth assert, that he never obtained an honour, nor progressed a step in public favour, which did not occasion, in my bosom, a sensation of delight, as perfect as if the merit had been my own. Every attraction that could induce a man of less exalted feeling, of patriotism less pure, to remain in England at the commencement of hostilities, were held out to him. Wealth, connection, preferments courted his acceptance. A living in the Established Church, of considerable amount, was his by inheritance; but, superior to every selfish consideration, and regarding the violated rights of his country, as injuries to his own honour, he nobly resolved, by the devotion of his life to her service, to become her defender, and ward off the exterminating blow, which the resentments of a merciless administration had denounced against her. Quitting Europe, and arriving safely on the American shores, he joined the Southern Army, and offering himself as a volunteer for promotion, speedily exhibited so many instances of gallantry, and so great an ardour for enterprize, as to be rewarded with a Cornetcy in the Legion. No youthful candidate for fame could ever, with greater success, have acquired the admiration of his superiors, the love of the troops serving under him, the perfect esteem and friendship of his brother officers. His career was short. He but lived to witness the expulsion of the enemy from our Capital, when seized by a mortal disease, he fell its victim. The regrets of every class of the community, affording the highest proof of his estimable character, his talents, and his virtues.

CLEMENT CARRINGTON,

OF THE LEGION INFANTRY.

Perhaps a more striking instance of the irregular action of fear upon the human mind, was never exhibited than at the battle of Eutaw. Early in the action, Mr. Clement Carrington, then a volunteer in the Legion, received a wound which incapacitated him from advancing with his corps, successfully charging the British with the bayonet. He was leaning on his spontoon, anxiously regarding the intrepid exertions of his companions, when a militiaman, flying from the field, appeared immediately in his front, rushing directly on him with the blind impetuosity of terror. Carrington, finding that he must be overturned, unless he could arrest his flight, crossed his spontoon over his breast, the more effectually to check his progress, and upbraiding his cowardice in an authoritative tone, commanded him to halt. The terrors of the fugitive were too highly excited to suffer control, he snatched the weapon opposed to him from the hands of Carrington, and passing the blade of it through his body, with redoubled speed ran on. To the satisfaction of his friends, the gallant volunteer recovered—was speedily commissioned in the Legion, and at the conclusion of the war, applying to the study of the Law, has since become a distinguished practitioner at the bar of Virginia.

DR. MATTHEW IRVINE.

It would be difficult to speak with encomium equal to his merit, of this excellent officer. This is no flattery; a cursory review of his services, will afford ample proof, that he stands in need of no such aid. He commenced his career, in the cause of Liberty, at the very dawning of hostilities, being one of that distinguished band, who, passing through the wilderness, and surmounting difficulties, such as had never before been encountered by man, appeared suddenly before the lines of Quebec. In the Middle States, he served with great distinction, being present at every action of consequence in the field, and participating in many partizan enterprizes, highly creditable to the American arms. But it was in the Southern war that he acquired the highest distinction, not only performing the duties of his profession with consummate skill, and exemplary tenderness and humanity, but frequently serving as an able negotiator with the enemy, and constantly employed as the confidential agent betwixt the General and the officers, on whose judgment he chiefly relied, in all consultations where important measures were contemplated, and secrecy regarded as essential to success. His great fault, if fault it can be called, was the too great exposure of his person. Possessing an intrepidity that could not be controlled, he was frequently to be found in the hottest of the fight; and it is well known that he was wounded at Quinby, at the head of Armstrong's troop, when his proper station was in the rear of the army. His military services ended, the celebrity he had acquired, as a skillful surgeon and physician, attended him in private life; and it is no exaggeration to say, that he continues the practice of his profession, with infinite advantage to the public, and constant increase of his own reputation.

DR. SKINNER.

I had, during the last campaign in the South, continued opportunity of witnessing the eccentricities of this extraordinary character; but while I admired his facetious and entertaining conversation, his exquisite humour, and occasional exhibition of sportive or pointed irony, I could not but consider him as a very dangerous companion. Colonel Lee has stated, that he had a dire objection to the field of battle, yet in private society always ready for a quarrel ; it might be truly asserted, that it required infinite circumspection not to come to points with him, since he really appeared to consider tilting as a pleasing pastime, and was (as an Irish soldier once said of him) " an honest fellow, just as ready to fight as eat." In his regiment, and among his intimates, he was regarded as a privileged man, and allowed to throw the shafts of his wit with impunity. This was a fortunate circumstance, as he would at any time rather have risked the loss of his friend, than the opportunity of applying a satirical observation in point. When first he appeared in the lower country, he wore a long beard and huge fur cap, the latter through necessity, the first from some superstitious notion, the meaning of which it was impossible to penetrate. An officer, who really esteemed him, asking him " why he suffered his beard to grow to such an unusual length," he tartly replied, " It is a secret, Sir, betwixt my God and myself, that human impertinence shall never penetrate." On a night alarm, at Ninety-Six, as Colonel Lee was hastening forward to ascertain the cause, he met Skinner in full retreat, and stopping him, said, " what is the matter, Doctor, whither so fast—not frightened, I hope?" " No, Colonel, no," replied Skinner, " not absolutely frightened, but, I candidly confess, most damnably alarmed." His strong resemblance to the character of Falstaff, which Colonel Lee has also noticed, was very remarkable. "He was witty himself, and the cause of wit in others." Like the fat knight, too, in the calculation of chances, not over scrupulous in distinctions betwixt *meum* and *tuum*; and, I should decidedly say, in his narrations of broils and battles, too much under the influence of Shrewsbury clock. I have seldom met with a man more fond of good and dainty cheer, or a more devoted idolater of good wine; but when they were not to be met with, the plainest food, and most simple liquor, were enjoyed with the highest relish. A lady of the lower country, addressing herself to a young officer who had been much accustomed to enjoy every species of luxury, asked, "how he had supported the privations experienced during the last campaign in the interior?" he replied—"That hunger made a simple rasher on the coals, as delicious as the most sumptuous fare, and where wine could not be obtained, he relished whiskey." "I am grieved, my young friend," said Skinner, with great gravity, "mortified, beyond expression, to hear such a declaration from your lips, since it has long been my opinion, that the man who would drink so mean a liquor as whiskey would steal."

In person, Skinner was not unlike the representation generally given of Sancho; in his government, exhibiting extravagant pretensions to state and self consequence. Nor was he insensible to the influences of the tender passion. He not only could love, but he believed himself possessed of every requisite to inspire passion, particularly priding himself upon a roguish leer with the eye, that he deemed irresistible. When disencumbered of his beard, he was presented at Sandy Hill, (the point of attraction to all the military) to Mrs. Charles Elliott, the amiable and benevolent hostess of the mansion. The facetious Captain Carns, who was his friend on the occasion, indulging his natural propensity to quiz, pointed her out to Skinner, as an object highly worth the attention of a man of enterprize. The bait was attractive, and he bit at it with the eagerness of a hungry gudgeon. On his first appearance, Skinner had shown evident marks of confusion, on account of the uncouth appearance of his cap. Mrs. Elliott had perceived it, and retiring for an instant, returned with an elegant military hat, which she placed on his head, and gracefully bowing, ran off. Skinner was mute with astonishment—he looked at the hat, and at the lady, and then at the hat again, and turning to his friend, seemed, in the language of Falstaff, to say—

"Her eye did seem to scorch me like a burning-glass."

The expression of his countenance was, to Carns, a sufficient indication of the agitation of his bosom. The hint was not lost. "Well," he feelingly exclaimed, "if ever a broad and palpable invitation was given, this, certainly, may be considered as such! Why, Skinner, what charm, what philter do you use to produce such havoc?" "Fie, fie," said the enraptured Doctor, adjusting his dress, and rising upon tip-toe, "Tempt me not, my friend, to make myself ridiculous. Mine is not a figure to attract the attention of a fair lady—it cannot, cannot happen!" "I will not," rejoined Carns, "compliment you, Skinner, on your personal attractions. You are a man of sense, a man of discernment, too wise to be flattered; but I certainly have seen men less elegantly formed than you are, and altogether without that *je ne sais quoi*, so fascinating, that you pre-eminently possess; besides, you have a fine, open, healthy countenance, a prepossessing smile, and a prodigiously brilliant and piercing eye." "Ah, ha," cried Skinner, "have you discovered *that?* You are a man of penetration! A man of taste! Yes, Carns, I *have* an eye, and if it has its usual trick, its tender expression, (you understand what I would say) I may, perhaps, be happy." Carns, for a time, gave indulgence to the effusions of his vanity, but would not suffer him to make himself completely ridiculous. Love was very speedily forgotten; and a kind invitation to feel himself at home, in the most hospitable mansion in the State, made Skinner the proudest and happiest of men.

Falstaff maintained, that it was proper for every man " to labour in his vocation." Skinner asserted, "that every man had his sphere of action, beyond the limits of which he ought never to emerge." "Mine," said he, "amidst the tumults of war, the conflicts of battle, is *in the rear.—There*, I am always to be found. I am firm at my post. What did Matthew Irvine get by quitting his?*—a wound—a villainous wound! Shall I follow his example, step out of my sphere, and set myself up as a mark to be shot at? O no! I am a stickler for the strict performance of duty, but feel no ambition to shine beyond it.

Being asked, which of the Ladies of South-Carolina possessed, in his estimation, the greatest attractions? he very readily replied, "The widow Izard beyond all comparison. I never pass her magnificent sideboard, but the plate seems ready to tumble into my pocket."

Arriving near the bank of the river, on the night of the contemplated attack upon John's Island, he was asked, whether he intended to pass the ford? "By no means," replied Skinner. "I am not fond of romantic enterprize, and will not seek for the perilous achievements where the elements, more than the enemy, are to be dreaded. The river is too deep, and my spirits are not buoyant; I should sink to a certainty and meet a watery grave. Death by water drinking! I shudder at the thought of it! I will remain and take care of the baggage; and as many of you as can boast a change, may be sure to meet, at your return, the comforts of clean linen, and the most cordial welcome that I can give you."

* After the gallant charge made by Captain ARMSTRONG at Quinby Bridge, both himself and his Lieutenant GEORGE CARRINGTON, having passed the gap made in it by the enemy, Dr. MATTHEW IRVINE put himself at the head of the dragoons who had failed in the attempt to cross, and made an entire company of the 19th Regiment prisoners, but in the conflict was wounded.

LIEUTENANT MANNING,

AND OCCURRENCES LEADING TO THE DEFEAT OF COLONEL PYLE.

That important consequences have resulted from accidental occurrences, and that achievements have been attributed to foresight and judgment, which originated in some fortuitous incident, cannot be doubted. The following anecdote may possibly be disbelieved by some, yet I must record it as doing honour to a fellow-soldier, to whom I was bound by the strictest ties of friendship. No man who knew Manning would question his veracity, and from his lips I received it. Nor is it credible, that *he* would wander into the regions of romance to exalt his reputation, when by the uniformity of his conduct, he was daily adding to the laurels universally acknowledged to be his due. I have besides, in my possession, a letter from my highly valued friend, Judge Johnson, of Abingdon, Virginia, at the period of its occurrence, an officer in the Legion, corroborating the principal fact, though slightly differing in the detail. With regard to the worth and abilities of Manning, his coolness and intrepidity, our sentiments are the same. His delineation of his talents and character I regard as perfect. "I never," says the Judge, "knew any man who was more remarkable for that quality, which is called presence of mind. The more sudden the emergency, the greater the danger in which he was unexpectedly placed, the more perfect was his self-possession, as related to the faculties both of body and mind. In corporal vigour and activity, he was exceeded by few; and there was an ardour about him, which characterized every thing that he said or did. If he had enjoyed the advantages of literary culture, he would have been as much the object of our admiration everywhere else, as he was in scenes of danger and military adventure."

Most of the settlers in North Carolina, in the neighbourhood of Cross Creek, now Fayetteville, were emigrants from Scotland, who had brought with them strong prejudices in favour of monarchy. Few among them had imbibed the spirit of Liberty, fostered with enthusiasm by almost the entire population in their adopted country; but, to the credit of such as professed attachment, it must be remembered, that having once declared in favour of the cause of America, none more courageously, zealously, and faithfully supported it. To Scotland, we owe many a gallant soldier. No other foreign nation contribute[d] so many distinguished officers in the line of our armies as Scotland. The intrepid *Mercer* sealed his devotion to our cause with his blood, and died in battle. Lord *Sterling*, Generals *M'Dougald*, *Sinclair*, *Stephens*, *M'Intosh* and *Davie*, were among the most gallant and strenuous champions of Independence. Knowing these facts, it cannot be imagined, that I could ever cherish or utter a sentiment injurious to a country to which I feel the strongest attachment, and from which I am proud to have derived my origin. A country, whose sons are brave, and daughters virtuous; where beauty is adorned with its most fascinating perfections, and manhood exhibits a vigour and activity that cannot be surpassed; where industry has produced an almost incredible influx of wealth, and the energies of mind an increase of literary acquirement, that places human knowledge on an eminence that it had never before attained; —a country where, as a student in a College of celebrity, I, for four successive years, listened with delight to the eloquence of the amiable and enlightened Miller, teaching, how far more congenial to the best feelings of the heart, and productive of happiness to man, is the purity of genuine Republicanism, than any system of government that the world has ever known. Where I studied the theory of morals, and witnessed the perfection of their practice, under the immediate protection and tuition of the first of Philosophers, and most virtuous of men, the immortal Dr. Thomas Reid. Where Jardine, the teacher of Eloquence, honoured me with his friendship; and the liberal kindness of other Professors, of the inhabitants of the city, generally, gave birth to sentiments of gratitude and affection, that can never be effaced. Truly, then, I can assert, that prejudices are unknown in the following narative:

The intrigues and efforts of Lord Cornwallis, to excite insurrection, backed by a very formidable force, had produced among the Highland emigrants a spirit of revolt, which it required all the energies of General Greene to counteract, before it could be matured.—The zeal and activity of Lieutenant Colonel Lee, whose usefulness exceeded calculation, united to his acuteness and happy talent of obtaining intelligence of every movement, and of the most secret intentions of the enemy, pointed him out as the fittest man for this important service. He was accordingly selected, with orders to impede the intercourse of Lord Cornwallis with the disaffected; to repress every symptom of revolt, and promptly to cut off every party that should take up arms for Britain. Constantly on the alert, and equally solicitous to give security to his own command, while he harassed the enemy. A secure position was, on one occasion, taken near a forked road, one division of which led directly to Lord Cornwallis' camp, about six miles distant. The ground was chosen in the dusk of evening; and to prevent surprise, patrols of cavalry were kept out on each fork during the night. An order for a movement before day had been communicated to every individual, and was executed with so little noise and confusion, that Lieutenant Manning, waking at early dawn, found himself, excepting one soldier, left alone. Stephen Green, the attendant of Captain Carus, lay near him, resting on the portmanteau of his superior, and buried in profound sleep. Being awakened, he was ordered to mount and follow, while Manning, hastening towards the fork, hoped to fall upon the track, and speedily rejoin his regiment. Much rain had fallen during the night, so that, finding both roads equally cut up, Manning chose at hazard, and took the wrong one. He had not proceeded far, before he saw at the door of a log-house, a rifleman leaning on his gun, and apparently placed as a centinel. Galloping up to him, he inquired if a regiment of horse and body of infantry had passed that way? "Oh, ho," cried the man, (whistling loudly, which brought out a dozen others completely armed, and carrying each a red rag in his hat,) " you, I suppose, are one of Greene's men." The badge which they bore, marked their principles. Without the slightest indication of alarm, or even hesitation, Manning pointed to the portmanteau carried by Green, and exclaimed —" Hush my good fellow—no clamour for God's sake—I have *there* what will ruin Greene—point out the road to Lord Cornwallis' army, for all depends upon early intelligence of its contents." " You are an honest fellow, (was the general cry) and have left the rebels just in time, for the whole settlement are in arms to join Colonel Pyle to-morrow, (naming the place of rendezvous) where Colonel Tarleton will meet and conduct us to camp." " Come," said the man, to whom he had first spoken, " take a drink—Here's confusion to Greene, and success to the King and his friends. This is the right road, and you will soon reach the army; or rather let me conduct you to it myself." " Not for the world, my dear fellow," replied Manning; " your direction is plain and I can follow it. I will never consent that a faithful subject of his Majesty should be subjected to the dangers of captivity or death on my account. If we should fall in with a party of rebels, and we cannot say that they are not in the neighbourhood now, we should both lose our lives. I should be hanged for desertion, and you for aiding me to reach the British army." This speech produced the effect he desired. The libation concluded, Manning rode off amid the cheers of the company, and when out of sight, crossed to the other road, and urging his horse to full speed, in a short time overtook and communicated the interesting intelligence to his commander. Lee was then meditating an attack upon Tarleton, who had crossed the Haw River to support the Insurgents; but, perceiving the vast importance of crushing the revolt in the bud, he informed General Greene of his plan by a confidential messenger, and hastened to the point of rendezvous, where Pyle, with upwards of four hundred men, had already arrived. It is unnecessary to detail the sanguinary scene which followed. Pyle completely deceived, and to the last believing the Legionary Dragoons the soldiers of Tarleton, was overpowered, and, with a considerable portion of his force, became victims of credulity.

It has been remarked, that "severity at first is often humanity in the end." Its policy, on this occasion, will scarcely be denied. As Lee permitted no pursuit, many escaped, and spreading universal alarm, so completely crushed the spirit of revolt, that opposition to government was put at once and effectually to rest. But had the Insurgents been cut off to a man, would not the act have been justified on the score of retaliation? The provocation would have sanctioned it. To Colonel Buford, but a little before, Tarleton had refused capitulation. Deaf to the voice of clemency, and intent on slaughter, a charge was made on an unprepared and unresisting foe. His heart was steeled against the claims of mercy, and, as Lee has forcibly said, "it needed but the Indian war-dance, and roasting fire, to have placed the tragedy which followed, first in the records of torture and death."

Many other proofs could be adduced of Manning's presence of mind, and cool intrepidity in action. It is grateful to me to mention one of these. At the battle of Eutaw, after the British line had been broken, and the *Old Buffs*, a regiment that had boasted of the extraordinary feats that they were to perform, were running from the field, Manning, in the enthusiasm of that valour for which he was so eminently distinguished, sprang forward in pursuit, directing the platoon which he commanded to follow him. He did not cast an eye behind him until he found himself near a large brick house, into which the York Volunteers, commanded by Cruger, were retiring. The British were on all sides of him, and not an American soldier nearer than one hundred and fifty or two hundred yards. He did not hesitate a moment, but springing at an officer who was near him, seized him by the collar, and exclaiming in a harsh tone of voice—"Damn you, sir, you are my prisoner," wrested his sword from his grasp, dragged him by force from the house, and keeping his body as a shield of defence from the heavy fire sustained from the windows, carried him off without receiving any injury. Manning has often related, that at the moment when he expected that his prisoner would have made an effort for liberty, he, with great *solemnity*, commenced an enumeration of his titles—"I am Sir, Henry Barry,

Deputy Adjutant General of the British army, Captain in the 52d Regiment, Secretary to the Commandant of Charleston." "Enough, enough, sir," said the victor, "you are just the man I was looking for; fear nothing for your life, you shall screen *me* from danger, and I will take special care of *you*." He had retired in this manner some distance from the brick house, when he saw Captain Robert Joiett of the Virginia line, engaged in single combat with a British officer. They had selected each other for battle a little before, the American armed with a broad sword, the Briton with a musket and bayonet. As they came together, a thrust was made at Joiett, which he happily parried, and both dropping their artificial weapons, being too much in contact to use them with effect, resorted to those with which they had been furnished by nature. They were both men of great bulk and vigour, and while struggling, each anxious to bring his adversary to the ground, a grenadier who saw the contest, ran to the assistance of his officer, made a longe with his bayonet, missed Joiett's body, but drove it beyond the curve into his coat. In attempting to withdraw the entangled weapon, he threw both the combatants to the ground; when getting it free, he raised it deliberately, determined not to fail again in his purpose, but to transfix Joiett. It was at this crisis that Manning approached—not near enough, however, to reach the grenadier with his arm. In order to gain time, and to arrest the stroke, he exclaimed in an angry and authoritative tone—"You damn'd brute, will you murder the gentleman?" The soldier, supposing himself addressed by one of his own officers, suspended the contemplated blow, and looked around to see the person who had thus spoken to him. Before he could recover from the surprise with which he had been thrown, Manning, now sufficiently near, smote him with his sword across the eyes, and felled him to the ground; while Joiett disengaged himself from his opponent, and snatching up the musket, as he attempted to rise, laid him dead by a blow from the butt end of it. Manning was of inferior size, but strong and remarkably well formed. Joiett, literally speaking, a giant. This, probably, led Barry, who could not have wished the particulars of his capture to be commented on, to reply, when asked by his brother officers, how he came to be taken, "I was overpowered by a huge Virginian."*

The reputation of a soldier, so highly distinguished both for valour and discernment, whose firmness enabled him, in all emergencies, to maintain a composure that neither difficulty nor danger could disturb, has caused the honour of giving birth to Manning to be claimed both by Ireland and America.

If my recollection is accurate, he certainly declared himself a native of Carlisle in Pennsylvania. Yet, when I remember the general tenor of his conversation—"the facility he possessed of involving in obscurity, the subject he meant to elucidate"— the accent on his tongue—the peculiar turn of his expression— his calling, for example, to his servant, walking with naked feet over ground covered by a heavy frost—"Shall I never teach you discretion, Drone!"—If you will go *bare foot*, why the devil don't you *put on* your blue stockings." And on another occasion, returning to camp, and looking at a bottle of spirits, *half emptied*, which he had left full—"Speak quickly, Drone, you big thief, and tell me what you have done with the remainder of my liquor!" My opinion is staggered, and I am inclined to acknowledge the superior claims of Ireland.

Manning, at the conclusion of the war, married into a highly respectable family, and settled in South Carolina. His attachment to a military life continuing unabated, he became a candidate for the appointment of Adjutant General of the Militia of the State, obtained it, and performed the important duties attached to it, with the applause of the public, till his death.

---

* HENRY BARRY was an eccentric character. He aimed at singularity in words as well as actions. He would send "his *bettermost* kind of compliments" to a lady; and, in a simple flower, present "the sweetest of *all possible* flowers." But in nothing was his conduct regarded as so farcical, as in his claim to delicate and liberal feelings. On one occasion, it has been stated, that reading a Poem, of his own composition, on the blessings of *Liberty*, a gentleman present asked him frankly, "How his actions could be so much at variance with the principles he professed?" "Because, Sir," he unblushingly replied, "I am a soldier of Fortune, seeking a snug and comfortable establishment. My feelings are as delicate as yours, or any other man's; but I never suffer myself to be *humbugged* by them." The day at Eutaw was certainly not his fighting day; but he is said to have distinguished himself in India.

SOLDIERS OF THE LEGION.

Having briefly sketched the characters, and detailed the services of several of the OFFICERS *of the Legion, I am confident that I shall gratify my readers, by recording a few interesting Anecdotes relating to the* SOLDIERS *of that corps. In proportion as they were removed from that rank in society, in which an enlargement of ideas, and expansion of mind was to be looked for, must be* THEIR *merit, who, under the exalted influences of military and patriotic enthusiasm, evinced a nobleness of soul, and chivalric intrepidity, increasing their own fame, and giving a higher stamp of celebrity to the American character. I fondly hope, that they will be received with cordiality by every patriotic bosom.*

SERGEANT WHALING.

WHEN the importance of wresting the possession of the Stockade Fort at Ninety-Six from the enemy, was clearly ascertained, Lieutenant Colonel Lee, to whom the charge of directing all operations against it, was intrusted by General Greene, adopted (it must be acknowledged too hastily) the opinion, that it might be effected by fire. Accordingly, Sergeant Whaling, a gallant non-commissioned officer, who had served with zeal and fidelity from the commencement of the war, and whose period of enlistment would have expired in a few days, with twelve privates, were sent forward in open day, and over level ground that afforded no cover to facilitate their approaches, to accomplish this hazardous enterprize. Whaling saw with certainty, the death on which he was about to rush, but by the prospect of which he was unappalled. He dressed himself neatly—took an affectionate but cheerful leave of his friends, and with his musket swung over his shoulder, and a bundle of blazing pine torches in his hand, sprung forward for the object of his attack. His alacrity inspired the little band with courage. They followed him closely up to the building around which the stockade was erected, before the troops within fired a shot. Their aim was deliberate and deadly. But one individual escaped with life. Whaling fell deeply lamented by every officer and soldier of the Legion. Instead of the rash and unavailing exposure to which he was subjected, all admitted his just claim to promotion—grieved that his valuable life was not preserved for those services he had so often shown himself so capable of rendering.

Poor Whaling!—the soldier's cherished hope was denied him,

"When all his toils were past,
"Still to return, and die at home at last."

SERGEANT MITCHELL.

It was at Ninety-Six also, that another soldier of distinguished merit lost his life, and unhappily under circumstances peculiarly distressing. Captain Michael Rudolph commanded the detachment of the infantry on duty on the night after the arrival of the Legion from Augusta, where the corps had been employed, during the early part of the siege of the post now threatened, in bringing Colonel Browne, and his command, to terms of submission. Sergeant Mitchell went the rounds with Rudolph, after having two hours before planted the centinels at their posts. Unhappily, among them were several militiamen, who had never before seen service. One of these, without challenging, fired at the relief with which Rudolph and Mitchell were approaching his position, and shot Mitchell through the body. He fell to the ground—told his Captain that he was mortally wounded—warmly pressed his hand—asked if he had ever neglected or omitted any of the duties of a faithful soldier and true patriot—regretted that he had not closed his life on the field of battle, and conjuring him to bear evidence that he died without fear, and without a groan expired! He was a Virginian from the County of Augusta. I fondly hope that this tribute to his memory, may reach his friends. Whaling was a Pennsylvanian.

BULKLEY AND NEWMAN.

Among the incidents in the Southern army, that excited the highest interest, was the singular and romantic friendship which united two of the most distinguished soldiers of the Legionary cavalry. Bulkley and Newman were natives of Virginia, born in the same neighbourhood, and from early infancy united by such a congeniality of sentiment, that it almost appeared as if one soul gave animation to both. Their attachment increased with their years—it strengthened with their strength. As school-fellows they were inseparable; their task was the same, and he who was first perfect in acquiring it, was unhappy till he had impressed it, with equal force, on the mind of his friend. When an appeal to arms, at the dawn of our Revolution, had called forth the youthful heroes of America to fight the battles of their country, and defend her violated rights, *both*, on the same day, and animated with the same enthusiastic devotion to her cause, were enrolled in the ranks of her armies. The officers of the Legion, who yet survive, can testify, that through all the perils and difficulties of the Southern war, each seemed more anxious for the safety and alleviation of the sufferings of his friend, than of his own. In action they invariably fought side by side; in the more tranquil scenes of encampment, they were constantly engaged in the same pursuits; their toils and their pleasures were the same. When at Quinby, the memorable charge was made on the 19th British Regiment, by the intrepid Armstrong, Bulkley and Newman were among the few dragoons, who, having leapt the gap in the bridge, which the enemy were industriously attempting to widen, were able to support their commander. The display of gallantry exhibited could not have been surpassed. Armstrong, seconded by George Carrington, his Lieutenant, his gallant Sergeant Power, the brave Captain M'Cauly, of the militia, and less than a dozen of his own troopers, actually cut his way through the entire regiment, when a heavy and fatally directed fire produced a most direful catastrophe. Power fell desperately wounded; and the youthful friends, Bulkley and Newman, closed their brilliant career in the path of glory for ever. Mortally wounded at the same instant, they fell on the same spot, and, with united hands, reciprocating kindness to the last, expired.

CORPORAL COOPER.

Making a tour to the North, in the year 1817, I was invited to visit the Franklin, then lying at Chester, in company with the Commodores Murray and Dale, and several other officers of distinction. On our passage to the ship, some mention being made of Carolina, a naval officer present, said, "I do not believe there exists at this day, an individual who has a more perfect knowledge of the Southern war of the Revolution than myself, particularly, all that relates to the battles fought in the Carolinas. I entered those States with the Legion, commanded by *Harry Lee*, and witnessed the conclusion of our toils at the evacuation of Charleston." "Under such circumstances, Sir," I immediately replied, "it must be my good fortune to be in company with an old companion, for I had the honour of holding a commission in the infantry of that regiment, and was, like yourself, attached to the command which took possession of Charleston, when given up by the British." "I am, Sir," rejoined the officer, "altogether at a loss, even to guess at your name; nor do I recollect ever to have seen you before. Attached to the Legion, you must have known Armstrong, who commanded the Sorrel Troop, and have probably heard of *Corporal Cooper*, who belonged to it." "Good heavens, Cooper," I exclaimed, with delight, "is it you? I now am astonished at my own forgetfulness, for I as thoroughly recognize you as if we had parted but yesterday!" I mentioned my name in turn, and was happy to find that I was not forgotten by him. I am confident that, on this occasion, the sensation of delight and good feeling to men who had served and suffered together, was strongly experienced by both. The surprise and satisfaction of the moment being at an end, Cooper, with a significant smile, said, "By the by, I believe you were one of the officers who sat on the court-martial when I was in jeopardy, and brought to trial at our encampment, near the Ashley River." "No, Cooper," I replied, "I was not; though I well remember, on another occasion, when we lay at M'Pherson's, that, in consequence of your——" "Hush, hush, my dear Sir," he exclaimed, "I find that you have an excellent and accurate memory, the less we say on *that subject* the better." I had known Cooper well; and it is no exaggeration to assert, that a more gallant soldier never wielded a sabre. The character, indeed, of consummate intrepidity, distinguished every individual of Armstrong's troop. Disciplined by him, and animated by his example, they were invincible. But there were particular traits that characterized Cooper, that entitled him to still higher commendation. If activity and intelligence were requisite to obtain information—if gallantry to strike a partizan blow, Cooper was always uppermost in the thoughts of Lee. He had a soul for enterprize, and by prompt discernment, and a happy facility of calculating from appearances of events to happen, of incalculable utility to the service. When Armstrong, by the falling of his horse, was made a prisoner, and a flag sent out from the British commander to say, that his servant and baggage would be expected, as he wished to show every civility to an enemy, whose bravery could only be exceeded by his generosity to all who fell into his power, Cooper was immediately directed by Lee, to act the part of a domestic, and sent forward for the purpose. I mentioned my recollection of the circumstance to Cooper, who replied, "and well I knew my Colonel's motives; and so perfectly was I disposed to second his views, that while taking the refreshment which was ordered for me by General Leslie, in the front of his quarters near the British lines, I was closely examining the course of a creek in his rear, by which I flattered myself, I should very speedily be able to conduct and introduce him at the Head-Quarters of our own army." He then went on to say—"The arts used by a Captain Campbell, who tried every manner of cajoling, to pick out of my conversation intelligence of our force and position, very highly amused me. I acted the simpleton's part so naturally, that I could clearly perceive, that he believed me completely entangled in his toils. When suddenly changing my manner, I gave him such a burlesque and exaggerated an account of troops of dragoons and regiments of infantry, that had no existence but in my own imagination, that perceiving my drift, he angrily exclaimed, " Damn you, you rascal, you are too cunning for me. Here, take a drink of grog and depart." I cannot conjecture why it was done; but finding that I was not to be deceived, I think that they might have done me the credit to suppose, that I was not to be intimidated ; but, instead of conducting me to my Captain, I was led to, and shut up in the Provost, when looking through the bars, I perceived Armstrong passing merrily along with several Naval officers, who seemed to vie with each other in civility to him. My situation forbid ceremony, so I called out lustily —" Hollo, Captain Armstrong ! pray have the goodness to tell me, is it *you* or *I* that am a prisoner?" My speech produced an explanation. I was immediately released; and profitting by every occasion to store my mind with useful intelligence, in a few days left the garrison, a partial exchange having freed my Captain from captivity. My fortunes have since varied very much. I have gained nautical information—have commanded a ship of my own—have, as a Naval officer, supported the flag of my country—and now the war being over, find a snug birth in the Navy Yard. My varied life would greatly amuse could I detail it, more especially, as its constant bustle but ill accords with *my religious principles;* for, though you might not suspect it, whenever my thoughts take a serious turn, I am professedly a member of the Society of Friends, a genuine homespun Quaker."

Although the expedition against Georgetown, conducted by General Marion and Lieutenant Colonel Lee, was not, from a combination of adverse circumstances, crowned with success. Although the flight of a guide, who had engaged to conduct Captain Armstrong and the dragoons of the Legion to a point, which would have effectually prevented the British soldiers, who had escaped the Legionary Infantry, from reaching a redoubt that afforded perfect security, had given ample grounds for the suspicion of treachery, and disconcerted the plans that had promised the most perfect triumph; yet, advantages arose from it of considerable consequence to the American cause. Colonel Campbell, the Commandant, was taken, and about seventy men either killed or made prisoners. It convinced the British, that however great the distance by which they were removed from their enemy, (the Continental army being, at the period of attack, on the borders of North Carolina) that they were still vulnerable, and at every moment subject to attack. It checked their marauding, predatory expeditions, gave comparative security to the oppressed inhabitants in their vicinity, and to themselves, full assurance, that to be safe, they must continue inactive, and remain within the limits of their garrison. It is pleasing to me to record the singular gallantry of a most meritorious soldier, who, on this occasion, gained high renown.

SERGEANT ORD.

In every instance where this heroic soldier was engaged in action, he not only increased his own reputation, but animated those around him by his lively courage. In camp, on a march, and in every situation he performed all his duties with cheerfulness and vivacity, preserving always the most orderly conduct, and keeping his arms, accoutrements, and clothing in the neatest possible condition. He might, indeed, be considered a perfect soldier.

At the surprise of Georgetown, being with a small party of the Legion infantry, in possession of an inclosure, surrounding a house from which they had expelled the enemy, the recovery of the position was sought by a British force, whose leader, approaching the gate of entrance, exclaimed—" Rush on, my brave fellows, they are only worthless militia, and have no bayonets." Ord immediately placed himself in front of the gate, and as they attempted to enter, laid six of his enemies, in succession, dead at his feet, crying out at every thrust—" No bayonets here—none at all to be sure!" following up his strokes with such rapidity, that the British party could make no impression, and were compelled to retire.

PERRY SCOTT.

There was no soldier in the Legion infantry, who appeared more completely to have gained the favour of Lieutenant Colonel Lee, than Perry Scott. His chief merit consisted in his consummate intrepidity, and readiness to engage in hardy enterprize. As often as a partizan expedition was in contemplation, he was invariably selected as one of the daring spirits to insure success. I am tempted to call for the pity of his countrymen for his untimely end, from the recollection, that in all the battles of the South, from the junction of the Legion with the army of General Greene, till the final retreat of the enemy, he was noticed for distinguished valour and activity. He was present at the evacuation of Charleston, and shortly after disbanded; but, devoted to a military life, again enlisted with his former commander, Michael Rudolph, then at the head of a Legionary Corps, under the orders of General Harmar, and as Sergeant Major acquitted himself with reputation.

The Indian war terminated, Scott knowing, that many of the officers of the Partizan Legion of Lee, and several of his old associates, had settled in Carolina and Georgia, resolved to visit them, and actually reached the Cheraws with that intention. Here, for the sake of repose, after a wearisome journey, he took up his quarters at a public house, kept by an old soldier, once attached to the volunteers of Ireland, the corps commanded by Lord Rawdon. An amicable intercourse, for a time, increased the attachment of these veterans to each other. Scott eulogized the bravery of the Irish, and his companion was lavish in his commendation of the soldiers of the Legion, when unluckily drawing comparisons relative to the merits of their respective corps, a serious quarrel ensued, which they immediately determined to settle by the sword. The conflict was maintained with spirit and obstinacy, and its result long doubtful, but Scott gaining a superiority and actively maintaining it, was about to triumph, when the wife of his adversary interfering, and putting a loaded pistol into her husband's hand, he discharged it at poor Scott, who fell dead at his feet. This conflict being considered as the settlement of a point of honour, no effort had been made to prevent it, but the survivor was now arrested, and being shortly after tried for murder, was condemned and executed.

PATRIOTS IN THE CIVIL LINE,

AND PRISONERS CONFINED AS SUBJECTS FOR RETALIATION.

WHILE such applause is bestowed on Revolutionary characters, distinguished in the field of glory, I consider it equally a duty, and it is altogether congenial to my inclination, to express my high admiration of the illustrious patriots, who, in defiance of the varied species of oppression by which they were incessantly goaded, adhered, with unshaken resolution, to the principles they had pledged themselves to support. History affords no example of magnanimity, that can surpass the firmness and patient suffering of the intrepid associates, who, selected as objects of peculiar severity, and more refined persecution, were accused of imaginary crimes, and, in violation of the capitulation of Charleston, and every principle of good faith, torn from their families, and exiled to St. Augustine. It has been said, that constancy will give place to despair, when suffering appears without end. To find them, therefore, firm in duty, and meeting their fate with that intrepid assurance which could alone result from greatness of soul, and a consciousness of correct and irreproachable conduct, must, as long as mankind possess sense to perceive, and virtue to approve, the beauty of patriotic worth and excellence, secure to them the gratitude and veneration of their country. This inhuman and unjustifiable measure is said to have been adopted expressly to ascertain the firmness and constancy of the American character. What was the result? Did tyranny produce submission? Did integrity lose its dominion in the patriotic heart? O, no! The reverses of fortune afforded a more ample field for the display of their exalted magnanimity; and they never appeared less appalled, nor inclined to bend with submission to the yoke, than at the period when not a ray gleamed in perspective, to cheer them through the dark terrors of the storm. Not an individual shrunk from his duty.

It is due to their exemplary firmness to be a little more particular relative to the suffering they were compelled to endure. When all the exiles (with the exception of General Gadsden, who steadily persisted in his resolution to enter into no new engagement with men who had once deceived him) had given their paroles to confine themselves within certain prescribed limits, and to withhold, until exchanged, all active opposition to the British authorities. The commanding officer of the garrison, as if distrustful of their sincerity, issued an order, that they should attend, at roll-call, thrice every day, in these insulting words:

"St. Augustine, September 16th, 1780.

General Orders.

"The Rebel prisoners are to appear at gun-fire in the evening, and at guard mounting in the morning, at the Town House, where the Commissary will attend, and call the roll of every name, and report to the Captain of the day if any be absent.

"They are to put some badge of distinction on their negroes and other domestics, so that they may be known.

"No Rebel uniform, or any coats in imitation of British or French Regimentals, to be worn by any of them.

"If any soldier is seen or known to associate with any of the Rebels, he shall be brought to a Court-martial, and tried for a disobedience of orders.

"By order of the Commanding officer,

"WM. FLOYER, Lieutenant,

"Acting Adjutant in 60th Regiment.

"To Wm. Brown, Esq.

"Commissary of Prisoners."

Additional severities were constantly imposed; but none that so highly aggravated misfortune, as an order which forbid the worship of the Deity. This was at first communicated by a verbal message, but was speedily followed by a direct order to Mr. Brown, the Commissary of Prisoners, to this effect:

"ST. AUGUSTINE, November 18th, 1780.

"SIR:
"HAVING been informed that the Rebel prisoners have very improperly held private meetings for the purpose of performing Divine Service, agreeably to their rebellious principles, and as such proceedings are thought highly injurious to His Majesty's Government, and of seditious tendency, and an infringement of their pledge of honour: I desire you will acquaint them, that such meetings will not be allowed, and that seats will be provided for their reception in the Parish Church, where it is expected they will observe the utmost decency. You are also to mention to these gentlemen, that I consider messages delivered by you of sufficient weight and authenticity, and that it is in compliance with your request, that I descend to this manner of satisfaction, which Lieutenant Colonel GLAZIER also desires may be understood to be expressive of his sentiments.

  (Signed)   "PAT TONYN.
"To WM. BROWN, Esq.
"Commissary of Prisoners of War."

It is unnecessary for me to comment on this outrageous insult both to God and man. I will content myself by giving an extract from the diary of the venerable Mr. Josiah Smith, which plainly, but *forcibly*, speaks its effect upon the mind of a pious man.

"Behold the act of a British Governor; an act neither charitable in its nature, nor pious in its intention. Totally unworthy of the Christian character, and even short of Heathen tenderness and forbearance. For we read in Scripture, Acts, chap. xxviii, ver. 30 and 31, 'that Paul, then a prisoner in Rome, dwelt for two whole years in his own hired house, and received all that came unto him, preaching the kingdom of God, and teaching those things which concerned the Lord Jesus Christ, with all confidence, *no man forbidding him.*' This only was our desire—and this we think was our duty; to spend a part of every Sabbath in holy adoration of the Divine Being who not only created, but daily preserveth us, and in tender mercy supplies all our wants. But we are charged with proceedings of a seditious tendency, and violation of our paroles and pledge of honour. This we absolutely deny, having carefully avoided to require any thing tending that way from our reader and preacher, either in sermons or prayers. Once, indeed, some expressions in the latter were made use of by the reader, contrary to the expectations of the company, but never again repeated; nor did we once court or enjoy the presence of any inhabitant in our Sabbath assemblies. But that we might not plead the entire want of religious worship, we are 'invited to attend the Parish Church, where seats will be provided for us, and where it was expected that we should observe the utmost decency.' This is, indeed, an insult upon our understandings; for, can it be expected, that we could, with the least sincerity, join in prayer for the daily destruction or disappointed efforts of our brethren and friends, or implore success for a man that had countenanced every kind of oppression and cruelty towards our friends and connexions, and all with a view of enslaving us and our posterity, and to whom we have sworn that we will never be subject while we can have the power of remaining free citizens of the United States of America. Such worship would indeed be no better than solemn mockery; therefore, rather than join in such hypocritical petitions, and perhaps be insulted with sermons calculated to affront us, we have resolved to refuse our attendance on Divine worship, at the Parish Church, and patiently put up with the loss of paying our devotions publicly, and at our own dwellings silently to spend our returning Sabbaths, in the best manner we can, by reading and meditation, until it shall please the Almighty disposer of all events, to restore us again to peace, and to our afflicted families and friends."

But how shall I find expression to do justice to the heroes, who, arrested as objects of retaliation, in the event of General Greene's carrying into effect his threat relative to the execution of Colonel Hayne, were shut up in prison-ships, and kept in momentary expectation of death. Allowed to forward an address to the American General, whose highly excited resentments the British commanders were anxious to deprecate. They urge not, as might have been expected, the adoption of measures which would ensure their safety, but raised by their magnanimity above the terrors of an infamous and public execution, alone lament, " that if it be the lot of *all* or *any* of them to be sacrificed, that their blood cannot be disposed of more to the advancement of the glorious cause to which they had adhered." Where, in the annals of the world, shall we find an instance of more exalted patriotism. The highly eulogized self-devotion of Regulus, which immortalized his name, and added lustre to the reputation of his country, when compared with such a display of magnanimity, shrinks into insignificance. The Roman had been remarkable for the severity of his manners, and would have been the last to excuse the failures of another; he therefore preferred a death which would obliterate from the minds of his countrymen the recollections of his misfortunes, and even exalt him in their opinion, to a life which could only subject him to neglect, and the severer pangs of self-reproach. But, in this instance, not a solitary individual, but a band of heroes, regardless of their own safety, bid defiance to the malignity of their persecutors, and calmly solicit, that no consideration of their sufferings, should alter the resolutions that the American General had adopted as necessary to the maintenance of the honour and interests of his country.

It must be acknowledged, that the conduct of the officers of the Continental Line, composing the army of General Greene, gives them a title to distinguished encomium. Regardless of the consequences to which, in case of capture, they would be exposed, they come forward with unanimity, and earnestly solicit that prompt retaliation should avenge the murder of a heroic soldier, and for ever put down the wish to renew such sanguinary proceedings. " We are not," they say, " unacquainted that such a measure will involve our lives in additional dangers, but we had rather forego temporary distinctions, and commit ourselves to the most desperate situations, than prosecute this just and necessary war, upon terms so unequal and dishonourable." This proceedure was highly gratifying to General Greene, but scorning to increase the miseries of the deluded loyalists who had joined the British standard, he resolved to retaliate on the regular officers alone. Fortunately for those who had been designated as the proper objects of resentment, no one of equal rank with Colonel Hayne was ever after made a prisoner. I well remember when Major Skelly, of the 71st regiment, was taken, report had given him higher rank—he was called Colonel Skelly. When ascertained that he was a really *a Major*, General Greene, whose mind was evidently extremely agitated, said, " I rejoice at the circumstance, as he has the reputation of having always conducted himself with humanity, and like a gentleman. Had he been a Colonel, he must have suffered."

My admiration of patriotism is such, that I make no excuse for giving the names of the persons, who, by their virtuous example, may teach the rising generation how to act and how to suffer for the honour and prosperity of our Republic.

EXILES TO ST. AUGUSTINE.

Edward Blake, John Budd, Joseph Bee, Richard Beresford, John Berwick, Robert Cochran, Benjamin Cudworth, Henry Crouch, John Splatt Cripps, Edward Darrel, Daniel De Saussure, John Edwards, Thomas Ferguson, George Flagg, Christopher Gadsden, Lieutenant Governor; William H. Gibbes, Thomas Grimball, G. A. Hall, William Hall, Thomas Hall, Thomas Heyward. Jun., Isaac Holmes, Richard Hutson, William Johnson, Noble Wimberly Jones, William Lee, Rev. John Lewis, William Logan, William Livingston, John Loveday, Richard Lushington, Arthur Middleton, William Massey, Edward M'Cready, Alexander Moultrie, John Morrall, John Neufville, Edward North, Joseph Parker, John Ernest Poyas, Samuel Prioleau, Jacob Read, Hugh Rutledge, Edward Rutledge, Benjamin Postell, John Sausum, Thomas Savage, Thomas Singleton, Josiah Smith, Philip Smith, James Hamden Thomson, Peter Timothy, John Todd, Anthony Toomer, Benjamin Waller, James Wakefield, Edward Weyman, Morton Wilkinson.

Of these distinguished citizens, five only survive, viz: Josiah Smith, Robert Cochran, George Flagg, W. H. Gibbes, and John Todd.

PRISONERS ON BOARD THE PRISON-SHIP TORBAY.

William Axson, Samuel Ash, George Arthur, John Anthony, Ralph Atmore, John Baddely, Peter Bommetheau, Henry Benbridge, Joseph Ball, Nathaniel Blundell, James Bricken, Francis Bayle, William Basquin, John Clarke, Jun., Thomas Cooke, Norwood Conyers, James Cox, John Dorsnis, Joseph Dunlap, Rev. James Edmonds, Thomas Elliott, Joseph Elliott, John Evans, John Eberley, Joseph Glover, Francis Grott, Mitchell Gargil, William Graves, Peter Gnerard, Jacob Henry, David Hamilton, Thomas Harris, William Hornby, Daniel Jacoby, Charles Kent, Samuel Lockhart, Nathaniel Lebby, Thomas Listor, Thomas Legare, John Lesesne, Henry Lybert, John Michael, John Minott, Sen., Samuel Miller, Stephen Moore, George Mouck, Jonathan Morgan, Abraham Mariett, Solomon Milner, John Neufville, Jun., Philip Prioleau, James Poyas, Job Palmer, Joseph Robinson, Daniel Rhody, Joseph Righton, William Snelling, John Stephenson, Jun., Paul Snyder, Abraham Seavers, Ripley Singleton, Samuel Scottowe, Stephen Shrewsbury, John Saunders, James Tousseger, Paul Taylor, Sims White, James Wilkins, Isaac White, George Welch, Benjamin Wheeler, William Wilkie, John Welch, Thomas You.

PRISONERS ON BOARD THE SCHR. PACK-HORSE.

John Barnwell, Edward Barnwell, Robert Barnwell, William Brandford, John Blake, Thomas Cochran, Joseph Gray, Robert Dewar, William De Saussure, Thomas Eveleigh, John Edwards, Jun., John W. Edwards, William Elliott, Benjamin Guerard, Thomas Grayson, Thomas Gibbons, Philip Gadsden, John Greaves, William H. Henry, John B. Holmes, William Holmes, Thomas Hughes, James Heyward, George Jones, Henry Kennon, John Kean, Stephen Lee, Philip Meyer, George Mosse, William Neufville, John Owen, Charles Pinckney, Jun. Samuel Smith, William H. Wigg, Charles Warham, Thomas Waring, Jun., Richard Waring, John Waters, David Warham, Richard Yeadon.

There are still other patriots to be added to the list of persons subjected to peculiar persecution. The dreary vaults of the Provost were assigned to them as a residence, and in some cases, with the additional incumbrance of heavy irons. The Colonels Stark and Beard, Captain Moore, Mr. Pritchard, Messrs. Peter Boquet, Samuel Legare, Jonathan Sarazin, Henry Peronneau, Daniel Stevens, and others, who, incapable of deserting the cause of their country, had shown no disposition to submission, were regarded as the proper objects on whom it was expedient to try the effect of coercion. They underwent the trial, the ordeal of persecution, without the slightest dereliction of principle, their patriotic virtue retained its purity to the last.

THE ANCIENT BATTALION OF ARTILLERY.

Wheresoever a display of patriotic devotion to the service of their country has distinguished any association of citizens, it has been peculiarly grateful to me to record it. I consider it a tribute justly due to the Charleston Ancient Battalion of Artillery, to state, that their patient endurance of difficulties, their active exertions in the field, gained them, throughout the war, a continued increase of reputation.—Their exemplary gallantry in the action near Beaufort, where a considerable British force under Gairdner, was defeated by General Moultrie, and steady conduct on the lines during the siege of Charleston, when the defence of the Horn-Work was particularly intrusted to them, must for ever redound to their credit. Nor is it less honourable to them to find, in the list of Exiles banished to St. Augustine, and persons selected for peculiar persecution, and sentenced to close confinement in the Provost and Prison-Ships, the names of all their officers without an exception, and very many of the non-commissioned officers and privates of the Battalion. They were the only volunteer corps of the militia that remained, at the conclusion of the war, unbroken; and after the evacuation of Charleston by the enemy, being speedily reorganized and recruited, have continued to preserve their high and merited reputation. It is a pleasure to me to give the names of the officers in command at the restoration of peace.

Thomas Grimball, *Major*.
Thomas Heyward, *Captain*.
Edward Rutledge, *do*.
Anthony Toomer, *do*.
William H. Gibbes, *Captain Lieutenant*.
Sims White, *Lieutenant*.
Edward Neufville, *do*.
Peter Bounthieau, *do*.
William Morgan, *do*.
John D. Miller, *do*.
Edward Weyman, *do*.
Daniel Stevens, *do*.
Charles Warham, *do*.

GENERAL GADSDEN.

The conduct of the British commanders towards this venerable patriot, in the strongest manner evinced their determination rather to crush the spirit of opposition, than by conciliation to subdue it. The man did not exist to whose delicate sense of honour, even a shadow of duplicity would have appeared more abhorrent than General Gadsden. Transported by an arbitrary decree, with many of the most resolute and influential citizens of the Republic, to St. Augustine, attendance on parade was peremptorily demanded; when a British officer stepping forward, said, "Expediency, and a series of political occurrences, have rendered it necessary to remove you from Charleston to this place; but, gentleman, we have no wish to increase your sufferings; to all, therefore, who are willing to give their paroles, not to go beyond the limits prescribed to them, the liberty of the town will be allowed; a dungeon will be the destiny of such as refuse to accept the indulgence." The proposition was generally acceeded to. But when General Gadsden was called to give this new pledge of faith, he indignantly exclaimed, "With men who have once deceived me, I can enter into no new contract. Had the British commanders regarded the terms of the capitulation of Charleston, I might now, although a prisoner, under my own roof, have enjoyed the smiles and consolations of my surrounding family; but even without a shadow of accusation proffered against me, for any act inconsistent with my plighted faith, I am torn from them, and here, in a distant land, invited to enter into new engagements, I will give no parole." "Think better of it, Sir," said the officer, "a second refusal of it will fix your destiny—a dungeon will be your future habitation." "Prepare it, then," said the inflexible patriot, "I will give no parole, *so help me God!*"

An opposition to the arbitrary mandate of the prevailing

authorities, was estimated as a crime too flagrant to pass unpunished. The rectitude of his character, the respectability of his age, afforded no plea in his favour; he was immediately separated from his companions in misfortune, and for the remaining period of his captivity, condemned to pass his days in solitary confinement. It was not, however, for persecution to daunt and overcome a mind as firm in patriotic virtue as his. Patient under every insult, he felt the pressure of tyranny, but bent not beneath its weight. He uttered no sigh, he made no rémonstrance, nor deigned to solicit a mitigation of the severities inflicted upon him; and for ever to his honour must it be remembered, that, superior to the dictates of resentment, however highly excited, at the memorable session of the Legislature at Jacksonborough, no individual advocated with greater ardor and humanity the cause of the unfortunates, who had incurred the public displeasure, nor more strenuously endeavoured to mollify the punishments denounced against them.

"*Les malheureux, qui ont de l'esprit, trouvent des resources en eux mêmes.*" Sensible that activity of mind would increase its energies, and better enable him to support oppression, he diligently engaged in the study of the Hebrew language, and was hourly increasing his reputation as a scholar, while his enemies vainly hoped that he was writhing under the penalties of his political offences.

The character of a disinterested patriot, pure in principle, and guided by the most honourable intentions, was allowed to him even by the most determined of his political opponents. The late Governor Boone, decidedly the man of the best information and correct judgment ever sent from Britain to preside over the province of South Carolina, was heard at the commencement of the Revolutionary War, to say—"God knows how this unhappy contest will end, or what the popular leaders in South Carolina can be aiming at—but Gadsden I know to be an honest man—*he* means well."

A writer of intelligence, immediately subsequent to his death, doing homage to his virtues, recommends, and in my opinion with singular propriety, a sentence from Cicero, as an appropriate epitaph:

"IN DIFFICILLIMIS REIPUBLICÆ TEMPORIBUS URBEM NUNQUAM DESERUI—IN PROSPERIS NIHIL DE PUBLICO DELIBAVI, IN DESPERATIS NIHIL TIMUI."

And to the still higher increase of his reputation, adds—"The first to raise the standard of opposition against the parent government, he was the first to recommend oblivion in favour of those who differed in opinion, and who were condemned to pay the penalty of their political offences, by the forfeiture of their estates."

An instance of his firm and decided character, which occurred in the year 1777, is highly worthy to be recorded. The Congress of the United States, not long after the Declaration of Independence, having recommended to the States, that such of the disaffected as were willing to take the oath of allegiance, should be permitted to do so; Mr. Lowndes, then President of the State, issued his Proclamation, extending the time for taking the oath allowed by the act of the State Legislature. This measure being reprobated by some of the whigs, a number of persons assembled, who, after tearing the Proclamation from the hands of the Marshal, proceeded with noise and tumult to the State House, where the President and Council were then in session. General Gadsden, who was one of the Council, came out to the people, and finding their resentments directed towards the President, told them that he, himself, was the man whom they should assail—that he had advised the Proclamation—that the public interest required the country should be united—and that all who were willing to embark in the common cause, should be received, though they came in at the last hour—that the recommendations of Congress, at such a crisis, should be received as law—that those who resisted them were little better than the enemies of the country—that for himself, whatever might be said, or done, he, as a Magistrate, would administer the oaths to any person, to the last moment of the time permitted by the Proclamation. In pursuance of this declaration, he sat up till twelve o'clock of the night of the last day appointed for the purpose of receiving the oaths, and did, actually, at a late hour, issue certificates to some who took the oaths before him.

When first shut up in the Castle at St. Augustine, the comfort of a light was denied him by the Commandant of the Fortress. A generous subaltern offered to supply him with a candle, but he declined it, least the officer should expose himself to the censure of his superior.

After Andre's arrest, Colonel Glazier, the Governor of the Castle, sent to advise General Gadsden to prepare himself for the worst—intimating, that as General Washington had been assured of retaliation, if Andre was executed, it was not unlikely that General Gadsden would be the person selected. To this message he replied—" That he was always prepared to die for his country; and though he knew it was impossible for Washington to yield the right of an independent State by the law of war, to fear or affection, yet he would not shrink from the sacrifice, and would rather ascend the scaffold than purchase with his life the dishonour of his country."

An election of a Governor of the State occurring shortly after his exchange, the suffrages of the majority of the Legislature were in his favour, but he declined the office, and in terms so highly honourable to him, that I fear not to offend by recording their purport.

"MR. SPEAKER AND GENTLEMEN:

"I have served my country in a variety of stations for thirty years, and would now cheerfully make one of a forlorn hope in an assault on the lines of Charleston, if it was probable that with a certain loss of life, you, my friends, would be reinstated in the possession of your capitol. What I can do for my country, I am willing to do. My sentiments in favour of the American cause have never changed. I consider it as the cause of liberty and human nature. The present times require the vigour and activity of the prime of life; the increasing infirmities of old age would prevent me from serving you to your advantage. For your sakes, and the sake of the public, I must beg your indulgence for declining so arduous a trust."

JOHN RUTLEDGE.

The extraordinary powers of John Rutledge, his extensive knowledge, and irresistible eloquence, can best be estimated by the high encomium bestowed on him by the celebrated Patrick Henry, of Virginia, who declared, that in the first Congress, where there was as brilliant a display of talent as was ever exhibited in a collected body of legislators, " that he shone with superior lustre." Being asked on his return to his native State, " what had been done by the representatives of the nation—what kind of men composed that illustrious body, and particularly whom he thought the greatest man," he replied, " If you speak of eloquence, *John Rutledge*, of South-Carolina, is the greatest orator; but, if you speak of information and sound judgment, *Colonel Washington* is unquestionably the greatest man on the floor." Of his decision of character there can exist no doubt. It was strongly exemplified at the very commencement of the Revolutionary contest. When the vote to appoint deputies to a Continental Congress was carried in the Assembly of South-Carolina, propositions were immediately introduced, for instructing the delegates to what point it was admissible for them to pledge the concurrence of the Province to such measures as might be proposed for general adoption. John Rutledge, with great ability, contended, that unless unshackled by restraint, and allowed to act at discretion, that their power to do good would be inadequate to the energies which the crisis demanded; and being asked, " what ought we to do then, with these men should they make a bad use of the power delegated to them, he replied, " *hang them.*"

But to his guidance of the helm of government, during the most calamitous scenes of the war within the State, is in a great degree to be attributed the successes ultimately obtained over a powerful and triumphant enemy. He, at a very early period, perceived the superior ability of General Greene to direct every military operation, and with, indefatigable industry, seconded his views with all the influences of the civil authority. His judicious promotion of the Generals *Sumter*, *Marion* and *Pickens*, did credit to his discernment, and proved of the highest utility to his country, while the well-timed proclamations, promising pardon and protection to all who had in an evil hour been tempted to make submission, awakened as by a charm the slumbering energies of patriotism, and roused the entire population of Carolina, as one man, to seek for conquest, or encounter death. In his speech, when advanced to the Presidential chair of the State, on the first formation of the Constitution, he declared, " I have always thought every man's best services due to his country ;" and to the last hour of the war, his entire conduct gave testimony of his sincerity. His zeal and activity never knew abatement. His decision in refusing to sanction the abandonment of the Fort on Sullivan's Island, on the approach of the fleet of Sir Peter Parker, must, for ever, redound to his honour, since it not only gave to General Moultrie, and his intrepid garrison, the opportunity to show how firm the resistence of men determined to be free; but so completely changed the sentiments of the enemy with regard to the opposition which they were to encounter, when engaged with Carolinians, that, though still formidable in force, and capable of doing much mischief, they at once relinquished the idea of further hostility, and precipitately withdrew to New York.

His exertions in collecting the militia of the interior country at Orangeburgh, on the invasion of Prevost, and expeditious movement to frustrate the attack on Charleston, by its happy results, increase his claim to applause. Above every other trait of character, (when I consider the propensity of man to indulge with wantonness in the exercise of delegated authority) it must redound to the honour of John Rutledge, possessing dictatorial powers, that the justice and equitable current of his administration, never engendered the slightest murmur, nor gave birth to a single complaint. So mild, indeed, and conciliating were all his actions, that obedience went hand in hand with command; and the ardour of zeal seemed rather to solicit service, than seek the means of avoiding it.

Though taxed by *Cassius*, a political writer of the day, as being the framer and advocate of the Confiscation Law, (now generally reprobated) it would be the height of injustice exclusively to censure *him*, when at the moment of its passing, there were not more than a dozen members of the Legislature who declared their sentiments, or gave their votes in opposition to it. The fact is, that the provocation to severity had been considered as excessive, and the irritation of the public mind excited beyond control. I was on the spot at the moment that the bill passed, and had strong reason to believe, that though certainly approved, it did not originate with him.

EDWARD RUTLEDGE.

As firmly attached as his brother, to every feeling and sentiment of patriotism, Mr. Edward Rutledge, with equal assiduity, devoted his time and his talents to the public service. If the Demosthenian eloquence of John Rutledge was more impetuous and commanding, the Ciceronian style of Edward was more persuasive. There was a suavity in his manner, and conciliating attraction in his arguments, that had frequently the effect of subduing the prejudices of the unfriendly, and which never failed to increase the ardour and inflexibility of steady friends. The eloquence of John Rutledge was as a rapid torrent; that of Edward as a gentle and smoothly gliding stream—the first hurried you forward to the point it aimed at, with powerful impetuosity—the last conducted to it, with fascinations that made every progressive step appear enchanting. Civil occupations engaged the attention of the elder brother. The younger in the field, as well as in the cabinet, obtained celebrity. In the well-contested action on Port Royal Island, he had the command of one of the field-pieces which essentially contributed to the victory, and justly received the thanks of the General who commanded. After the capture of Charleston, the influence both of his talents and example, did not escape the penetration of the British Commanders. They plainly saw, how much a man of such superior ability, would be looked up to by the suffering multitude; and to destroy the effect, by an act of as great tyranny as ever was exercised, removed him to St. Augustine. The cheerfulness of his natural disposition, his conciliating attention to his companions in this situation of unmerited persecution, contributed in no trifling degree, to cherish hope, and oppose intrepid resistance to every encroachment of despondency. After his exchange and freedom from captivity, he was elected a Member of the Legislature of the State; and at the conclusion of the war, served in the Council aiding the administration of Governor Matthews. The act of his life that exalts him to the highest honour, is still to be mentioned. He was one of the signers of the Declaration of Independence, on the 4th of July, 1776. This is a sublime test of patriotism, that can never be disputed; and which, as long as the liberties of America shall endure, will secure to him the admiration and blessings of his country.

HUGH RUTLEDGE.

The talents of Mr. Hugh Rutledge were not, perhaps, equally brilliant, nor of so distinguished a cast as those of his brothers; but, for solidity of judgment, and strong manly sense, he was not inferior to either of them; and as a firm and intrepid patriot, was pre-eminently distinguished by the cheerful performance of every duty to his country. He too, like his brother Edward, was deemed of sufficient consequence, to be made an object of peculiar persecution; and being sent into exile, supported all the trials of long confinement, and irritating restrictions, with unshaken constancy. After his exchange, he filled the Speaker's Chair in the Legislature greatly to the satisfaction of its members, and finally advanced to the Chancery Bench, closed a life of usefulness with the applause and sincere regrets of his grateful country.

DR. DAVID RAMSAY.

The literary character of Dr. Ramsay does honour to his country; his political conduct during the Revolutionary war no less honour to himself. The dawn of hostility found him with a reputation for talents, integrity, and patriotism, which his conduct throughout the contest seemed to extend and embellish. It was the peculiar characteristic of the American Revolution, that the men the most distinguished for genius and virtue were its advocates. In the ranks of *the Rebels* (as the English delighted to call them) were found almost all the orators, statesmen, and philosphers, of whom the country could boast. Lawyers who had attained the highest distinction in the Legislature, and at the bar; Physicians who had become eminent for their science and professional skill; Merchants who had acquired wealth and honour by commercial enterprize; and even ministers of the Gospel, who, by their learning and piety, had endeared themselves to the people, all united their efforts in the common cause. Thus was dignity given to the contest, and the public feeling was excited to a state of the most noble enthusiasm. The influence of Dr. Ramsay's example was felt and acknowledged by all. He was universally esteemed as a man of professional learning, and of the purest patriotism, and he was known to be governed in all his actions by a deep sense of moral and religious duty. The purity of his life was considered as the best evidence of the uprightness of his views. The zeal with which he espoused the cause of freedom, could not fail then to produce a powerful effect on the minds of the timid and scrupulous. Dr. Ramsay never hesitated a moment as to the part he should take in the struggle.

With an earnestness and ardour which no danger or difficulty could impair, he embarked his life and fortune in the cause of liberty and his country. He was one of the earliest advocates for independence, and in every period of the war he wrote, and spoke, and acted, with the greatest zeal and ability for the accomplishment of that glorious object. As a member of the Council of Safety, of the Provincial Legislature, and finally of the Continental Congress, he was always distinguished for his eloquence in debate, his wisdom in council, and his promptitude and energy in action. Having engaged in the contest from principle, Dr. Ramsay pursued his course with a devotion and perseverance, which proved that his heart was in the work. The press teemed with the ingenious productions of his pen; and at all public meetings his eloquence was exerted to sustain the pride and spirit of the people. Regardless of his private interests, he never hesitated to perform any labour, or to incur any risk, which the general welfare seemed to require. When his professional services were called for he constantly joined the army, and was present with the Charleston Ancient Battalion of Artillery at the siege of Savannah. It was natural that such a man should become the peculiar object of the vengeance of the enemy. He was accordingly one of the victims selected by Lord Cornwallis to be banished to St. Augustine. After an exile of eleven months, in consequence of an exchange of prisoners, he was released and returned to Carolina, joining Governor Rutledge at the Hills of Santee, and shortly after took his seat as a member of the Legislature, convened at Jacksonborough. Though he had just suffered great indignity from the injustice and violated faith of the enemy, yet always superior to bad passions, and incapable of revenge, he exerted his great talents and influence in the Assembly to prevent the passage of the Confiscation Acts, and to lessen the punishments denounced against political offenders. These honourable exertions were not crowned with success, yet still the praise is due to Dr. Ramsay of having sacrificed his personal feelings, and made a noble effort to stem the torrent of public indignation, which was then sweeping before it many of the wisest and best men of the State.

During the Revolution he was carefully treasuring up materials for a history of its eventful scenes, his ardent character never permitting him to doubt the final success of his countrymen, and the establishment of American Independence. In the year 1785, he published his History of the Revolution in South Carolina, and in 1790, he gave to the world his general History of the American Revolution. No man could have brought to the composition of such works, higher qualifications or a more valuable stock of information. He was aware, that his feelings as an American patriot, might affect his impartiality and bias his judgment; and he also knew, that a faithful detail of facts, would probably be received at that period, by both parties, with dissatisfaction. He set out, therefore, with a firm resolution, as he himself declares, " to decline the fruitless attempt of aiming to please either party, and to follow the attractions of truth whithersoever she might lead." In the prosecution of this honourable determination, " I declare (says he) " that in the whole course of my writing, I have carefully watched the workings of my mind, lest passion, prejudice, or party feeling should warp my judgment; and I have endeavoured to impress on myself, how much more honourable it is to write impartially for the good of posterity, than to condescend to be the apologist of a party." No higher praise can be bestowed on Dr. Ramsay, than to say, that he acted on these noble principles in the composition of all his works. By the histories above alluded to, and those which he afterwards published, Dr. Ramsay acquired the distinguished appellation of *The American Historian*, and erected for himself a monument as lasting as time.

The character of Dr. Ramsay's eloquence was altogether striking and peculiar. I never heard on the floor of our Legislature, a Speaker whose harrangues were better calculated to impress on his audience the truths which he wished to inculcate. His arguments always forcible, and admirably arranged, were brought forward with peculiar effect: for, so strong was his expression of feeling, that it was impossible not to believe him sincere. His biographer on this subject, expresses himself as follows:—" Dr. Ramsay was a remarkably fluent, rapid, and ready speaker; and though his manner was ungraceful—though he neglected all ornament, and never addressed himself to the imagination, or the passions of his audience, yet his style was so simple and so pure, his reasoning so cogent, his remarks so striking and original, and his conclusions resulted so clearly from his premises, that he seldom failed to convince."* Dr. Ramsay retained his style of speaking, in all its original ardour, purity and force, to the period of his death.

As a politician, Dr. Ramsay was always remarkable for his candor and liberality. As an instance of this, it may be here mentioned, that he had on one occasion, expressed doubts of the correctness of the principles on which the association of the Cincinnati is founded; and in common with many others, entertained fears of the tendency of that Society, to build up an aristocracy in this country. Experience, "the best test of truth," fully convinced him of his error; and the late war with Great Britain having brought the patriotism of its members to the test, gave occasion to Dr. Ramsay, voluntarily, to assure the author, that he was so fully convinced of the Republican virtues of the Cincinnati, that should he publish another edition of his history, he would acknowledge the error of the opinions he had formerly entertained on the subject. This expression of his sentiments, induced the submission to his perusal of an admonitory address to a youthful member, recently admitted into the Society, when with great expression of feeling he exclaimed—" I will venture to assert, that this young man never heard a sermon which did him so much good. While such your lectures, and such the principles inculcated into the youthful mind, I know of no association more likely to benefit society than the Cincinnati." From a man of so serious a turn of mind, a higher compliment could not have been paid; and I have ever lamented that his untimely fate prevented the display of a liberality which would have done him the highest honour.

* Vide the Biographical Memoir of Dr. RAMSAY, prefixed to his History of the United States. That Memoir was written by Colonel ROBERT Y. HAYNE, of this city, being the substance of an oration delivered by him, on the occasion of Dr. RAMSAY's death, before the Literary and Philosophical Society of South Carolina, published by the request of that Society, in the Analectic Magazine, and afterwards prefixed to Dr. RAMSAY's History.

WILLIAM HENRY DRAYTON.

It had long been a source of mortification to the Colonists, that no attention had been paid to native talents, and that as often as a post of trust or emolument became vacant, that instead of being filled up by a choice from the candidates for distinction, with whom both the Courts and the Legislature abounded, some needy adventurer, or parasitical sycophant, was seen to arrive, whose only merit consisted in the art of bowing with humility to his superiors, or whose favour was derived from the fascinating influence of some pretty relative, who had skill to impress on an influential minister, the conviction that he was qualified to support the dignity of Britain in her Colonies. There were few communities in which a greater display of ability was shown than in Carolina. What country could boast of superior talents to those exhibited by Peter Manigault, William Wragg, John, Edward and Hugh Rutledge, Charles Cotesworth and Thomas Pinckney, Rawlins Lowndes, William and William Henry Drayton, Thomas Bee, John Matthews, David Ramsay, Jacob Read, and very many others; but these were characters too honest and proud in spirit, implicitly to obey the dictates of a power daily encroaching on the liberties of the people, and alone intent to reduce them to a submission that would have led them to lick the dust beneath the foot that spurned them. Their talents and their virtues appeared but feeble claims to distinction, and their being natives, an insurmountable bar to success. Twice had the respectable Lieutenant Governor Bull been insulted by a cruel departure from the regular routine of succession, having men of the very meanest capacities put over him. It is certainly no scandal to say, that the two last Governors under the royal administration, were deficient even in common understanding, owing their promotion entirely to their rank, and the powerful influence of their families. There were among the judges some men of ability, but the majority of them were miserably deficient in political and general information, and of professional knowledge altogether ignorant. It has often been said of Chief Justice Shinner, that he never opened a law book till he was actually on his passage to America. Of the qualifications of Judge Futerel, a little anecdote will give an adequate idea. At a dancing assembly, having too freely sacrificed to Bacchus, he lay extended on a bench, in a retiring room, confused with liquor, when perceiving a gentleman pulling off his coat for the purpose of changing a waistcoat that had been accidentally soiled, he leapt up, and putting himself into a boxing attitude, exclaimed, "O damn you, if you are for that sport, I'm at home —come on." Such were our Governors, such the men sent from the Parent State to administer justice.

A reference to an interesting debate in the British House of Commons, more fully illustrates the extent to which such insult towards the Colonists were carried. George Grenville, exclaiming, " Shall these Americans, our own children, planted by our cares, nourished by our indulgence, dare to resist our decrees," &c. &c. &c. Colonel Barré caught the words, and with manly eloquence said, " They nourished by our indulgence! They grew up by our neglect; and as soon as you began to care about them, that care was exercised in sending persons to rule over them, in one department and another, who were perhaps the deputies of the deputies of some members of this House, sent to spy upon their liberty, to misrepresent their actions, and to prey upon them. Men whose behaviour, on many occasions, has caused the blood of these sons of liberty to recoil within them; men promoted to the highest seats of justice, some of whom, to my knowledge, were glad, by going to foreign countries, to escape the vengeance of the laws in their own."

At the commencement of the Revolution, William Henry Drayton, who officiated as one of the Assistant Judges, was the only member of the bench who was a native American.

His part was promptly taken, and with decision. His ardour to support the liberties of his country was so highly estimated, as to cause his immediate nomination to the Presidency of the Provincial Congress. His abilities were confessedly great, and popular talents considered so well calculated to conciliate the wavering and unfriendly, and effect their adherence to the cause of their country, that, in conjunction with the Rev. Mr. Tennant, he was sent into the interior expressly to effect the union of parties, and to excite a general and firm opposition to British tyranny. The seeds of disaffection, however, were already too generally sown. The enemies to Revolutionary principles temporized, but as speedily as the hope revived of being supported by a competent British force, broke out in open hostility, and it was quickly found that the swords of Sumter and of Pickens more effectually produced the performance of their duties, than the persuasive eloquence of Tennant, and commanding oratory of Drayton. His letters published expressly to controvert the machinations of the British commissioners, holding out the fallacious hope of conciliation, have been considered as replete with irresistible arguments, and written in the best style of composition. His strictures also on the conduct of General Charles Lee disobeying orders at the battle of Monmouth, and calling in question the military capacity of General Washington, have been, by a great majority of the Union, very highly approved.

MR. JOHN EDWARDS.

It must appear both injudicious and unjust, that Mr. John Edwards has been so little noticed. This name has been scarcely mentioned in the records of our Revolution; yet, there was no citizen of the republic, in whose bosom the love of liberty glowed with more generous enthusiasm. Possessing wealth beyond any other mercantile man of the day, he was the first individual in Carolina who tendered his fortunes in support of the American cause. His friend, the venerable Josiah Smith, was no less liberal in his loans to Government; and it cannot be doubted, but that their example must, in a great degree, have contributed to give stability to public credit, and to induce many of less sanguine hopes, to risk their fortunes for the public good. Warned by his more prudential friends, that he placed too much at hazard; that the success of America, opposed to the power of Britain, could scarcely be expected; and that the total loss of his ample possessions might follow: With a feeling of patriotism that cannot be too highly appreciated, he replied—"Be it so! I would rather lose my all, than to retain it, subject to British authority." His subsequent conduct gives ample testimony, that this was no vain boasting. Shortly after the fall of Charleston, invited to a conference by Admiral Arbuthnot, who was quartered on him, and occupied the principal apartments of his house, a conversation took place, the purport of which, immediately after the conclusion, was communicated by him to his son-in-law, Mr. John Bee Holmes, from whom I received it. "Nothing, Mr. Edwards," said the Admiral, "has appeared more extraordinary to Sir Henry Clinton and myself, than that *you*, a native of Great Britain, should have taken part with the Rebels, and appeared, throughout the contest, a strenuous and decided advocate of revolutionary principles. How, Sir, is it to be accounted for?" "Because," replied Mr. Edwards, "I conscientiously approved and have solemnly pledged myself to support them." "But, Mr. Edwards," rejoined the Admiral, "as a *man of sense*, however, you may have been heretofore deluded, your eyes must now be opened to the futility of resistance; and as a *man of honour*, you are bound, by every means in your power, to aid in promoting the submission of the people, by a reconciliation with the merciful Government, that would obliterate every recollection of past offences, and again receive them with favour and forgiveness. We know that your influence can do much—that many look up to you for the regulation of their own conduct—we know too, that no individual has suffered such heavy pecuniary loss, by the depreciation of the paper currency, as *yourself*. Reject not, therefore, the liberal and advantageous proposition which I am about to make you. Take protection yourself—recommend it to your friends to follow your meritorious example—use your best endeavours to put down opposition to the British authorities, and you shall be forthwith, not only remunerated for every loss that you have sustained, but for the good effected through your means, a pecuniary reward shall be granted you, equal to your most sanguine desires." "Admiral Arbuthnot," said Mr. Edwards, "it is not the temptations of wealth that shall ever induce me to forfeit my honour. I cannot hesitate to choose, where duty, inclination, and every virtuous principle point out the course which it becomes me to pursue. My losses have been great, but they cost me not a sigh. My monies were lent, to support a cause which I consider that of justice and humanity. I have a wife, tenderly beloved, and ten children worthy of my most ardent affection. They are all dependent upon me, and I may probably have little to leave them but good principles and an untarnished reputation; but, were a gallows to be raised by your order, in my view, and you were to say—*Your fate depends upon your resolve—take protection or perish*—I would, without a moment's hesitation—*die!*"

If the traits of character which I have exhibited, are acceptable to public sentiment, and have a claim to applause, how much must admiration of his patriotic conduct be increased, when it is remembered, that hearing in council the magnanimous proposition to await the the event of an assault, and to devote the lives of the garrison of Charleston to the attainment of general good, rather than surrender to the enemy, he nobly supported the opinion, and heroically declared for death in preference to submission. "I would rather," he exclaimed, "that my breast should meet the British bayonet, than that my signature should be given to any proposition recommending the surrender of the city."

Supporting all the severities of exile and persecution at St. Augustine, with unshaken fidelity to his country, he was sent with the companions of his misfortunes, after the happy negotiation of Major Hyrne for the exchange of prisoners, to Philadelphia. There, his virtues gained him respect—his misfortunes, friends. He died in exile, and was interred amidst the regrets of an admiring people, whose pity for his sufferings could only be surpassed by their applause and admiration of the firmness with which he supported them.

GOVERNOR MATTHEWS.

To this distinguished patriot I have ever considered the citizens of the Southern States as peculiarly indebted. It might at this late period be difficult to prove the fact, it must indeed at any time have excited astonishment, but I have heard him repeatedly declare, that after the defeat of General Gates near Camden, when the cloud that overshadowed the prospects of America wore its darkest hue, and even to the Revolutionists the most sanguine of success, the enfeebled rays of hope were scarcely perceptible, that through the intrigues, and at the suggestion of the French Ambassador, it was contemplated to bring forward a proposition in Congress to purchase from Great Britain, *Peace, and the independency of a large portion of the United States, by the sacrifice of the Carolinas and Georgia.* Nor did he conceal the name of the individual who had engaged to introduce and advocate the measure. Fired with resentment, indignant that even in the private circles of society a proposal so base and disgraceful should have been whispered —that it should have been admitted into an American bosom, he determined at once to put the virtue of the Delegated Representatives of his country to the test. Repairing to Congress, he forcibly reminded them of their bond of union; that the several States were pledged to each other, through every variety of fortune, to accomplish the end of their association, or to fall together. " I will regard the man," he exclaimed, " who would attempt to weaken these sacred ties as the fit object of universal execration ; and in the event that the members of Congress should so far debase themselves, as to listen to his nefarious proposal, after having, in conjunction with my colleagues, protested against the measure, and pointed out the source of the evil, I will say to my constituents, make your own terms with the enemy—no longer regard as associates, nor put your trust in men, who appalled by their fears, and under the influence of a foreign power, to secure themselves from harm, make no scruple to doom their friends to destruction." Happily for our country the energetic conduct of our Delegates, crushed the intrigue in embryo. It never saw the light. Mr. Bee and Colonel Eveleigh very nobly supported Mr. Matthews on this momentous occasion.

Sometime subsequent to the writing of the anecdote above recorded, I learnt from General Thomas Pinckney, that while with Governor Rutledge at Camden, subsequent to the fall of Charleston, he was informed by him that he had received a letter from a member of the South-Carolina Delegation in Congress, (probably Mr. Matthews, to whom he was allied by the strictest ties of friendship,) informing him, that despondency for the fate of the Southern States was the universal sentiment, but that he still *indulged the hope* that Carolina would remain a member of the Union. But that some discussion had occurred in Congress, corresponding with the representation made by Governor Matthews, is more clearly demonstrated by the copy of a declaration made by that respectable body, June 25th, 1780, and extracted from Rivington's New-York Royal Gazette, September 13th of the same year, which, under other circumstances, would have been altogether superfluous, and inconsistent with common sense.

"Whereas, it has been reported in order to seduce the States of South-Carolina and Georgia from their allegiance to the United States, that a treaty of peace betwixt America and Great Britian was about to take place, and that these two States would be ceded to Great Britain.

Resolved unanimously, That the said report is insidious, and utterly void of foundation. That this confederacy is most sacredly pledged to support the liberty and independency of every one of the members; and in a firm reliance on the Divine blessing, will unremittingly persevere in every exertion for the establishment of the same, and for the recovery and preservation of any and every part of the said United States that have been, or may hereafter be invaded or possessed by the common enemy.

"Extract from the minutes.

"CHARLES THOMPSON, *Sec'ry.*"

BENJAMIN GUERARD.

The distresses of the Patriotic Citizens of South Carolina, transported to Philadelphia, were sufficient in their nature to engender the most gloomy despair. Hospitality opened the doors of the inhabitants to many families, who were kindly sheltered, and treated with the most cordial affection. But there were many unfortunates, accustomed through life to possess every essential comfort, who were destitute of common necessaries, and not a few who actually wanted bread. I record it to the honour of Mr. Benjamin Guerard, a gentleman of extensive property, that he, upon this occasion, generously stepped forward, and offered to pledge his estate as a security, to raise a sum to be exclusively appropriated to the maintenance of his suffering countrymen, demanding no greater share for himself, than that which should be allowed to every other individual. Carolina estates, however, were regarded as castles in the air, and his generous intentions proved altogether abortive.

It would be painful to me, to neglect to mention names where just claims to humanity existed. My information is limited. Such individuals as I knew pre-eminently distinguished by their efforts to give relief, I am proud to speak of. Dr. Bond, Mr. Wikoff, Colonel Pettit, Mr. Ingersoll, Dr. Logan, and many others, were liberal with delicacy, and doubled the obligation by bestowing their favours without ostentation. Nor should it ever be forgotten in Carolina, that Colonel John Mitchell, so much the victim of misfortune in his latter years, who lived in Philadelphia at that period, in ease and affluence, never failed, as occasion required, to sooth the afflictions of the exiles, by every attention that benevolence could bestow.

I AM sensible, that to many of my readers a considerable portion of the anecdotes which I record, may appear uninteresting, but as they relate to men, to recollect whom, gives pleasure not only to myself, but to all who remember their constancy and exemplary good conduct in times "that tried men's souls," I am inclined to persist.

JUDGE BURKE.

THROUGHOUT the whole of the Revolution, acted a very conspicuous part. He was a steady and inflexible Patriot, and zealous supporter of the Laws. The people had not an *advocate more ready* to maintain their *just* rights, nor a more prompt opponent, whenever they manifested the slightest disposition to *licentiousness*. He always meant well, though he frequently took an awkward way of showing it, and secured confidence by his unremitted endeavours to deserve it.

It had been much the fashion, towards the close of the war, for persons wishing to avoid militia service, to attach themselves as volunteers to the regular Continental regiments, engaging to take the field whenever called upon; but it speedily appeared, that self-indulgence was much more their *real* object, than public good. To counteract this practice, a bill was introduced into the Legislature at Jacksonborough, to compel every man to serve in the militia regiment in which he was enrolled. Judge Burke, on this occasion, after using many arguments in support of the bill, concluded by saying—"I shall give but one reason more, Mr. Speaker, against the volunteer system, and that is a very powerful one. Your volunteers are a set of very shabby fellows, and I have a good right to say it, I am a volunteer myself." Travelling the Circuit some years previous to the period, when an improved system of education had completely extinguished a ferocity of character, which tolerated gouging, biting, and other disgraceful practices, and being asked why he carried pistols of unusual size and calibre: he replied—"As the best specific for the preservation of my eye-sight—country frolics too frequently producing blindness."

The system of espionage, however disgraceful to the party who undertakes to betray, being resorted to in every war, has been regarded as altogether justifiable on the part of the officer who seeks intelligence. To individuals communicating information relative to the movements of the enemy, both General Greene and General Marion had promised protection, and release from the penalties attached to their political offences. This was a measure, in the highest degree, revolting to a large proportion of the Members of the House of Representatives, who steadily maintained—"that to men so lost to every honourable feeling, the rights of citizenship should never be granted." The singularity of Judge Burke's reasoning on this subject, occasioned much amusement. He briefly said—"I am at a loss, Mr. Speaker, to conjecture, what the gentlemen would be at. The Generals were authorized to engage spies, who would be tempted to betray the secrets of the Government they professed to honour; and having done so, this House is bound to fulfil every contract that they have made. They proudly assert, what in my conscience I have little inclination to deny—that such men would be bad citizens anywhere. But, spies are confessed to be a necessary evil; and I should be glad to know, if the gentlemen ever expect to find honest men, who will undertake the dirty work required of them, and act the part of villains, to promote the public good? No, Mr. Speaker. You are at liberty to despise the traitors, while you profit by their treason. You may cut their acquaintance—you may withhold the compliment of your hat, your hand, and your heart; but, protected by the pledge given by the Generals, that they should be restored to their rights, and pardoned for their political criminality, the less that is said on the subject the better, since these *Scoff's*, *Yahoos* as they are, are as truly citizens as any of us."

Sending a challenge to a person who had grossly offended him, he thus expressed himself:—Sir, I must insist upon your giving me immediate satisfaction, for having so far imposed on me, as to make me believe for a single moment, that you were a man of honour, or a gentleman."

I myself remember to have heard him relate the circumstances contained in the anecdote which follows:

When, to give permanency to, and increase the strength of the Union, the adoption of the Federal Constitution was strongly recommended by the most enlightened of our citizens, Judge Burke stood forth its strenuous opposer, using his utmost efforts to render it hateful to the people; but, when he found that a great majority were of a different sentiment, and that its acceptance was sanctioned by their applauses, he gave up opposition, and studiously endeavoured to give energy to all its operations.

Returning from a Circuit in the interior, he happened on one occasion, to fall in with a long train of wagons near Nelson's Ferry, conveying produce from North Carolina to Charleston. With their conductors he immediately engaged in conversation, and wishing to ascertain their opinions of passing events, asked—" If they thought the recently adopted Constitution of the United States, would prove useful and acceptable to the People." The reply was unanimous—" By no means. We abominate it, and to such a degree, that should the President think proper, on any emergency, to call us into the field, we would refuse obedience to a man." " Tell that," said the Judge, " to some one that does not know you. Refuse to obey the call of your Chief Magistrate, when your country is in jeopardy!—impossible! Look to the discipline which every mother's son of you keep up on your farms, when you wish to know the extent and condition of your stock. Do you not blow your conchs, and do not your cattle, and your sheep, your pigs, and your poultry gather about you, as it were to ask your commands? And when danger threatens, and the President blows his conch, to call you to your duty, would you have me believe, that you would be more insensible than the beasts of the field? The protection which the government which he administers affords, is to you what feed is to your hogs; and at the first blast, not one of the swinish herd would be more nimble in seeking his rations, than you would be in the opportunity of repelling aggression." "You are a very free spoken man," said one of his auditors, "and may, perhaps, be a clever one; but, for your want of civility in comparing us to our hogs, be pleased to pass to the rear; you cross not the river till the last of our wagons has reached the opposite shore." The Judge was forced to comply; but, recollecting that his presence was required by a particular time in another quarter, he, at the risk of his life, swam his horses, and paddled himself across the river, admiring the independency of character in men, who would not tolerate incivility even from a Judge.

Shortly after the evacuation of Charleston, Judge Burke, under the signature of Cassius, attacked with much point, and decided effect, the acts of the Jacksonborough Assembly against those who had submitted and taken British protections. I have always thought that the censures which he lavished on this occasion would not have been received so favourably, if obnoxious individuals had been allowed to plead in justification of their conduct, or if particular penalties had been attached to particular crimes. But contrary to every principle of justice, prejudice reigned with unlimited sway, and under the protection of influential friends, many escaped even censure, for the very acts for which others were banished, and fined to the full extent of their possessions. Wealth was too frequently regarded as an indication of crime; and in committee, on the reading over the names of the accused, the cry of "a fat sheep—a fat sheep—prick him! prick him!" was followed by immediate condemnation unless some man of influence, or friend to humanity, in pity, undertook to palliate the misconduct of the offender, and by his eloquence averted the blow which was to destroy him. In his last hours he exhibited the same humour and eccentricity that had distinguished him through life.

On the day previous to his death, having been tapped by

Dr. Irvine for a dropsy, he said, " well Irvine, what am I to expect; is the decree life or death." " Life, my good fellow," said Irvine. " You are an Irishman, and will yet last a long time." " Then, by Jasus," said Burke, " I shall be the first thing that ever lasted long in this house, after being once put on tap."

CAPTAIN RICHARD GOUGH.

It is a tribute justly due to the independent spirit of Captain Richard Gough to record, that having in vain opposed proceedings so abhorrent to justice, as those already mentioned, he vacated his seat in the Jacksonborough Assembly, declaring, "that he could never remain a witness to the condemnation of a man who was not allowed the privilege to state, in his own defence, the motives which had decided his conduct."

The magnanimity of this gentleman on another occasion, is highly deserving of praise. Having been a prisoner, he had been thrown into irons, and treated with peculiar indignity. A change in the political occurrences of the time, highly favourable to America, having taken place, many of the adherents of Britain, repenting the imprudence of their conduct, wished, by a full confession of error, to be admitted to the rights of citizenship. An American, who had interested himself very highly in favour of an individual subjected to the penalties of the Confiscation Law, making an appeal to the humanity of Captain Gough, said, "I am sensible that it is only necessary for you to oppose the petition in his behalf, which will be presented to the Legislature, to ensure its failure." "Make yourself easy then," was the generous reply. "Give me the petition, I will present and support it, and shall be happy if that prevents opposition from any other quarter. The war is brought to a happy conclusion—my resentments are no more." It gave additional lustre to this act of generosity, that a little before, while at supper with his aged mother, he had been fired upon and desperately wounded by a tory party from the British garrison.

EXEMPLARY CONDUCT OF THE CLERGY.

It is a highly gratifying circumstance to perceive, from the perusal of the interesting " History of the Episcopal Church in South-Carolina," by the Reverend Dr. Dalcho, that five only out of twenty of the Clergy of that persuasion, adhered to the British cause.

BISHOP SMITH.

THE late Bishop Smith shouldered his musket, and amidst scenes of the greatest danger, both by precept and example, stimulated to intrepid resistance. Made a prisoner at the surrender of Charleston, immediate banishment followed his captivity. Such was the apprehension of his influence, that, though ill and confined to his bed, a centinel placed over him, was not allowed to quit his chamber, till he was taken from it under a guard, to be transported to Philadelphia.

The nature of the work permits me to speak of his political conduct alone. To his credit, however, I must state, that blessed with opulence, his charities were unbounded. The poor and the needy wept his departure with unfeigned sorrow. Benevolence was enthroned in his heart. His Clerical Brothers found in him a friend, and mourned in him a Father. Many charitable institutions were benefitted, both by his exertions and by his liberality; but the Clergy Society, which, with utility beyond the reach of praise, gives relief to the bereaved widow, and rescues the helpless orphan from the pangs of want and misery, originating with him, was, to his latest hour, fostered with peculiar delight.

THE REV. DR. PERCY,

FREQUENTLY preached to the troops, encouraging them to intrepid exertions, and a patient endurance of the privations necessarily connected with their situation. He was the first orator who addressed the people on the Anniversary of our Independence. His steady conduct being highly offensive to the British authorities, he was ordered to relinquish his clerical duties, as soon as Charleston fell, under the penalty of a dungeon; and to avoid persecution, retired to Europe.

THE REV. MR. LEWIS,

OF St. Paul's, was a firm advocate for independence, and an indefatigable agent in promoting its accomplishment. Delivering a patriotic discourse on the text—" The Lord forbid that I should give the inheritance of my fathers unto thee;" he became particularly obnoxious to the British commanders, was exiled to St. Augustine with many other patriots, but was speedily separated from them, and shut up in the Castle, and till the period of his exchange, condemned to solitary confinement.

THE REV. DR. PURCELL,

Was equally firm in his principles; and acting as Deputy Judge Advocate in the field, supported all the difficulties and dangers of campaigning, with exemplary patience and intrepidity.

THE REV. PAUL TERQUAND,

Served as a member in the First Provincial Congress, and distinguished himself, not only in his legislative capacity, but by his oratorical powers, and his animating address to that respectable body from the pulpit, and for which he received their unanimous thanks.

THE REV. SAMUEL WARREN,

Called by interesting concerns to Europe at the commencement of the Revolution, was tempted by all the arts of persuasion, and offers of liberal preferment, by a brother, a Dignitary in the established Church, to remain in England; but with a soul superior to all selfish consideration, he thought only of the good that might flow from his exertions in the cause of Liberty; returned to America; with unremitted zeal performed every duty, braved every danger, and both by precept and example, to the conclusion of the contest, pointed out the road to honour and renown.

Nor is less praise due to the Clergy of other denominations, who, with unshaken zeal and firmness, were reckoned among the most strenuous supporters of the Revolution.

THE REV. JOSIAH SMITH,

Pastor of the Independent Church, though advanced to his 77th year, disdaining to receive the favour which would have been allowed him, of remaining in Charleston, from an enemy who had wantonly violated the terms of capitulation, granted to the inhabitants, went into banishment with his family, and died an exile.

THE REV. MR. TENNANT

Stands pre-eminently distinguished. He was born in New-Jersey, in the year 1740, and educated at the College of Princeton, where, in 1758, he received a bachelor's degree, and was two years after licensed to preach. He first settled in Connecticut, but after a lapse of ten years, accepted, on invitation, the pastoral charge of the Independent Church in Charleston, and arrived there in 1772. As a man of learning, eloquence, and piety, he was held in high estimation. It is my province to speak more particularly of his revolutionary services; and here there is an ample field for praise. His life, from the earliest dawn of hostility, was devoted to the service of his country, and the whole tenor of his conduct gave unequivocal proof that he considered religion, liberty, and happiness, implicated in her success. The vigour of his mind would not suffer him, under such circumstances, to act an inferior part. He boldly stepped forward the champion of Liberty and Independence—with zeal and eloquence preached resistance, nor failed to support it with all his energies. As a member of the Provincial Congress, and afterwards of the House of Assembly, he, in his legislative capacity acquired great celebrity, and so forcibly impressed upon the minds of his colleagues, the conviction of his superior and persuasive talents, that in conjunction with the Honourable William Henry Drayton, he was delegated to visit the disaffected districts of the interior country; by the exercise of his abilities, to demonstrate to the misguided both the weakness and wickedness of their conduct; and by dint of reason, to reconcile them to those patriotic measures which could alone save their country from destruction. This was a service of extreme difficulty and danger. Suspicion had exerted its baneful influence. Motives and designs were reciprocally attributed by the opposite parties to each other, of the most ungenerous nature and mischievous tendency. Camps were formed preparatory to open contention, and the whole country breathed the spirit of war. A conference, however, betwixt the leaders, put a temporary stop to hostility. The Loyalists engaged to remain in a state of neutrality, and both parties retired to their homes. The good that was expected from the commission of the Delegates, was not as extensive as the government had anticipated; but their eloquence was not without its effect. Many men of character and influence, were induced to sign the Association, and renouncing their errors, became the steady supporters of the popular cause.

To sum up his character as a politician, it is no exaggeration to say, that resistance to oppression, and firmness in supporting the just rights of the people, were the cherished doctrines of his heart; and to have attained their accomplishment, he would have laid down his life rejoicing.

The respect to his memory, by the Congregation over which he presided, is feelingly demonstrated by the inscription on his monument, erected by them in their Archdale-street Church:

In memory
Of the Reverend WILLIAM TENNANT, A. M.,
Pastor of this Church,
and principally instrumental in the
erection of this building,
dedicated to the worship of
Almighty God,
who died at the High Hills of Santee,
August 11th, 1777,
in the thirty-seventh year of his age.
He was distinguished for
quickness of perception,
solidity of judgment,
energy and firmness of mind,
for inflexible patriotism
and ardent public spirit,
for the boldness with which he enforced
the claims of the Deity,
and vindicated the rights of Man.
As a Preacher, he was prompt, solemn,
instructive and persuasive—
of every social virtue, he was a bright example.
"*Blessed are the dead who die in the Lord.*"

His valuable life terminated while discharging a filial duty, bringing his aged and recently widowed mother from New-Jersey to Carolina.

THE REV. DR. FURMAN.

With great delight I mention a faithful servant both of God and the Republic, who still lives, an ornament and blessing to society. In the field a hero; in private life I know no man, that by the uniform display of talent and of virtue, does greater honour to humanity than Doctor *Furman*. Strenuous in opposition to the invaders, he fought and he preached with energy and effect, and the recollection of his zeal to promote unanimity and steady resistance to the encroachments of an enemy, who but a little time since, would again have disturbed the tranquility of his country, demonstrated that the patriot fire that warmed his youthful bosom, burns even in advanced life with all its pristine purity and effulgence.

ADDITIONAL ANECDOTES,

ILLUSTRATIVE OF

GARDEN'S

REVOLUTIONARY ANECDOTES.

BROOKLYN, N. Y.
1865.

ADDITIONAL ANECDOTES,

ILLUSTRATIVE OF

GARDEN'S REVOLUTIONARY ANECDOTES.

I. Page 5.

GOVERNOR JOHN RUTLEDGE.

Gov. Rutledge had not that great elevation of mind which prompts to the endurance of personal slights when great public interests are at stake, nor was he one of those in whom self-love is always subservient to a country's good.

He resigned his office of President of South Carolina, because the Legislative Council and General Assembly passed an act which gave the elective franchise, which they had not before possessed, to the citizens of the State; created the office of Governor with limited powers; instead of that of President with undefined authority; declared the republic perpetual, instead of a temporary expedient in the interim of an accommodation with Great Britain.

Gov. Rutledge was an aristocrat,—detested universal suffrage with all the *hauteur* of a Venitian Doge, and admired a monarchical government with its attachment of an established Church; and in his veto message offered as an objection to the new constitution that it precluded the hope of an accommodation with the mother government, which of course included submission to it.

The fatal act of Gov. Rutledge's life, which should consign his name to infamy, was the pusillanimous proffer to the British General Provost, during a temporary investment of Charleston, of neutrality of the State during the war.

The investure of that place, was a bold experiment of an irregular body without seige guns, of whom Gen. Moultrie received trustworthy information that fixed their numbers at 3,600 of all arms, while his own army numbered at 3,180, with the advantage of lines of defence.

Most of the Southern annalists carefully avoid reference to this humiliating affair. Dr. Ramsay is weak enough to defend it as a "*ruse de guerre*" for the purpose of gaining time for Gen. Lincoln to arrive, but honest Gen. Moultrie shows, by documentary evidence, that Gov. Rutledge and his Council were governed by an uncontrollable panic.

It is altogether probable that Gov. Rutledge, who as we have already seen, was not averse to an accommodation with the British, seized upon the occasion of universal fear to bring about the result which he had foreshadowed, in his resignation of the office of President of South Carolina.

Gov. Rutledge seemed to waver between officious and misjudged zeal, and feeble despondency. The former induced him to assume military powers, while Gen. Moultre commanded at the seige of Charleston, by Provost, and induced him to send Col. Benjamin Huger with a scout on a service, which of all others, the commanding officer should not have been left ignorant of, and which cost that brave officer his life by the hands of his comrades, as will be found narrated under the notice of that ill-fated man. The latter trait forced him into that sad error which history has suspended on the borders where misfortune and crime blend into one. The narrative of this unfortunate affair will be found under Note XIII.

II.

Page 10.

LIEUT.-COL. ISAAC MOTTE.

This officer commanded in the unresisted attack on Fort Johnson, Sept. 16th, 1775, having entered it after great preparations for an assault some hours after its abandonment by the British, by whom it had been dismantled.

This, the first overt act of the Revolution in the South, was performed on the very spot where, after a lapse of ninety years, another and a vaster Revolution had its birth. Almost a century expires, and the descendants of these insurgents engage with hotter zeal, and a fiercer *patriotism* in an assault upon the same walls, once more abandoned and undefended from their valor.

Soon after the possession of the fort by Col. Motte was discovered, Gov. Campbell, who had taken refuge upon the Tamer, British sloop-of-war, "despatched Mr. Innis, his Secretary to Fort Johnson, but he was not allowed to enter it; and Capt. C. C. Pinckney was sent by Col. Motte to receive at the water side any communications which the Governor's Secretary had to make. Upon this he delivered the message he had for Col. Motte to Capt. Pinckney, which was, 'The Governor desires to know by what authority he had possession of the fort, and by what authority he held it.' And he desired Capt. Pinckney to be very exact in delivering this communication to Col. Motte, 'as much depended upon it.' How the turbid brain of this ex-functionary must have laboured to produce this feebly threatening message, which could provoke nothing but scoffing laughter, unless it were a bewildered incredulity at the exhibition of such weak anger.

"To this Col. Motte replied, 'that he had taken possession of the fort and held it by the express command of the Council of Safety,' upon which Secretary Innis made his bow, and the man-of-war's boat carried him back to the Tamer. This message must have afforded Governor Campbell exceeding satisfaction, for his Excellency sailed away with his little squadron the next morning, doubtless rejoicing greatly in the dignity of the title of Commander-in-Chief, which he had managed to preserve from the wreck of his honors. He sailed away, but returned with Sir Peter Parker; acting as volunteer aid to him at the attack on Fort Moultrie, only however to perish in sight of the land he had governed."

III.

DAVID FANNING,

THE TORY COLONEL.

Page 19.

Marion's politic clemency secured the citizens of the Carolinas from the midnight ravages and assassinations of this monster, for only the short period intervening between the 17th of June and the 5th of Sept., 1782. We have the advantage of perusing the journal in which this tory bandit narrates his horrible atrocities with the self-complacency of a Thug, after it has slept for eighty years.

The incident to which Major Garden refers on page 260, and which took place immediately after Marion's clement act is narrated by Fanning, with the additional horror of the abduction of Hunter's wife, the treatment of whom by that bandit a husband would prefer to forget.

"On the 1st of May, 1782, I heard of a wagon being in the road, I imagined it was going down to market, as I heard of a number of wagons which was to proceed down with liquor to market. On the 2d, I mounted and pursued the wagon which I heard of the day before; as I was about setting out for Charleston I concluded to have a frolic with my old friends before we parted.

"After riding about ten miles I overtook the said wagon which belonged to a certain man who had been taken prisoner and paroled by the British, and had broken his parole. In the meantime I was examining his papers, I set a sentinel over him. He knowing himself guilty, expected nothing but death.

He took the opportunity and sprung upon my riding mare, and went off with my saddle, holsters, pistols, and all my papers of any consequence to me.

"We fired two guns at him, he received two balls through his body, but it did not prevent him from sitting in his saddle, and make his escape. I took the other man, and caused him to take me to the man's plantation, where I took his wife and three negro boys, and eight head of horses.

"I kept his wife for three days in the woods, and sent the man to see if he would deliver up my mare and property, containing my papers, for which he wrote me an insolent letter. On the 7th of May, finding I could see no opportunity of getting my mare, notwithstanding she was one of my principal creatures, and a mare I set great store by, and gave one hundred guineas for her. I was obliged to let loose all his horses except one, as they were of no account to me in the situation I was in, the negroes I kept; I then proceeded to a Major Gayner's truce land in Pedee, South Carolina, where I made my truce with the Rebels *some time before*, and I continued there until June, when I left my wife, horses, and negroes; as I was entirely a stranger to the situation of the country and the roads, I was obliged to procure a pilot to Charleston; I could not get one for less than twenty guineas. I continued in Charleston until the 5th of September, and my horses having got recruited, and one of my negroes having made his way good through the country, came down to me; I then set out for the country again, on account of my misfortune of losing my mare, which was of great value to me. I went up to the settlement again, to the man I sent to Hunter before, and he informed me that Hunter refused five negroes for the mare, and would not return her. He also went where I left one of my negroes and took him, and sent him over the mountains to keep him out of my way. I continued in the settlement until the 22d of the month, trying to get her, but was disappointed in my hopes. Knowing that Charleston was to be evacuated I was obliged to return, and as I was on my way I understood my mare was at a certain place about 125 miles from Charleston; being about half the distance from where I then was, toward Charleston. I instantly pursued on my journey to the place I heard she was, and my riding horse was so particularly known I sent a man up to the house, and he was known; they directed us the wrong way, and immediately sent word to where my mare was; I found out we was wrong, and took through the woods, and to a house within half a mile where they had word of my coming, and was making ready to go to their assistance. On seeing us come up, he immediately left his horse and was running off through a field, then turned round and presented his piece and snapped, but she missed fire; with this I ordered one of my men to fire at him, who shot him through the body, and despatched his presence from this world.

"The other two men that was at the house did not run, and informed me that they had received word of my coming a half an hour before I arrived, and also that these men were lying in ambush ready to attack me. With this, as the man who had my mare had gone off with her and having only two men and my negro that set out with me from Charleston, also two little negroes that I had for my mare, I thought it was best to proceed to Charleston; and on the 28th of September I arrived at Charleston, where the shipping was ready for me to embark for St. Augustine." Thus did this sanguinary wretch requite the clemency of Marion.

It will be seen that Fanning's narrative differs in some particulars from Garden's statement of the same affair, but in none of moment, or which are greater than would appear in the narrative of an event by two observers of it.

IV.

Page 19.

KOSCIUSKO.

CHARGE OF INHUMANITY AND INCAPACITY.

The incident to which Major Garden refers, found under the paragraph entitled Wilmot and Moore, does not by any means sustain the grave charge of inhumanity. It certainly adds testimony to the reputation for high personal courage which Kosciusco has always possessed. But Garden, on every occasion where the mention of Kosciusko's name becomes necessary in his reminiscences, exhibits an animus of dislike, and indulges in detraction unsustained by any attempt at evidence. He denounces his attack on a detached party at the seige of Charleston as a rash expedition, and decries his abilities as an engineer at Fort Ninety-Six. The Carolina historians, some of whom were participants in the dangers of these actions, by no means corroborate all of Garden's opinions of Kosciusko's ability and humanity.

Lee questions his talents as an engineer, but confirms the general belief in his bravery and humanity.

"Col. Kosciusko, a Polish officer at the head of the engineers in the Southern army, was considered to possess skill in his profession, and much esteemed for his mildness of disposition, and urbanity of manners. Never regarding the importance which was attached to depriving the enemy of water, for which he depended entirely on the rivulet on his left, Kosciusko applied his undivided attention to the demolition of the star, the strongest point of the enemy's defence."

"Taught by a successful rally of the enemy that he was of a

cast not to be rashly approached with impunity, Kosciusko *was directed* to resume his labors under cover of a ravine, and at a more respectful distance."

" Kosciusko was extremely amiable, and I believe a truly good man, nor was he deficient in his professional knowledge, but he was very moderate in talent—not a spark of the etherial in his composition. His blunders cost us Ninety-Six, and Gen. Greene, much as he was beloved and respected, did not escape criticism for permitting his engineer to direct the manner of his approach." This criticism, it must be borne in mind, is the utterance of an impatient and disappointed partisan, who knew no other warlike craft than to 'fight on.' Ninety-Six was defended by a brave, sleepless and skillful officer, Colonel Cruger, and was early relieved by the approach of Lord Rawdon with an overwhelming force, which, if they were not reasons sufficient to console Lee for his defeat, ought to have been enough to have made him more candid.

V.
COLONEL PETER HORRY.

The regiment of Colonel Horry, composed of 200 South Carolinians, encamped on Haddrell's Point, in June, 1776, could not have been a source of great satisfaction to a brave and impetuous soldier. Secured from the dangers of an attack from British ships, by such a fortification as General Moultrie, successfully resisted one without serious loss of life; these brave and chivalrous Carolinians, refused to leave its shelter for more hazardous service. General Charles Lee, under the above date, writes to Moultrie: " I have ordered General Armstrong to ease Colonel Thompson's regiment of their heavy duty, for I find that a part of Colonel Horry's regiment had most *magnanimously* refused to take this duty upon them; we shall, I hope, live to thank them." Colonel Thompson was employed in the harrassing service of night reconnoissances on Long Island, in Charleston Harbor, where the British were expected to land; but there was too much danger and fatigue in such affairs for these brave Carolinians.

Marion's memorable conversations with this companion of his exile from the Carolinas, on the causes of the decline of the Patriot cause in those States, is worthy of attention at this hour of their humiliation.

VI.
COLONEL MAHAM.

Page 22.

LIEUTENANT COLONEL Watson, an active and able officer of Lord Rawdon's Corps, had deposited the baggage of his regiment in a post which he had established at Wright's Bluff, on the Santee, while he proceeded by rapid marches in pursuit of Marion. The latter was enabled, by an unexpected juncture with Colonel Lee, to strike a blow at this post. The investiture was commenced by cutting off the ordinary supply of water, and this, it was believed, would alone compel the surrender of the fort in a few hours.

In Lee's Memoirs, vol. 2, p. 51, we find a graphic description of the novel device referred to by Major Garden. "The ground selected by Colonel Watson, for his small stockade, was an Indian Mount, generally conceived to be the cemetery of the tribe inhabiting the circumjacent region; it was at least thirty feet high, and surrounded by table land. Captain McKoy, the Commandant, saw at once his inevitable fate unless he could devise some other mode of procuring water, for which purpose he immediately cut a trench from his fosse (secured by abattis), to the river, which passed close to the Indian Mount. Baffled in their expectation, and destitute both of artillery and intrenching tools, Marion and Lee despaired of success, when Major Maham, of South Carolina, accompanying the Brigadier, suggested a plan, which was no sooner communicated than gratefully adopted. He proposed to cut down a number of suitable trees in the nearest wood, and with them to erect a large, strong, oblong pen, to be covered on the top with a floor of logs, and protected on the side opposite to the fort, with a breastwork of light timber.

"To the adjacent farms, the Dragoons were dispatched for axes, the only necessary tool, of which a sufficient number being soon collected, relays of working parties were allotted for the work; some to cut, some to convey, and some to erect. Major Maham undertook the execution of his plan, which was completely finished before the morning of the 23d., effective as to the object, and honorable to the genius of the inventor. The besieged was, like the besieger, *unprovided with artillery*, and could not interrupt the progress of a work, the completion of which must produce immediate submission.

"A party of riflemen being ready, took post in the Maham tower the moment it was completed; and a detachment of musketry, under cover of the riflemen, moved to effect a lodgment in the enemy's ditch, supported by the legion infantry with fixed bayonets; such was the effect of the fire from the riflemen, having thorough command of every part of the fort from the relative supereminence of the tower, that every effort to attempt to resist the lodgment was crushed. The Commandant finding every resource cut off, hung out the white flag. It was followed by a proposition to surrender, which issued in a capitulation.

"This incipient operation, having been happily effected by the novel and effectual device of Major Maham, to whom the Commandants very gratefully expressed their acknowledgments."

This experiment was again resorted to in the reduction of Fort Cornwallis, when commanded by the Tory Colonel Brown, and contributed greatly to the success of the Whigs, in obtaining possession of Augusta.

VII.
GENERAL SUMTER.

Page 23

It was the misfortune of this brave officer, as it was that of Marion and other Southern partisan generals, to command some of the most undisciplined and reckless marauders, who were ever held together by that only tie of such wretches—the hope of plunder or revenge.

It is in vain for the Southern annalists, to attempt to conceal or disguise the fact; the traits which Major Garden attributes to irregular troops in general, were characteristic of Southern militia, whig or tory, republican or monarchist, and will be sought in vain in the history of the Northern militia.

The subsequent defeat of Sumter's corps, was the natural result of the undisciplinable character of his men.

The sentry left his post and resumed it at pleasure, camp guards communicated his numbers and plans to the enemy for pay, and the men fought or fled as the whim of the hour dictated, or their cowardice or hope of plunder preponderated.

Harsh as these charges seem, they are substantiated by almost every account of a close contest, in which reliance was placed upon them. On those occasions, when they were successful, as at King's Mountain, the men were mountaineers, who fought in the same wild manner, to which they had been accustomed in their warfare with the savages.

VIII.
GOVERNOR PICKENS.

Page 16.

When Lord Rawdon, by rapid marches, and with an overwhelming force, was pursuing General Greene, Governor Pickens exhibited an illustrious instance of republican virtue.

On the announcement of the order for retreat, General Pickens' family and private property, were sent off with the baggage of the army. This precaution, though wished for by all, and justified on every principle of prudence, gave an alarm to many who either had not the same means of transportation, or who could not have attended to it without deserting the American Army. To encourage the men to remain on their plantations, General Pickens ordered his family and property back again to his house, within twenty miles of the British garrison.

His example, saved the country in the vicinity from depopulation, and the army under Greene, from sustaining a great diminution of their numbers, by the desertion of the militia to take care of their families.

IX.
LIEUTENANT-COLONEL HENRY LEE.

Page 52.

WITH all the splendid qualities for a partisan officer, which Henry Lee undoubtedly possessed, he was not the perfect military hero which Major Garden's partiality and Carolinian pride has clothed him with. Notwithstanding the vigilance for which he was most remarkable, he was, as he has the candour himself to narrate, twice surprised, and but for slight obstacles to the enemy's progress, his legion would have been cut to pieces. In all the qualities of an officer of light troops, where vigilance and sagacity are essential requisites, and rapidity of movement is not less necessary than quickness of decision, Colonel Otho Williams was greatly his superior.

Fatigue somewhat dulled his sagacity, and passion sometimes obscured his judgment.

At Irwin's Ferry, during the long and harrassing retreat of Greene's Army, Colonel Lee, who formed part of the rear guard commanded by Colonel Williams, believed himself secure for a few hours from the tireless pursuit of the van of Cornwallis, under General O'Hara.

"Lieutenant Colonel Lee having discerned from conversation with his guides, that a bye-way in front, would lead him into William's rear before the close of evening, and save a considerable distance, determined to avail himself of the accommodation. A subaltern's command of dragoons was left to proceed on the route taken by Colonel Williams, with orders to communicate any extraordinary occurrence to the Commandant, and to Colonel Lee.

"The Cavalry who met Miller in the morning, had lost their breakfast, and Lee's chief object in taking the short course, was to avail himself of an abundant farm, for the refreshment of his party. As soon as he reached the proposed route, the infantry were hastened forward with directions to halt at the farm, and prepare for the accommodation of the corps, while the cavalry continued close to the enemy. In due time afterwards they were drawn off, and passed through the woods, leaving in front of the British van, the detachment which had been selected to follow the route of the light troops. The obscurity of the narrow road taken by Lee, lulled every suspicion with respect to the enemy, and a few videts only were placed at intervals, rather to give notice when the British should pass along, than to guard the legion from surprise. This precaution was most fortunate, for it so happened that Lord Cornwallis, having ascertained that Greene had directed his course to Irwin's Ferry, determined to avail himself of the nearest route to gain the road of his enemy, and took the path which Lee had selected.

"Our horses were unbridled, with abundance of provender before them, the hospitable farmer had liberally bestowed his meal and bacon, and had given the aid of his domestics in hastening the much wished repast. To the surprise and grief of all, the pleasant prospect was marred by the fire of the advanced videts—certain signal of the enemy's approach. Before the farm was a creek, which in consequence of incessant rains, could be passed only by a bridge, not more distant from the enemy than from our party. The cavalry being speedily arrayed, moved to support the videts; while the infantry were ordered in full run to seige and hold the bridge. The bridge was gained and soon passed by the corps of Lee. The British followed. The road over the bridge leading through cultivated fields for a mile, the British army was in full view of the troops of Lee, as the latter ascended the eminence, on whose summit they entered the great road to Irwin's Ferry.

"Thus escaped a corps, which had been hitherto guarded with unvarying vigilance, whose loss would have been severely felt by the American General, and which had been just exposed to imminent peril, from the presumption of certain security—criminal imprudence. A soldier is always in danger, when his conviction of security leads him to dispense with the most vigilant precautions." (Lee's Mem. vol. 1, p. 288.)

Colonel Lee's candour disarms criticism, but the criminality of other occurrences in his military life is not so easily palliated. He was not capable of the noble magnanimity and self-control of Gen. Marion, who instead of punishing the murderer of his nephew, when the wretch was a prisoner in his power, severely reprimanded the Captain of the Guard, for not killing a militia officer who took upon himself the punishment of the murderer, by shooting him through the head.

Colonel Lee himself relates the efforts he made to slay the British Captain Miller, whose drunken dragoons the latter had been unable to prevent from massacreing Lee's bugler, and admits that although the truth of Captain Miller's denial of complicity in the slaughter was probable, yet that nothing prevented his murder of the Captain in revenge, except the officious zeal of Colonel Williams, in forwarding the prisoners to headquarters.

Stedman relates an incident of Lee's parade of prisoners, taken at the capture of Augusta, before Colonel Cruger's besieged garrison in Fort Ninety-Six, with a severity of language, which is warranted by the occasion, if all its incidents narrated by him are true.

Another incident narrated by the same author, as occurring during the seige of that post, reflects as little credit on his humanity, as the other, and would have afforded Major Garden a juster opportunity for criticism, than the affair in which Kosciusko was so severely blamed by him. Colonel Lee's chagrin, at the unexpected resistance of Colonel Cruger, so far clouded his better judgment, that he ordered a forlorn hope to advance and fire the abattis, under a fire which destroyed the whole detachment, long before they reached that obstruction.

X.
GENERAL WILLIAM WASHINGTON.

Outshone by the lustre of the character of his great relative, this noble officer has not received full justice from the plaudits of his countrymen. To excite this reticence of praise to loud applause, the great modesty so remarkable in his character; the moderation of his ambition; and the quiet self repose of his mind, have contributed little.

But there is much in his character, as in that of Marion, which generous minds love to dwell upon. In neither is the valor of the soldier stained by inhumanity, or the ardor of success permitted to degenerate into imprudence.

There was a chivalry in the conduct of both, which the Carolinians were fonder of boasting the possession of, than practising. At the battle of Eutaw, the fortune of war had thrown him a prisoner into the hands of the enemy, to whom he had given his parole. "After the battle, the British Lieutenant-Colonel Stuart, ordered all the arms belonging to the dead and wounded to be collected, which was accordingly done. When the army had marched off the the ground, this pile of arms was set on fire by the rear-guard.

Many of the muskets being loaded, an irregular discharge took place, resembling the desultory fire which usually precedes battle. The retreating British army, at once presumed that Greene was up, and had commenced an attack on its rear.

Dismay and confusion took place; wagoners cut their horses from the wagons and rode off, abandoning their wagons. The followers of the army fled in like manner, and the panic was rapidly spreading when the firing in the rear ceased. Colonel Washington, who had been taken, though indulged with his parole, was accompanied by two officers. These gentlemen abandoned the Colonel and galloped off, not liking present appearances, but as soon as the mistake was discovered, returned to their charge. During their absence, Colonel Washington, who might have made good his escape, remained, calmly awaiting the event. After his exchange, he communicated the facts to his friend Major Pendleton, aid-de-camp to General Greene.

XI.
GENERAL NATHANIEL GREENE.

ONE of the highest qualities of this General, was the combination of great prudence, with an undaunted courage that bordered on temerity. Ramsay says that General Greene often risked his person at considerable distance from his army, to incite the militia of the Carolinas to action, and it is sad to learn from the same source that his peril and labor were in vain.

When Greene and Cornwallis had approached so near that battle was inevitable, each seemed to feel that his great rival needed only a moment's weakness on his part, the neglect of an unguarded portion of his force for a single instant, to accomplish his overthrow.

"Never did two Generals exert themselves more, than did these rival leaders upon this occasion. Long withheld from each other by the sagacious conduct of Greene until he acquired sufficient strength to risk battle, they seized with ardour the opportunity at length presented of an appeal to the sword. This decision was wise in both, and every step taken by the one and by the other as well in preparation for battle, as in the battle demonstrated superior abilities. Greene's position was masterly, as was the ground selected for the combat peculiarly adapted to his views and troops.

Cornwallis saw the difficulties thrown in his way by the skill of his antagonist, and diminished their weight by the disposition of his force as far as it was practicable. Having done all that was possible to accomplish their purpose, no attention was omitted, no peril avoided by the leaders.

They exposed their persons unconscious of danger, and appeared self-devoted to national triumph. Upon one occasion, Greene was nearly passed by a body of the enemy within thirty paces of him, when Major Pendleton, one of his aids, discovered them. Luckily a copse of woods intervened, which covered Greene's return to our line.

Soon afterwards Cornwallis, seeing the discomfiture of one battalion of the guards, repaired in person to direct the measures for the recovery of the lost ground; when, by the dauntless exposure of himself he was placed in extreme danger. It was upon this occasion that he ordered his artillery to open through his flying guards to stop Washington and Howard. Brigadier O'Hara remonstrated by exclaiming that the fire would destroy themselves. True, replied Cornwallis, but this is a necessary evil which we must endure, to arrest impending destruction. (Lee, vol. 1, p. 353.)

XII.
COLONEL JOHN LAURENS.

Page 73.

There was a quixotic spirit in this young officer which could not be disciplined into the dull routine of military utility. His was an order of ability, (if his adventurous temerity can be dignified with the term) which is not only difficult to control, but most dangerous to the military commander, who relies upon it for aid. Appalled by no danger, men of his class take no precautions, and by treating the prudent as cowards, they become as inhuman as they are rash, and more dangerous to their friends than their foes. General Moultrie, in his journal of May 3d, 1779, narrates the affairs to which Garden alluded, as follows :

"As the enemy was so near I was desiring one of my aids to go and bring off our rear guard from Coeshatchie to join us immediately ; but Colonel John Laurens (who joined me two days before) being present, he requested me to permit him to go on that service, which I readily consented to, thinking him to be a brave and experienced officer ; I told him at the same time that I would send 150 good riflemen to cover his flanks, lest the enemy should be too close upon him ; I accordingly sent Capt. James, with one hundred and fifty picked men, and one hundred men of the out picket to join him, these altogether made a body of three hundred and fifty men, which was one-fourth of my little army, but instead of Colonel Laurens bringing off the guard, as he was desired, he very imprudently crossed the river to the east side, and drew them up on the opposite bank of the river, taking those one hundred and fifty men who were sent to cover his flanks, and the one hundred men of the out picket, and joined them to the guard, while he left the houses on the hill for the British to occupy; in this situation did he expose his men to their fire, without the least chance of doing them any injury; after remaining some time *he got* a number of the men killed and wounded, and was wounded himself. He desired Capt. Shubrick, who commanded after he left the field, to stay a little longer, and then to bring off the men; had not Capt. Shubrick moved off at the very instant he did, his party would have been cut off from their retreat, and every man of them would either have been killed or taken prisoners. We heard the firing very distinctly at Tullifiny, and supposed it was our retreating guard coming in, but presently Colonel Laurens came to me wounded in the arm; I said to him, "Well Colonel what do you think of it." "Why, sir, said he, your men won't stand," upon which I said, "If that is the case I will retreat," and immediately after our rear guard came in I ordered the bridge broken up, and begun my retreat about 12 o'clock. *Had not Colonel Laurens discouraged the men by exposing* them so much and unnecessarily, I would have engaged General Provost at Tullifiny, and perhaps have stopped his march to Charlestown; we were all at our posts on a very commanding ground, and expected every moment to be engaged. Colonel Laurens was a young man of great merit and a brave soldier, but an imprudent officer; he was too rash and impetuous." (Moultrie's Mem. vol. 1, p. 402.)

XIII

COLONEL CAMPBELL.

Page 62.

THE circumstances of the death of Colonel Campbell, as narrated by Ramsay, Johnson and Lee, offered ground for some sharp criticism, bordering on angry recriminations by Henry Lee, in his work entitled Campaign of 1781.

Colonel Lee, in his declaration of Dr. Ramsay's error in his narration of this officer's death, leaves it to be inferred that he fell by a shot from the Virginia Militia—his narrative of the fall of Colonel Campbell we quote in full. "Of six commandants of regiments (in the battle of Eutaw Springs) bearing continental commissions, Williams' and Lee only were unhurt. Washington, Howard and Henderson were wounded, and Lieutenant Colonel Campbell, highly respected, beloved, and admired, was killed.

"This excellent officer received a ball in his breast in the decisive charge which broke the British line while listening to an interrogatory from Lieutenant Colonel Lee, then on the left of the legion infantry adjoining the right of the Virginians —the post of Campbell. He dropped on the pummel of his saddle speechless, and was borne to the rear in the arms of Lee's orderly dragoon, in whose arms he expired the moment he was taken from his horse."

"Doctor Ramsay has represented the death of this highly respected officer differently, from information which no doubt the Doctor accredited. But as the writer was personally acquainted with the transaction, he cannot refrain from giving it exactly as it happened."

"The Virginians had begun to fire, which was not only against orders, but put in danger Rudolph and his party, then turning the enemy's left. To stop this fire, Colonel Lee galloped down the line to Campbell, and while speaking to him on the subject, the Lieutenant Colonel received his wound, of which he soon expired *without uttering a word*." Doctor Ramsay says, "while with great firmness Colonel Campbell was leading on his brigade to that charge which determined the fate of the day, he received a mortal wound. After his fall, he enquired, 'Who gave way,' and being informed 'The British,' he added 'I die contented,' and immediately expired."

If dying heroes are to be so constantly robbed by history of their last speeches, for which they become as famous as for their fighting, it is to be feared that half the illusion of glory, (which is the milk on which heroes are nurtured) will be forever destroyed. Wolfe and Montcalm may yet lose their hard-earned glory at the stroke of a learned historian's pen,— some curious Dryasdust, who has unearthed a dingy manuscript more potent than their swords.

XIV.
MAJOR BENJAMIN HUGER.

Page 82.

THE death of this brave officer was the result of the officious meddlesomeness of Gov. Rutledge, a trait in the character of that gentleman, which many times exhibited itself to the obstruction of the military service, and the great embarrassment of the commanders in South Carolina.

At the seige of Charleston by General Provost, this disposition was rampant and uncontrollable. Without consultation with Gen. Moultrie, or notification of any kind to the troops holding the lines, he had sent out Major Huger in the night on a hazardous service, and the continental troops observing a force moving on in the darkness as if to surprise them, opened a heavy fire, by which Major Huger and several others were killed and wounded.

XV.
SCOTCH LOYALISTS.

Page 90.

THE earliest collision of armed forces in the Carolinas in which blood was shed, occurred at Ninety-Six,—afterwards so memorable for its seige of Nov. 19,(1775),—between these Highland Loyalists and South Carolina Militia under Major Williamson. The district between the Broad and Saluda rivers was occupied by a population almost entirely devoted to the interests of Great Britain. Moses Kirkland, who had accepted the commission of Captain in the provincial forces, disgusted by the promotion of a neighbor and rival to a majority, threw his influence on the side of the monarchists. Hostile camps of the roused and angry inhabitants were soon formed against each other. Temporary adjustments of the growing discord were followed by an almost immediate rearming for the expected fray. Robert Cunningham, a royalist leader of great energy, was at length imprisoned, and his friends instantly assembling for his release, were headed by Patrick Cunningham, who had the good fortune to seize a thousand pounds of powder belonging to the commonwealth. Major Williamson who attempted its recovery was soon obliged to retreat before their superior numbers to a stockade near Ninety-Six. The royalists possessing themselves of the jail, fired into the fort and killed Monsieur St. Pierre, a French gentleman, who was the pioneer of grape cultivation in the Carolinas, and probably a few others were wounded, but the seige was not sanguinary, nor had the assailants yet become vindicative, and in a few days the latter tendered terms of accommodation, which were accepted, and the parties marched unmolested to their several homes. (Ramsay's His. of Rev. in S. C., vol. 1, p. 66.)

XVI.

Page 91.

GENERAL DONALD McDONALD, AND McLOUD.

The bitterness of partisan warfare, in the participants of the revolutionary struggles; and the bigotry of what is termed patriotism in later generations; has so clouded the reason and better sensibilities of historians, that they have never permitted themselves to utter one word of defence of those noble men, who from the highest principles of honour retained their fealty to the British government.

That splendid fidelity for which their race is renowned, lost none of its lustre in the husband of Flora MacDonald, who accompanied the chieftain of his clan, and fought by his side. Her daring and faithfulness to a proscribed and fugitive prince, have won her imperishable fame, and Donald MacDonald would have proved unworthy of his race, had he been recreant to a government, from which he had received nothing but favor.

Gov. Martin had fled from the State to a British Man-of-War. From this secure position, he issued mandates and commissions, which imperilled the lives of others; without much troubling himself with the results.

Among the recipients of these favors, was Donald McDonald, who was made a Brigadier General, while McLeod received a commission of Lieutenant-Colonel, and Governor Martin armed them with a proclamation, commanding all persons on their allegiance, to repair to the Royal Standard.

A council of Regulators and Highlanders, was also formed to aid this service, by whose advice the subordinate officers were generally appointed; and thus organized, they awaited the coming of a British force on the coast. The accidental, and temporary appearance of a fleet off the coast of Georgia, caused them to appear in arms, before they could be supported by British troops.

Termed insurgents, they were at once looked upon as outlaws, and Colonel Moore, with a provincial regiment, reinforced by militia, with five field pieces marched against those Highland loyalists, who were directing their course from Cross Creek to Wilmington. Each force declined a contest of arms, and commenced one of negotiations, at Rockfish Creek, which terminated in confirming each in his former views and demands, when they separated. Moore's forces, joined by Colonel Lillington and Colonel Caswell, with a thousand men, fortified themselves at Moore's Creek Bridge, on the route which MacDonald must pursue to reach Wilmington, where he hoped to be reinforced from the British fleet. On the morning of Feb. 27, 1776, Colonel McLeod pressed forward with the advance, in an attack upon the strong entrenchments at the bridge, and charging sword in hand, was with many of his men killed at the first fire. Thrown into disorder by a galling discharge of musketry and cannon, the loyalists recoiled and fled. General MacDonald was taken prisoner, and the loyalist enterprise quelched. (Drayton 2, p. 216.)

LEE'S LEGION. Page 107.

THE dashing exploits of this partisan corps, and the celebration of them in romance and history, have contributed to the fame of Carolinian patriotism, without a particle of truth to give historic solidity to the reputation. Not a single Carolinian was a member of the corps, for a long period after its formation. Johnson, himself a South Carolinian, in the life of General Greene, gives the following account of it.

"The legionary corps, commanded by Colonel Henry Lee, of *Virginia*, was perhaps the finest corps that made its appearance on the arena of the revolutionary war.

"It was formed expressly for Colonel Lee, under an order of General Washington, whilst the army lay in Jersey. It consisted at this time, of about three hundred men, in equal proportion of infantry and horse. Both men and officers *were picked from the army,* the officers with reference only to their talents and qualities for service, and the men by a proportionable selection from the troops of each State, enlisted for three years, or the war. Virginia contributed twenty-five as her quota. No *State South of Virginia* contributed any, as they had no troops in the field."

"Colonel Lee had been expected to march early in October, from Philadelphia, but the equipping, disciplining, (and perhaps exhibiting) his command, had rendered his movements very slow, his journey from Fredericksburgh to Richmond, for instance, required a fortnight, not a little to the distress of his commander."

"In Maryland, General Greene had made a requisition of seventy-five cavalry horses, and sundry equipments for the legion, and the liberal spirit in which the requisition was complied with, gave Lee an opportunity of equipping his cavalry in a brilliant style." It was thus, that Northern soldiers won such fame on Southern fields.

XVIII.

CAPTAIN ARMSTRONG.

An incident in the life of this brave and honorable officer, occurring at the battle of Eutaw Springs, illustrates the maxim, that neither courage or honour are sufficient to conquer fate.

Colonel Lee had halted in the edge of a wood, impatiently awaiting the arrival of his dragoons, in order to make the final charge on Coffin, and turn the head of the ravine. Observing the approach of Captain Armstrong, (the leading officer of the day,) and not doubting that the entire corps was following, Colonel Lee advanced into the field, directing Captain Armstrong to follow.

He had gone but a little way, when Captain Armstrong volunteered the information that only his own section of the corps was at hand, having never seen the rest of it since its discomfiture on the left some time before. This unlooked for intelligence was fatal, not only to the enterprise in hand, but to Colonel Washington and his troops. Some officious field-officer, on seeing the other section commanded by Captain Eggleston, standing in reserve, had ordered it into action, where unsupported by infantry, it was foiled and routed. Had the legion cavalry all been up at this crisis, Coffin would have been cut to pieces; the enemy's left occupied in force, and Washington would have awaited the movement of Majoribanks to close the enemy's broken line, and fallen on his retiring column, and the victory made complete. (Lee, vol. 2, 290.

XIX.
COLONEL THEODORICK BLAND.

COLONEL Bland had the misfortune to be the cause of obstructing a blow, with which Washington could, on the 11th of September, 1777, have crushed the forces of General Knyphausen on the Brandywine. General Howe was advancing in two columns at something more than supporting distance, when Washington was informed of their separation, and that the left and superior force had diverged widely from the other. Persuaded of this fact he wisely determined to pass the Brandywine and strike at Knyphausen's unsupported column. The unfortunate Colonel Bland arrives at the very moment of his final disposition for the attack with a confused report apparently contradictory of that which declared the weakness of Knyphausen's position. The caution of Washington which permitted no action based on conjecture, was aroused by this information, and before it could be corrected, the opportunity was lost.

' The narrow escape of Lee, while a captain in Bland's regiment, and of Colonel Alexander Hamilton is thus narrated by the former. "A violent storm, accompanied by a deluge of rain stopped the renewal of the battle of the Brandywine on the following day. Contiguous to the enemy's route lay some mills stored with flour for the use of the American Army. Their destruction was deemed necessary by the Commander-in-Chief, and his aid, Colonel Alexander Hamilton, attended by Captain Lee, afterwards Colonel Lee of the Legion Cavalry, with a small party of his troop of horse, were despatched in front of the enemy with the order of execution. The mill or mills, stood on the bank of the Schuylkill. Approaching, you descend a long hill leading to a bridge over the mill race. On the summit of this hill two videts were posted, and soon after the party reached the mills, Lieutenant Colonel Hamilton took possession of a flat bottomed boat for the purpose of transporting himself and his comrades across the river should the sudden approach of the enemy render such retreat necessary. In a little time this precaution manifested his sagacity, the fire of the videts announced the enemy's approach. The dragoons were ordered instantly to embark. Of the small party, four with Lieutenant Colonel Hamilton jumped into the boat, the van of the enemy's horse in full view, pressing down the hill in pursuit of the two videts. Captain Lee, with the remaining two, took the decision to regain the bridge, rather than detain the boat.

Hamilton was committed to the flood, struggling against a violent current increased by the recent rains, while Lee put his safety on the speed and soundness of his horse.

The attention of the enemy being engaged by Lee's push for the bridge delayed the attack upon the boat for a few minutes, and thus afforded to Hamilton a better chance of escape.

The two videts preceded Lee as he reached the bridge, and himself, with the four dragoons, safely passed it, although the enemy's front section emptied their carbines and pistols at the distance of ten or twelve paces. Lee's apprehension for the safety of Hamilton continued to increase, as he heard volleys of carbines discharged upon the boat, which were returned by guns singly and occasionally. He trembled for the probable issue, and as soon as the pursuit ended, which did not long continue, he despatched a dragoon to the Commander-in-Chief, describing, with feelings of anxiety, what had passed, and his sad presage.

His letter was scarcely perused by Washington, before Hamilton himself appeared, and ignorant of the contents of the paper in the General's hand, renewed his attention to the ill boding separation, with the probability that his friend Lee had been cut off, inasmuch as instantly after he turned for the bridge, the British horse reached the mill, and commenced their operations on the boat. Washington relieved his fears by giving to his aid-de-camp the Captain's letter. Lieutenant Colonel Hamilton escaped unhurt, but two of his four dragoons, with one of the boatmen, were wounded.

XX.
JOHN MIDDLETON.

In the memorable pursuit of Greene by Lord Cornwallis, Colonel Lee having ascertained that the baggage of the British army had become separated from it, and was accompanied by only a small escort, made a bold push for its capture, but in the night pursuit the legion missed its road, and became lost in the woods, and Cornwallis's baggage escaped.

Upon Lee's junction with Clarke, he found a packet from General Greene to Lord Cornwallis, which he sent off by Cornet Middleton of South Carolina, with a flag. The cornet reached the British piquet just after the Captain had breakfasted, and was politely invited to take breakfast, while the packet for his Lordship should be sent to headquarters, from whence a reply would be forwarded if requisite, which Middleton could convey. Cornwallis was on his rounds, agreeable to his custom, and soon after Middleton had finished his breakfast, called at the piquet, when he was informed by the Captain of the packet from General Greene, with the detention of the bearer for the answer, if any was requisite. His Lordship dismounting, entered the Captain's headquarters, where Cornet Middleton was introduced to him. Presuming from his dress that he belonged to Lee's legion, he asked if he did not belong to that corps, and being answered in the affirmative, with a smile he significantly inquired where the corps had been the preceding night.

The amiable Middleton, somewhat surprised and confounded at a query so unexpected, with evident confusion replied that it had not been far off. Upon which Lord Cornwallis familiarly said, the object of the inquiry was unimportant, the matter to which it related being passed, and that he asked to gratify his curiosity. Middleton blushing, then told him, that Colonel Lee had received intelligence of his lordships escort, with his baggage and stores being lost in the night, and so had instantly proceeded in the expectation of putting them on the right course. This idea tickled the British General, he laughingly asked, "Well, why did he not do it."

"Because said Middleton, we got lost ourselves traversing the roads all night, and as it appeared, within two miles of our much desired prize." Turning to his aids, Cornwallis said, "You see I was not mistaken."

XXI.
DR. SKINNER.

Page 120.

This person was an example of the truth of the maxim that the duelist fights because he is a coward, and is afraid it will be discovered if he does not.

Another Anecdote of this doughty surgeon, is narrated by Lee. The legion was passing through a defile, so narrow as to admit of proceeding only in single file. When the troops in the centre had entered the defile, we were alarmed by beating to arms in the camp of the infantry, which was soon followed by their forming in line of battle. This unexpected event was felt by all, but most by our amiable surgeon of the infantry, who was at that moment leading his horse through the defile. Not doubting but that battle must instantly take place, and believing the surer course was to avoid, not to meet it, the surgeon turned his horse with a view of getting out of danger, never reflecting that the passage did not admit of turning his horse.

Ductile to the force of the bridle, the horse attempted to turn about, but was brought upon his head athwart the narrow passage, from which position he could not possibly extricate himself. The troops which had passed the defile, instantly galloped up the hill and arrayed with the infantry, while the remaining troops were arrested by the panic of an individual. Eggleston, who commanded the troop so unhappily situated, dismounting several of his strongest dragoons pulled the horse back again lengthwise of the defile. He then had space to use his limbs, and soon stood upon his feet, and our deranged and distressed cavalry were enabled to pass the defile.

This accident interrupted the progress of the horse for ten minutes, ample time for their destruction, had the enemy been at hand.

XXII.

Page 169.

JOHN EDWARDS.

The name of this gentleman should be preserved in hallowed remembrance, as one of the Council of South Carolina, whose assent was not given to the pusillanimous proffer of neutrality. Gen. Moultrie narrates an incident, which exhibits the high tone of this gentleman's character.

"When the question was carried for giving up the town upon a neutrality, I will not say who was for the question, but this I well remember, that Mr. John Edwards, one of the privy Council, a worthy citizen, and a very respectable merchant of Charleston, was so affected as to weep, and said, 'What! are we to give up the town at last.'"

INDEX TO VOLUME ONE.

A.

	PAGE.
ADAMS, David, 4; *John*, 32; *Pres.*	
John,	94, 98
ANDRE,	155
ANTHONY, John,	149
ARBUTHNOT, Admiral,	169, 170
ARCHER, Capt.,	107
ARMSTRONG, 108, 134, 136, 139; *Capt. James*, 109, 110, 119, 123, xxvii. Ap.	xxviii. Ap.
ARNOLD,	46
ARTHUR, George,	149
ARTILLERY, The Charleston Ancient Battalion of,	151
ATMORE, Ralph,	149
AXSON, William,	149

B.

BADDELY, John,	149
BAKER, Capt. Richard Bahon,	4
BALFOUR, Col.,	18, 93
BALL, 58; *Joseph*,	149
BARNWELL, Gen., 37-52; *John*, 41, 149; *Edward*, 41, 149; *Robert*,	41, 149
BARRE, Col.,	167
BARRY, Major, 93; *Henry*,	128, 130
BASQUIN, William,	149
BAYLE, Francis,	149
BAYLOR'S Regiment,	51
BAXTER, Col.,	21
BEE, 173; *Joseph*, 148; *Thomas*,	166
BENBRIDGE, Henry,	149
BERESFORD, Richard,	148
BLAKE, Edward, 148; *John*,	149
BLAND, 111; *Bland's Regiment*, 56, 57; *Col.*,	xxviii. Ap.
BLOUNT, Gov.,	100

	PAGE.
BLUNDELL, Nathaniel,	140
BOLMAN, Dr.,	85-88
BOND, Dr.,	175
BOONE, Gov.,	153
BOUNNETHEAU, Peter, Lt.,	151, 119, 151
BOYD,	26
BRADDOCK, Gen.,	46
BRANDFORD, William,	149
BRICKEN, James,	149
BROWN, 28; *Col.*, 108, 109, 133, xii. Ap.; *William*,	144, 145
BROWNE,	22, 27
BRUSH, Lieut.,	6
BUDD, John,	148
BUFORD, Col.,	128
BULKLEY and NEWMAN,	134, 135
BUONAPARTE, 32, 33; *Joseph*,	32
BURKE, Judge,	176-180
BURNETT, Major,	67
BUTLER, Capt.,	17
BUYSSEN, Chevalier de,	191, 192

C.

CAMPBELL, Lt.-Col., 82; *Col.*, 139, xxii.; *Capt.*, 137; *Gov.*	lii, iv. Ap.
CARLISLE, Mr.,	60
CARNS, Capt.,	101, 122, 126
CARRINGTON, 67, 134; *St. George*, 107, 123; *Maj. Gen.*, 106; *Clement*, 118; *Col.*	51
CASWELL,	xxvi. Ap.
CLAY, Mrs.,	9
CLARKE, John, Jr.,	149
CLERGY, Exemplary Conduct of the,	182
CLINTON, Gen., 92; *Sir Henry*,	169
CHARACTER AND CONDUCT OF OFFICERS OF THE LEGION,	107

25A

INDEX.

CHARLESTON, Ancient Artillery Battalion,..........151
CIVIL LINE, Patriots in the.......143
COCHRANE, Thomas.......149
COCHRAN, Robert,..........148
COFFEE, Brig. Gen.,..........104, 105
COMMANDERS OF MILITIA, the Partisan,..........23
CONTINENTAL OFFICERS, Distinguished,..........43
COFFIN,..........xxvii. Ap.
CONYERS, Norwood,..........149
COOKE, Thos.,..........140
COOPER, Corporal,..........136, 137 138
COX, James,..........149
COTESWORTH, Charles,..........166
CORNWALLIS, Lord, v., 24, 27, 29, 44, 48, 52, 58, 65, 68, 126, 127, ...163, xxxi., xx. Ap.
CRAFTS, William,..........63
CRIPPS, John, 63; *John Splatt*,..........148
CROUCH, Henry,..........148
CRUGER, 128; *Major*, 55; *Col.* xvii., ix. Ap.
CUDWORTH, Benjamin,..........148
CUNNINGHAM, Robert and Patrick, xx. Ap.
CUTHBERT, Gen. John,..........38
Cyane, The,..........68

D.

DALCHO, Rev. Dr.,..........182
DALE, Commodore..........136
DAQUINS, Mayor,..........104
DARREL, Edward,..........148
DRAYTON, William Henry, 166-168, 186; *William*,..........166
DAVIE, 67; *Gen*..........28-31, 125
D'ESTAING,..........66
DE KALB, Baron,..........83
DESAUSSURE, 65; *Daniel*, 148; *William*,..........150
DENAR, Robert,..........150
DISTINGUISHED CONTINENTAL OFFICERS,..........43
D'OYLEY, Col..........96
DONNOM, John,..........149
DUNLAP, Joseph,..........149
DUVAL, Lieut.,..........82

E.

EBERLY, John,..........149
EDWARDS, John, 148, 169-170, xxxii. Ap.; *John, Jr.*, 150; *John W.*..........150
EDMONDS, Rev. James,..........149
EGGLESTON, xxxii.; *Capt. Joseph*, 101, 108, 149, xxviii. Ap.; *Thomas*, 149
ELLIOTT, William, 42, 150; *Mrs. Charles*, 121; *Mrs. Bernard presents Colors to the 2d Regt.*..........6

ELLSWORTH, Gov. Oliver,..........32
EVANS, John,..........149
EVELEIGH, Thomas, 150; *Col.*,..........173
EXILES TO ST. AUGUSTINE, Fla.,..........148

F.

FANNING,..........18, 19, v. Ap.
FENNICKE..........42
FERGUSON, Thomas,..........39, 148
FITZPATRICK, Gen.,..........85
FLOYER, Lieut. William,..........144
FRANKLIN, Dr., 76; *The Ship*,..........136
FREER, Capt. Charles,..........38
FULLER, William,..........78
FURMAN, Rev. Dr.,..........188
FUTEREL,..........167

G.

GADSDEN, Gen., 152-155; *Christopher*, 148; *Philip*,..........150
GAGE, Gen..........90
GARDINER,..........151
GANET, Mayor,..........17, 18
GARDEN, v., xiii. Ap.; *Major*,..........xv. Ap.
GARGIL, Mitchell,..........149
GATES, Gen.,..........24, 29, 46, 48, 57, 66, 97, 172
GERRY, E.,..........97
GIBBES, John, 79; *Miss Mary Anna*, 41, 79; *Capt. William H.*..........148, 151
GIBBON, Lieut.,..........195
GLAZIER,..........155
GLOVER, Joseph,..........149
GOUGH, Capt. Richard,..........181
GORDON, Lieut.,..........60
GRAHAME, Major,..........29
GRAVES, William,..........149
GRAY, Joseph,..........149
GRAYSON, Thomas,..........150
GRIMBALL, Thomas, 148, 151; *Major*,..........151
GREAVES, John,..........150
GREENE, Gen., v., xix., Ap., 27, 30, 39-42, 44, 50-55, 58, 64-71, 82, ...126, 127, 131, 141, 151, 147, 177
STEPHEN,..........126
GUENVILLE, Geo.,..........167
GREY, Lieut.,..........6
GRIERSON, Col..........109
GROTT, Francis,..........140
GUERARD, Peter, 149; *Benjamin*,..........150, 175
GUNBY..........50

H.

HALL, Mrs. Daniel, 78; *G. A.*, 148; *William*, 148; *Thomas*,..........148

HAMILTON, Gen., 94; *Colonel*,
xxix, xxx. Ap., 25; *David*, ... 149
HANDY, Capt., ... 114
HARMER, Gen., ... 141
HARRIS, Thomas, ... 149
HARRISON, ... 107
HAYNE, Colonel, 39, 41, 93, 147,
148; *Lt.-Col.*, 102, 103; *Col. Robt. B.*, 165; *Inspector Gen.*,
103; *Col. Anthony P.*, ... 103
HENDERSON, Col., ... 95
HENLY, Capt., ... 104, 105
HENRY, Jacob, 149; *Wm. H.*, 150;
Patrick, ... 156
HEYWARD, Capt. Thomas, 151;
Thomas, Jr., 148; *James*, ... 150
HINDS, Major, ... 104
HOLMES, Isaac, 148; *John B.*, 150;
Wm., ... 150, 169
HORNBY, William, ... 149
HOWARD, 67; *Col.*, ... 58
HORRY, 5, x.; *Col. Peter*, ... 20, 21
HUCK, Capt., ... 23
HUGHES, Thomas, ... 150
HUGER, xxiv., 67; *Major Benjamin*, 83; *Col. Francis K.*, 83,
86, 87, 88, ii., Ap.; *Isaac*, 43,
44, 45; *Daniel*, 43; *John*, 43;
Francis, 43; *Benjamin*, 34;
Isaac, ... 43
HUNTER, ... v., vi., Ap.
HURD, Capt., ... 107
HUTSON, Richard, ... 148
HYRNE, Major, ... 67, 93, 171

I.

INNIS, ... iii., iv. Ap.
INTRODUCTION, ... iii.-vii. Ap.
INGERSOLL, ... 173-5
IRVINE, Dr. Matthew, ... 52, 119, 123, 180
IZARD, Ralph, 36, 74; *Walter*, ... 74

J.

JACKSON, Gen., ... 98, 99, 10, 103, 125
JACOBY, Daniel, ... 149
JARDINE, ... 125
JAMES, Capt., ... xxi. Ap.
JASPER, Sergeant, ... 6, 77
JEFFERSON, ... 74
JOHNSON, William, ... 148
JOHNSTON, Lt. Peter, 116; *Judge*, 53, 123
JOIETT, Capt. Robert, ... 129
JONES, Noble Wimberly, 148; *George*, ... 148
JORDAN, ... 107

K.

KEAN, John, ... 150
KEMPER, Col. Reuben, ... 105

KENT, Charles, ... 149
KENNON, Henry, ... 150
KING, Lt., ... 60
KIRKLAND, ... xx, Ap.
KNOX, Gen., ... 65
KNYPHAUSEN, Gen., ... xxviii. Ap.
KOSCIUSKO, ... viii. Ap., 19, 52, 78, 79

L.

LAFAYETTE, his escape from Olmetz, ... 83-89
LATOUR, Mr., ... 103
LAURENS, Lt.-Col. John, 73-76;
Col., 37, 38, 192, xxi., xxii, Ap.
LEACH, Ensign, ... 106
LEBBY, Nathaniel, ... 149
LECHMERE, Col., ... 41
LEE, 69, 27, 22, 67, 107, 109, 112, 114,
2; *Col.* xxix, xxvii, xvi, xxiii,
ix, x., xi. Ap., 126, 128, 129,
121, 79; *Lt.-Col. Henry*, 52-56,
131, 136-139, 141; *Gen. Charles*,
73, 168; *Capt. Henry*, 111;
William, 148; *Stephen*, ... 150
LEGARE, St. James, 6; *Thomas*, ... 149
LEGION, Soldiers of the, ... 131, xxv. Ap.
LESESNE, John, ... 149
LESLIE, Gen., ... 71, 137
Lerant, The Ship, ... 68
LEWIS, Rev. John, ... 148, 183
LILLINGTON, Col., ... xxvi. Ap.
LINCOLN, 28; *General*, ... 57, 96, ii., Ap.
LISTON, Thomas, ... 149
LIVINGSTON, William, ... 148
LOCKHART, Samuel, ... 149
LOGAN, William, 148; *Dr.*, ... 175
LOVELL, ... 107
LOVEDAY, John, ... 148
LOWNDES, ... 154
LUMSFORD, ... 107
LOUNDEN, 154; *Rawlins*, ... 166
LOYALISTS, Scotch, ... xx. Ap.
LUSHINGTON, Richard, ... 148
LUZERNE, Chevalier de la, ... 65
LYBERT, Henry, ... 149

M.

MAHAM, Col., ... xi. Ap.
MAJORIBANKS, Major, John, ... 60
MANNING, Lieut., ... 124, 130
MANIGAULT, Peter, ... 166
MARION, Gen. Francis, v., 5, 11-20,
21, 54, 67, 70, 139; estimate of
his character, 11, 12, 13; invites a British officer to dinner, 14; his humanity, 14; activity, 15, 16; his protection of
Butler, ... 17

INDEX.

MARRIETT, Abraham. 149, 157, 177,
  .... iv., x., xi., xvii., xviii., Ap.
MARSHALL, ... 97
MARTIN, Governor .... 90, 91, xxv. Ap,
MATTHEWS, Gov., 16, 17, 40, 160-
  172-174; *John*, ... 166
MAYHAM, Col 14, 22
MAYNARD, Capt., ... 79
McCLELLAND, Lieut., ... 104
McCAULEY, Capt., ... 134
McCREADY, Edward, ... 148
McDONALD, Sgt., 6, 91; *Gen.*,
  xxv. Ap.; *Flora*, ... xxv. Ap.
McDOUGALD, Gen., ... 125
McGIRTH, ... 38
McINTOSH, Gen., ... 125
McKAY, Capt. .... xi. Ap.
McKEY, Mrs. 110
McLEOD, 91; *Col.*, ... xxv Ap.
MERCER, ... 125
MERRIWEATHER, Lieut. 71
MEYER, Philip, ... 150
MICHAEL, John, ... 149
MIDDLETON, xxx., xxxi. Ap.: *John*,
  117; *Arthur*, ... 148
MILLER, 125; *Lieut. John D.*, 151;
  Samuel, 149; *Capt.*, ... xvi. Ap.
MILITIA, Partisan Commanders of ... 23
MILNER, Solomon, ... 149
MINOTT, John, Sr., ... 149
MITCHELL, Sgt., 133; *Col., John*, ..175
MONTAGUE, Lord Charles, 3, 8, 9;
  Letter to Moultrie, ...7
MONTGOMERY, ... 46
MORGAN, 67, 68; *General*, 27, 44-47,
  58; *Lieut. Wm.*, 151; *Jonathan*,
  149
MOORE, 20; *Judge Alfred*, 31; *Gen.*,
  91; *Stephen*, 149; *Col.*, ...xxvi. Ap.
MORRIS, 69; *Col.* 67
MORRALL, John, ... 149
MORSE, George, ... 150
MOTTE, Lieut.-Col., Isaac, 5, 10,
  .... iii., iv., Ap.
MOUCK, George, ... 149
MOULTRIE, 20, 37, 38, 43; *General*,
  1-7, 75, 81, 151; *Capt. S.*, 81;
  Alexander, 148, ii., x., xxi.,
  .... xxiv., Ap.
MOYLAN's Regiment 57
MURRAY, Mr. 32; *Commodore*, ... 136
MUSSEY, William, ... 148

N.

NEUFVILLE, ;Lieut. Edward, 151;
  John, 148; *John, Jr.*, 149; *William*, ... 150

NEW ORLEANS, Col. A. P. Hayne's
  Account of the Battle of, ... 103
NETLE, Capt. Philip, ... 81
NORTH, Edward, ... 148

O.

OFFICERS, Distinguished Conti-
  nental, 43; who fell in the
  Southern War, ... 72
O'HARA, Gen., ... xv. Ap.
O'NEAL, Capt. 74, 111
ORD, Sgt., ... 139, 140
OWEN, John, ... 150

P.

PALMER, Job, ... 149
PARKER, iv. Ap.; Sir Peter, 10, 15; *Lt.-
  Col. Richard*, 80; *Joseph*, ... 148
PARSONS, Capt., ... 60
PARTISAN COMMANDERS of Militia ... 23
PATRIOTS IN THE CIVIL LINE, ... 143
PATTERSON, Commodore, ... 104, 105
PENDLETON, xix., xx. Ap.; *Capt.*, 67;
  Judge, ... 67
PERCY, Rev. Dr., ... 183
PETTIT, Col., ... 175
PICKENS, Gen., ... xiv. Ap.
PICKNEY, iii, Ap.; *General*, 26,
  27, 32, 100; *Gen. Thomas*, 95-98,
  166, 173; *General C. C.*, 90-94,
  Charles, Jr., ... 150
PICKERING, Col., ... 64
PIERCE, Major, ... 67
PLANCHE, Major, ... 104
POSTELL, Benjamin, ... 149
POYAS, John Ernest, 148; *James*, ..149
POWER, Sgt., ... 107, 134, 135
President, ... 68
PRIOLEAU, Samuel, 148; *Philip*, ...149
PROVOST, 37, 75, 83; *Gen.*, i., ii.,
  .... xxii., xxiv., Ap.
PYLE, Col., ... 124, 127
PURCELL, Rev. Dr., ... 184

R.

RAMSAY, Dr. David, 110, 162-167,
  .... ii., xix., xxii., xxiii., Ap.
RAVENEL, Daniel, ... 60
RAWDON, Lord, ... 93, 141, x., xiv. Ap.
READ, Jacob, ... 148, 166
REGIMENT, THE SECOND, ... 5
REGULATORS, The, ... xxvi. Ap.
REDDY, Daniel 149
RIGHTON, Joseph, ... 149
ROBERTS, Col., Owen, ... 72
ROBINSON, Joseph, ... 149
RODGERS, Commodore, ... 68

INDEX.

	PAGE.
ROUPELL, George,	41
RUDOLPH, Major, John, 107; *Capt. Michael,*	112, 133, 141
RUGELY, Col.,	58
RUTLEDGE, xxiv., *Gov.,*	i., ii., Ap.

S.

SAUNDERS, John,	149
SAUSUM, John,	149
SAVAGE, Thomas,	149
SCOTCH LOYALISTS,	xx. Ap.
SCOTT, Perry,	141
SCOTTOWE, Samuel,	149
SEAVERS, Abraham,	149
SECOND REGIMENT, The,	5
SHREWSBURY, Stephen,	149
SHUBRICK, Capt., 4, 67, xxii. Ap.; *John S.,* 68; *William, Sr.,* 68; *Lieutenant Edward,* 68; *Irvine,*	68
SIMMONS, Lieut.	60
SINCLAIR, Gen.,	125
SINGLETON, Benjamin, 81; *Thomas,* 149; *Ripley,*	149
SKINNER, Dr., 120, 121, xxxi. Ap.; *Chief Justice,*	167
SKOLLY, Major,	148
SMITH, Josiah, 145, 149, 169, 185; *Philip,* 149; *Samuel,* 150; *Bishop,*	182
SNELLING, William,	149
SNOWDEN,	107
SNYDER, Paul,	149
SOLDIERS of the Legion,	131
STAEL, Madame de,	32
STEADMAN,	xvii. Ap.
STERLING, Lord,	125
STEPHENS, Gen.,	125
STEPHENSON, John, Jr.,	149
STEVENS, Lieut. Daniel, 151; *Lieut. J. H.,*	14
STEWARD, Col.,	58
ST. PIERRE,	xxv. Ap.
STUART, Lieut., 60; *Col.,*	xviii. Ap.
SUMTER, 29, 56, 51, 67, 70, 157, 168; *General,*	23-25, xiii. Ap.
SURVIVORS of the Revolution,	80
SWEENY, Commodore,	110

T.

TARLETON, 21, 110; *Lieut.-Col.,* 57,	58, 127, 128

	PAGE.
TATAM, Major,	103
TAYLOR, Paul,	149
TENNANT, Rev. Mr.,	168, 185-187
TERQUAND, Rev. Paul,	184
THOMPSON, Col., alias Count Rumford,	110, 174, x. Ap.
THOMSON, James Hamden,	140
TONYN, Pat.,	145
TOWNER, Capt. Anthony,	149, 151
TOUSSEGER, James,	146

W.

WAKEFIELD, James,	149
WAINWRIGHT, Mr.,	74
WALLER, Benjamin,	149
WARREN, Rev. Samuel,	184
WARHAM, Lieut. Charles, 150, 151; *David,*	150
WARING, Thomas, 150; *Richard,*	150
WASHINGTON, vi. Ap., 10, 36, 56, 67, 83, 168, xxx. Ap.; *General,* 57-63, 65, 66, 73; *Col.,* 50, 69, 156; *William,*	xviii. Ap.
WATSON,	xi. Ap.
WATTS, Capt.,	60
WEBSTER,	58, 59
WELCH, John, 149; *George,*	149
WEMYSS,	24
WEYMAN, Lieut. Edward,	151, 149
WHALING, 55; *Sgt.,*	131, 132
WHEELER, Benjamin,	149
WHITE, Lieut.,	140, 151
WIGG, Capt., 75; *William H.,*	150
WILLIAMS, 67; *Col. Otho H.,* 48,	70, xv., xvii. Ap.
WILLIAMSON,	xx. Ap.
WILKIE, William,	149
WILKINS, James,	149
WILKINSON, Morton,	149
WILMOTT, 20; *Capt. and Lieut. Moore,*	78
WILSON, Daniel,	81
WINSTON,	107, 111
WITHERSPOON, Rev. Dr.,	28
WRAGG, William,	166

Y.

YEADON, Richard,	150
YOU, Thomas,	149

END OF VOLUME I.

www.ingramcontent.com/pod-product-compliance
Lightning Source LLC
Chambersburg PA
CBHW020805230426
43666CB00007B/862